With the signing of the Moscow Treaty in 1970, West German–Soviet relations came to the forefront of world politics. Two decades later, the historic opening of the Berlin Wall and German reunification has once again focussed world attention on the Federal Republic's relations with the USSR. This timely book explores the development of this relationship from the perspective of West Germany.

Dr Avril Pittman outlines the main events after the Second World War and then focusses on four issues central to this relationship in the 1970s and early 1980s. She explores family reunification and emigration rights for ethnic Germans living in the Soviet Union; the central role of Berlin and the reasons why the city persisted as a serious bilateral problem; the triangular relations between West Germany, the Soviet Union and East Germany; and the significance of the Soviet intervention in Afghanistan with its ensuing sharp deterioration in East–West relations. In her concluding chapter, the author outlines recent events and assesses the extent to which they represent a continuity in West German–Soviet relations.

This is the first book to examine the recent history of German–Soviet political relations. It will therefore be widely read by students and specialists of Soviet and German studies, European history and politics as well as by diplomats and foreign correspondents.

FROM OSTPOLITIK TO REUNIFICATION: WEST GERMAN–SOVIET POLITICAL RELATIONS SINCE 1974

Soviet and East European Studies

Series list continues on page 223

FROM OSTPOLITIK TO REUNIFICATION: WEST GERMAN–SOVIET POLITICAL RELATIONS SINCE 1974

AVRIL PITTMAN
Research Fellow, University of Nottingham

CAMBRIDGE
UNIVERSITY PRESS

PUBLISHED BY THE PRESS SYNDICATE OF THE UNIVERSITY OF CAMBRIDGE
The Pitt Building, Trumpington Street, Cambridge, United Kingdom

CAMBRIDGE UNIVERSITY PRESS
The Edinburgh Building, Cambridge CB2 2RU, UK
40 West 20th Street, New York NY 10011–4211, USA
477 Williamstown Road, Port Melbourne, VIC 3207, Australia
Ruiz de Alarcón 13, 28014 Madrid, Spain
Dock House, The Waterfront, Cape Town 8001, South Africa

http://www.cambridge.org

© Cambridge University Press 1992

First published 1992
First paperback edition 2002

A catalogue record for this book is available from the British Library

Library of Congress Cataloguing in Publication data
Pittman, Avril.
From Ostpolitik to reunification: West German-Soviet political relations
since 1974 / Avril Pittman.
          p.   cm.   – (Soviet and East European studies: 85)
Includes bibliographical references (p.   ) and index.
ISBN 0 521 40166 6 (hardback)
1. Germany (West) – Foreign relations – Soviet Union.   2. Soviet Union –
Foreign relations – Germany (West).   3. Soviet Union – Foreign relations –
1975–1985.   4. Soviet Union – Foreign relations – 1985–
I. Title.   II. Series.
DD258.85.S6P58   1992
327.43047–dc20   91-880   CIP

ISBN 0 521 40166 6 hardback
ISBN 0 521 89333 X paperback

Contents

Tables

Preface

With the signing of the Moscow Treaty in 1970 which led to the rapid and historic accommodation with the East (earning Willy Brandt the Nobel Peace Prize) and to the Allied Quadripartite Agreement on Berlin, FRG–USSR relations were very much to the forefront of world politics. The recent historic opening of the Berlin Wall and the reunification of Germany has meant that the world's attention has once again been fixed on the Federal Republic's political relations with the USSR.

This study is an examination of FRG–USSR political relations between 1974 and 1982. The study concentrates on the West German side of FRG–USSR relations in the 'follow-on' period to the innovatory 'treaty' period of Ostpolitik. It was a period when the overall climate of détente began to deteriorate, culminating in the Afghanistan crisis.

This was a period in which Chancellor Schmidt consolidated the achievements of the Brandt period, steering FRG–USSR relations through the difficult time of the late 1970s and early 1980s and developing FRG–USSR relations, putting them on the solid basis that they have today. It is a measure of the success of the period that when Schmidt fell from office in 1982, the CDU/CSU more or less continued Schmidt's foreign policy with no change, no change sometimes even in style. Indeed, whilst much credit must be given to the diplomacy of Chancellor Kohl and particularly to his FDP coalition partner, Foreign Minister Hans-Dietrich Genscher, the rapidity of accommodation with the Soviet Union in 1990 leading to the reunification of Germany – although due in large measure to the Soviet Union's desperate economic situation – must also be seen as a reflection of those foundations laid during the Schmidt period.

There is a large literature covering the beginnings of Ostpolitik (Grand Coalition), the Brandt or 'treaty' period and on Ostpolitik in general. Although there are numerous short studies and serialised reports (for example those by the Bundesinstitut für ostwissenschaftliche und internationale Studien and Radio Liberty Research), and an excellent comprehensive study of the political economy of West German–Soviet relations from 1955 to 1980 (Angela Stent), there has so far been no major study or overview dealing specifically with West German–Soviet political relations in the 'follow-on' period to the 'treaty' period of Ostpolitik. Given the past and present importance of this topic and its interest not only to the expert but also to the general reader, the author felt that such a study would be both interesting and worthwhile – both for its own sake and as a contribution to our understanding of the continuum of FRG–USSR political relations.

Two additional chapters have been included to put the study into context – a general chapter aimed at being particularly helpful to the non-expert reader and providing a summarised account of the background and events after the Second World War leading up to the Schmidt period; and a final chapter providing a summary analysis of FRG–USSR political relations after 1982 and the events leading up to the historic reunification of Germany.

The author wishes to express her appreciation to the people who have assisted her during the course of the research and writing of this study.

In particular the author wishes to thank the following: Professor David Childs (Institute of German, Austrian and Swiss Affairs, University of Nottingham), Mr Jens Fischer (Head of the Office of Former Chancellor Helmut Schmidt, Bonn), and Professor Hans-Adolf Jacobsen (Seminar für Politische Wissenschaft der Universität Bonn) for their expert support and advice; Mr Fred Oldenburg, Diplompolitologe, and the Bundesinstitut für ostwissenschaftliche und internationale Studien, Cologne, for providing some extremely useful bibliographic assistance; all those who kindly gave up their time to be interviewed; and to Karen Watson for her skillful typing of the manuscript.

The author also wishes to acknowledge the Department of Linguistic and International Studies, University of Surrey for the excellent grounding she received there; and Mr Anthony de Reuck, formerly Senior Lecturer in the Department of Linguistic and Regional Studies, University of Surrey for his continued interest.

The author's especial thanks are due to her supervisor, Professor Ian Bellany (Department of Politics and International Relations, University of Lancaster) for his unfailing professional advice and for his continued generous support; and to Mr Rainer Dobbelstein (Foreign Office of the Federal Republic of Germany, Bonn), for the invaluable help and advice which he has given in a non-official capacity. Mr Dobbelstein checked the first draft of all chapters on the grounds of his experience as a desk officer in the East–West relations and CSCE department of the FRG Foreign Office from 1978 to 1982. All aspects on which he was not able to comment have been checked for accuracy by other civil servants with special expertise, also in a non-official capacity.

Whilst the author gratefully acknowledges the help of those named and those who for various reasons are unnamed, final responsibility for all errors and omissions remains the author's.

Selected quotes from Klaus Bölling *Die Fernen Nachbarn: Erfahrungen in der DDR*, (Hamburg: STERN-Buch im Verlag Grüner und Jahr, 1983), have been included in the study by permission of the publishers. Figures for Western–Soviet high-level meetings for the period 1974–82 have been reproduced on p. 139 of this study from Roland Smith, 'Soviet Policy Towards West Germany', *Adelphi Papers* (no. 203, 1985) by permission of the International Institute for Strategic Studies.

Note on text

Interviews were mainly conducted during three field visits made to the FRG during the period 1984–85. Details of name, date and place of interview have not been given in the study as the interviews were conducted on the understanding that this would not be done. The term 'government official' has been used for both FRG foreign office and FRG government officials.

With regard to the presentation of the material in this study, the reporting of the contents of some interviews inevitably has a clumsy appearance. This occurs where the author has felt that accounts of these interviews should be given in full as they were with people who had expert knowledge of a particular point not available to the author (i.e. they had access to classified documents, were present at top-level talks or were long-term observers), or because they represented informal surveys of informed Bonn opinion on a particular question – but where, of necessity the interviewees had to remain anonymous. The author feels that the price exacted by the anonymity requirement in presentational terms, was a price well worth paying for the material that was obtained.

Where the titles of books, articles in journals, magazines or newspapers and of publications by research institutes are given in German or French, translations of quotations are the author's own (see relevant footnotes). Translations of quotations are also the author's own where they are taken from sources listed in German in the Bibliography under the headings 'FRG government publications and documents', 'Pressedienst der Freien Demokratischen Partei (FDP news service)', and 'Deutschland Archiv. Dokumentation' as are all translations of quotes from *Jahresbericht der Bundesregierung*.

In the case of references to reports in the annual and bi-annual publication *Sowjetunion*, edited and published by the Bundesinstitut für ostwissenschaftliche und internationale Studien, references have initially been given in full and thereafter for the sake of clarity restricted to individual author and title and date of publication. References to *Jahresbericht der Bundesregierung* have in every case been given in full.

Chronology

(Chronology lists only those main events either mentioned in the study or of immediate relevance to it. After 1982, the chronology provides a less exhaustive but more descriptive list of events and is intended for orientation purposes only.)

6 May 1974	Willy Brandt resigns as Chancellor
16 May 1974	Helmut Schmidt becomes Chancellor at the head of the SPD/FDP coalition with Hans-Dietrich Genscher as Foreign Minister
9 August 1974	President Nixon resigns. Vice-President Ford sworn in as President of USA
28–31 October 1974	Helmut Schmidt visits Moscow
14 January 1975	USSR rejects trade/credit agreement with USA because of the Jackson–Vanik Amendment
28 July 1975	Summit in Helsinki of Conference on Security and Co-operation in Europe
2 November 1976	Jimmy Carter elected President of USA
28 October 1977	Helmut Schmidt gives Alastair Buchan Memorial Lecture to IISS, London, pointing to the West's security gap in the medium range nuclear missiles area
4–7 May 1978	The Second Official Visit by Soviet Party Leader and Head of State L. I. Brezhnev to the FRG
18 June 1979	SALT II Agreement signed by Carter and Brezhnev in Vienna
21–24 November 1979	Foreign Minister Gromyko visits Bonn
12 December 1979	NATO double-track decision taken
24 December 1979	First wave of Soviet troops begins to arrive in Afghanistan

30 June – 1 July 1980	Helmut Schmidt visits Moscow
19 July – 3 August 1980	FRG joins US boycott of Moscow Olympic Games
17 October – 17 November 1980	First round of talks in Geneva between the USSR and the USA on the limitation in Europe of medium-range nuclear weapons
4 November 1980	Ronald Reagan elected President of the USA
1–2 April 1981	Foreign Ministers Gromyko and Genscher meet in Moscow
22–25 November 1981	The Third Official Visit by Soviet Party Leader and the Head of State L. I. Brezhnev to the FRG
30 November 1981	Talks begin in Geneva between the USSR and the USA on the limitation in Europe of medium-range nuclear weapons
11–13 December 1981	Helmut Schmidt visits the GDR
13 December 1981	Martial Law declared in Poland
1 October 1982	Helmut Schmidt loses his office as Chancellor through a constructive vote of no confidence
10 November 1982	Death of Brezhnev
12 November 1982	Yu. V. Andropov becomes General Secretary of the Central Committee of the CPSU
6 March 1983	Election of Chancellor Helmut Kohl at the head of the CDU/CSU/FDP coalition, with Hans-Dietrich Genscher as Foreign Minister
5 July 1983	Summit meeting between Helmut Kohl and Yu. V. Andropov in Moscow, the first meeting between Andropov and a Western leader
22 December 1983	Federal Government ratifies the decision to install 108 Pershing II missiles and 96 cruise missiles
13 February 1984	K. U. Chernenko becomes General Secretary of the Central Committee of the CPSU
May 1984	Soviet Union begins 'revanchism campaign'
11 March 1985	M. S. Gorbachev becomes General Secretary of the Central Committee of the CPSU
20–22 July 1986	Genscher visits Moscow. Both sides agree to open a new page in relations

27 October 1986	Kohl gives an interview linking the public relations abilities of Gorbachev with those of Nazi propaganda minister Goebbels
6–11 July 1987	State visit of Federal President Richard von Weizsäcker to the USSR
7–11 September 1987	SED General Secretary Honecker visits the FRG
8 December 1987	US–Soviet INF treaty signed
17–19 January 1988	Foreign Minister Shevardnadze visits the FRG, marking a new dynamic phase in FRG–USSR relations
24–27 October 1988	Helmut Kohl makes an official visit to Moscow with the aim of beginning a new future-orientated chapter in FRG–USSR relations
20 January 1989	George Bush sworn into office as President of the United States
May 1989	Hungary begins to dismantle its border with Austria
12–15 June 1989	M. S. Gorbachev makes an official visit to the FRG, the first Soviet leader to do so since the Brezhnev visit in 1981
10 September 1989	Hungary opens its border with Austria
18 October 1989	Honecker resigns
4 November 1989	Czechoslovakia opens its border with the FRG – mass exodus of GDR citizens begins
7 November 1989	East German government resigns, followed twenty-four hours later by the East German Politburo
9 November 1989	GDR declares all citizens can leave East Germany for visiting purposes through all crossing points in the Berlin Wall and the border with West Germany
28 November 1989	Kohl presents ten point programme for overcoming the division of Germany and Europe to the Federal Parliament in Bonn
10–11 February 1990	Kohl and Genscher pay lightning weekend visit to Moscow which, after breakthrough in talks, results in the Soviet Union giving the go-ahead for German reunification later in the year

5 May 1990	First 'two plus four' meeting
21 June 1990	GDR and FRG give formal recognition to the post war border between Germany and Poland
2 July 1990	FRG and GDR ratify treaty introducing monetary union
14–16 July 1990	Kohl visits Moscow, and Stavropol and Zheleznovodsk in the Caucasus. At the end of the visit the announcement is made that the last significant obstacles to reunifying Germany by the end of the year have been removed; eight point reunification plan is agreed
31 August 1990	FRG and GDR sign political unification treaty
12 September 1990	'Treaty on the Final Settlement with Respect to Germany' is signed by the foreign ministers of the FRG and the GDR and the four wartime allies Britain, the United States, France and the Soviet Union
13 September 1990	FRG and USSR sign 'Treaty on Good Neighbourliness, Partnership and Co-operation' in Moscow
24 September 1990	East Germany leaves the Warsaw Pact
3 October 1990	Germany is reunited, with Chancellor Kohl becoming the first all-German Chancellor since the end of the Second World War in 1945

Introduction

This study is an examination of FRG–USSR political relations between 1974 and 1982. The study concentrates on the West German side of FRG–USSR relations in the 'follow-on' period to the innovatory 'treaty' period of Ostpolitik. It was a period when the overall climate of détente began to deteriorate, culminating in the Afghanistan crisis.

The study is chiefly grounded on the West German side of FRG–USSR relations, though chapter 7 is a partial exception where events after 1982 are dealt with and where the focus inevitably shifts to the USSR.

Three main types of sources are used in the study: interviews with West German government and party officials; West German official public documents; and West German, British, United States, and French literature and press sources. No interviews of Soviet officials were conducted, nor were original Soviet sources used. However, where the Soviet side is brought in, the author has striven to produce as accurate a picture as possible using Western sources (particularly those having access to Eastern sources not open to the author)[1] and interviews with West German government and party officials.

With regard to the reliability of public statements made by the Chancellor during this period, Schmidt is one of those politicians who seem to put 'a lot of themselves' into their speeches and his speeches are generally acknowledged to be very valuable and informative. Certainly Chancellor Schmidt is very much associated with the terms *Berechenbarkeit, Glaubwürdigkeit, Stetigkeit,* and *Vorhersehbarkeit* ('calculability', 'credibility', 'constancy', and 'predictability'). Furthermore, even if Schmidt – as he surely did – spoke in public with an eye to creating a certain effect, there is a limit to how far any political figure required to operate in private and in public can keep to two entirely different 'sets of books', i.e. the private 'real' ideas and opinions of the politician, if he has any – as Schmidt certainly had – keep on breaking through his public discourses. A well-known contemporary instance of this is Kissinger.[2]

FRG government and party officials were, when interviewed, generally reluctant to discuss German–German relations in the context of FRG–USSR relations (see pp. 63, 94–5) and although Günter Gaus and Klaus Bölling, the FRG's Permanent Representatives in East Berlin during the 1974–82 period, have both published books on their terms of office (see bibliography), that of Günter Gaus is not, as he himself states, the sort of memoir in which he exhaustively traces such aspects as the development of negotiations.[3] More frequent use of the single source, Klaus Bölling, has been made therefore in chapter 4 than would normally have been the case and a certain reliance has had to be put on his statements. However, the author took the precaution of sending a draft of chapter 4 to the FRG Foreign Office, inviting comments, thus balancing out any potential over-reliance on Klaus Bölling.

The survey of FRG–USSR relations in this study is a broad range one, focussing in detail on four main subject areas: ethnic Germans; Berlin; the Federal Republic of Germany's relations with the German Democratic Republic; INF, Afghanistan and the post-Afghanistan period. The study examines each of the four topics in the context of FRG–USSR relations and the major issues which occurred. A short treatment only of FRG–USSR economic relations is presented in two appendices (A and B) summarising the main points which the author wishes to make and giving essential background information as it pertains to this study, as there has already been a major study in bilateral economic relations.[4] Appendix C consists of a number of extracts, made by the author, from the official FRG document *Aspekte der Friedenspolitik: Argumente zum Doppelbeschluss des Nordatlantischen Bündnisses*, which add up to an official, declaratory version of what FRG foreign policy was in the early 1980s.

Chapter 1 is aimed at putting the study into context. It provides a summarised account of events after the Second World War as they related to FRG–USSR political relations – the division of Germany; the descent of the Iron Curtain; the Cold War; the new Ostpolitik; the beginnings of disillusionment with Ostpolitik and détente; the changeover from Brandt to Schmidt.

Family reunification and emigration rights for ethnic Germans living in the Soviet Union is an issue to which the FRG attaches great importance and one which is given high priority. Indeed, the situation of the ethnic Germans in Eastern Europe, including the Soviet Union, and their wish to emigrate has been one of the major planks of the FRG governments' Ostpolitik right from the sixties to today, regardless of who was in power. This issue has been brought up time and again in the CSCE process and at all CSCE follow-up meetings. Chapter 2 gives an overview of the background to the problem, including a brief history of the ethnic Germans, their situation as of 1982 in the Soviet Union and their demands for emigration. It deals with the bilateral issue of emigration and examines the reasons for the decline in emigration in the five years from its high-point in 1976/7.

Despite the fact that the international situation of Berlin was one of comparative calm after 1972 – the Quadripartite Agreement having regulated the most troublesome questions and having brought great practical improvements to the city – Berlin was a major stumbling block in FRG–Soviet relations until 1978 and the summit meeting between Brezhnev and Chancellor Schmidt. The chapter on Berlin, therefore, examines the reasons why the city remained a serious bilateral problem through an introduction to the background and provisions of the Quadripartite Agreement, the differing Soviet, Allied and FRG positions on Berlin, and the early history of its implementation. It analyses the conflict after 1973 and Schmidt's 'breakthrough' in 1978 and its consequences.

Given the divided state of the nation, FRG–GDR relations were of prime importance to the FRG. Chapter 4 firstly examines three areas: the triangle FRG–USSR–GDR; the FRG's policy towards the GDR; the question as to whether German–German relations were demoted during the Schmidt period (a view that was held both in Bonn and in certain circles of the GDR). The second part of the chapter traces FRG–GDR relations from 1974 to 1982 in the context of the Soviet dimension.

Chapter 5 deals with FRG–USSR relations during the very difficult, 'crisis' period of East–West relations. It examines the FRG's position after the Soviet forces' entry into Afghanistan; the validity of the widely held view that Chancellor Schmidt performed a mediator/interpreter role between East and West; the FRG and the NATO double-track decision; and FRG–USSR relations in the immediate and post-Afghanistan period. Not much space is given to the Polish crisis as FRG–USSR relations were relatively unaffected by it and it did not achieve the significance that the Soviet intervention in Afghanistan did. The sharp deterioration in East–West relations occurred in 1979/80, after the NATO double-track decision and the Soviet intervention in Afghanistan. The chapter therefore concentrates on the FRG's position and the state of FRG–Soviet relations after Afghanistan and the very important visit which Chancellor Schmidt made to Moscow in June 1980 when he was able to obtain Soviet agreement to go to the negotiating table, thus getting the superpower dialogue going again.

In her assessment of FRG–USSR political relations the author examines the view that has been held both in the FRG and abroad that during the Schmidt period Ostpolitik was demoted, that Ostpolitik and FRG–Soviet relations began to stagnate and that the great 'visionary' period of Brandt was over. It assesses the concrete achievements and disappointments in FRG–USSR relations during the 1974–82 period; the extent to which the FRG was able to influence the Soviet Union; and the extent to which the FRG modified its foreign policy out of consideration for (or as a result of Soviet pressure arising from) her bilateral relations with the Soviet Union. The chapter is concluded with a summary of the Federal Republic of Germany's political relations with the USSR, 1974–82.

Chapter 7 is also aimed at putting the study into modern context. It provides a summary analysis of FRG–USSR political relations after 1982 and the events leading up to the historic reunification of Germany. The date of reunification, 3 October 1990, has been chosen as the natural cut-off point for this study. Although many aspects will remain constant, FRG–USSR political relations are obviously entering a new era and one in which the third element, the GDR, no longer exists.

1 The Second World War and its aftermath, 1945–1974

Allied wartime co-operation was born out of the need to defeat the Axis Powers, Anglo-Russian military co-operation beginning in June 1941 when Germany attacked the Soviet Union, and the United States becoming the Soviet Union's ally after the attack on Pearl Harbor. Internal strains were present based on mutual mistrust and Allied differences over the nature and form of a postwar Germany and Europe. These differences, however, were largely subdued and concealed due both to the need to defeat the Axis and to reach Allied agreement.

The Allies met three times at the conferences of Teheran (28 November–1 December 1943), Yalta (4–11 February 1945) and Potsdam (17 July–2 August 1945) which resulted in the following territorial provisions: the eastern part of Poland was given to the Soviet Union; East Prussia was divided up and the southern half put under Polish, the northern area under Soviet administration; and the Oder-Neisse river was declared the provisional border between Germany and Poland pending a peace treaty and final settlement. The Oder-Neisse border meant the loss of German territory to Poland comprising Danzig, large parts of Silesia and Pomerania, and part of Brandenburg and entailed the expelling of 7 million Germans from these areas.

The remainder of Germany was temporarily, i.e. pending a final settlement, divided into four zones of military occupation, and allotted to the Allies, including France. A Four Power control council, the Allied Control Council, was set up to co-ordinate affairs during the occupation period. Berlin, an enclave within the Soviet zone of occupation, was set aside as a special area and divided into four zones under joint administration.

It was not long before East–West tensions, previously for the most part concealed, began to surface. The Allied Control Council was unable to fulfil its intended function. The Eastern and Western zones began to develop along separate lines with the foundations for a communist system being laid in the Soviet zone and moves towards self-government in the three Western zones. In May 1947 the Western zones were amalgamated into the 'Bizone'. By 1947 Europe itself had split into two armed camps leading Churchill to speak of an 'Iron Curtain' dividing East and West. Within two years a state of Cold War existed between the Soviet Union and its wartime allies.

In March 1948 the Soviet Union withdrew from the Allied Control Council and the Berlin Kommandatura, thus bringing to an end formal Four Power co-operation in Germany. In June 1948 a single currency for the Western sectors was introduced. The Cold War was intensified with the Soviet blockade of Berlin aimed at forcing the Western Allies out of the city. It had been preceded by Soviet efforts throughout 1947 to restrict access to the city but on 24 June 1948 all land routes into West Berlin were closed by Soviet troops. The blockade was lifted in April 1949 as a result of the successful Allied airlift to the city. It was, however, a precursor of the future disputes and endless wrangles over the status of Berlin and of the building of the Berlin Wall in 1961.

In September 1949 the three Western Powers handed over their zones to the newly created Federal Republic of Germany under the leadership of Konrad Adenauer. Its provisional constitution, the 'Fundamental Law' (*Grundgesetz*), was designed to include the whole German nation, including the Eastern zone. The Soviet Union proclaimed the German Democratic Republic in October 1949. The preamble to the constitution called upon the whole German people to unite through free self-determination.

On 10 March 1952 Stalin proposed in his famous peace note that there should be a peace treaty with a sovereign, reunited, rearmed but neutralised Germany. The proposal was rejected by Adenauer and the Western Powers. Up until 1959 there were a number of Four Power meetings which were unsuccessful in finding an overall peace settlement for Germany.

Despite reunification being the declared aim of the FRG's constitution, Adenauer's first priority was integration with the West. Integration with the West provided the FRG with international rehabilitation, economic recovery and security. FRG policy towards the Eastern Bloc under Adenauer consisted of the following:

claims on territory in the Eastern Bloc, i.e. GDR; Oder-Neisse territories;

solution of the 'German Question' only through free and democratic elections in the GDR;

refusal of Bonn to recognise the legality of the communist government in the GDR and in the other Warsaw Pact countries (except the Soviet Union), and the insistence on Bonn's sole right to speak for all Germans (*Alleinvertretungsrecht*);

usage of the term 'East Zone' (*Ostzone*) for the GDR;

insistence that any step towards reducing tensions in Europe must be accompanied by progress towards reunification;

the Hallstein Doctrine of breaking off diplomatic relations with any state which recognised the GDR. The aim was to isolate the GDR in the hope that the Soviet Union would find it too much of a burden.

Normalisation of relations was regarded as a consequence of the resolution of the German problem. Adenauer's 'policy of strength' based on the position that only a strong West would cause the Soviets to capitulate was supported by the Western Allies – at least in words.

Adenauer did, however, make some gestures towards the Soviet Union. In 1955 he visited Moscow and diplomatic relations were established. In 1958 a trade agreement between the FRG and the USSR was signed and a Soviet trade mission was opened in the FRG. An agreement on the exchange of culture, science and technology was signed for the period 1959–60.

After the FRG became a member of NATO in 1955, the Soviet Union insisted that the only acceptable basis for a solution to Europe was the recognition of the GDR. The Soviet Union saw the FRG as revanchist and used the 'FRG threat' to secure hegemony over the Eastern Bloc.

In November 1958 the second Berlin crisis occurred when Khrushchev threatened that the Soviet Union would sign a separate peace treaty with East Germany unless his demands were met. These were the withdrawal of all foreign troops from Berlin on the grounds that the Potsdam agreement was no longer in operation and that access to the city should be controlled by the East German government. The Americans held out and the issue eventually was left unresolved. In 1961 the Berlin Wall was erected. Up until that date an estimated 2 million East Germans had used West Berlin to escape to the West.

The Berlin Wall signalled the end of Adenauer's policy of strength, i.e. the position that a policy of strength would lead to the reunification of Germany. Indeed, it seemed that the policy of strength had resulted in a threat to the very substance of the nation. Up until this point the divided East and West Germans had at least been able to meet in Berlin. Now this opportunity of maintaining the *Zusammengehörigkeitsgefühl* (the sense of belonging together) had been closed off.

Demands began to be made in West Germany for a more active foreign policy.

The world background to the German Question had also changed. With the new administration came a change in American policy with the United States pursuing a policy of détente *vis-à-vis* the Soviet Union. The emphasis was on a global dialogue with Moscow centring on arms control negotiations. There was a change in Soviet policy too, with the Soviet Union attempting to seek a relaxation of tensions with the West. President Kennedy, newly elected, became increasingly impatient with Adenauer's negative position towards the East. With the United States and France pursuing policies of *rapprochement* and bridge-building with Eastern Europe, Bonn could not afford to remain a cold war island and risk isolating itself from its Western partners with the possibility that political accommodation might be achieved at the expense of the FRG's interests.

Adenauer resigned in 1963 and was replaced by Ludwig Erhard whose foreign minister, Gerhand Schröder, was more Atlanticist in his foreign policy than Adenauer. Schröder began to seek a 'new opening' to the East. It was, however, below the level of official recognition and was intended to isolate the GDR from her East European allies and in fact led to them imposing a 'reverse' Hallstein Doctrine of official relations in return for recognition of the GDR. Nevertheless, trade missions were established in several Eastern Block states. Schröder's 'policy of movement' advocated strengthened relations in all areas from trade to sport. A general revision of policy, however, and even further measures of relaxation were blocked by opposition within the CDU (Christian Democratic Union)/CSU (Christian Social Union). Nevertheless, it did lay the groundwork for the new Ostpolitik of the Grand Coalition.

On 25 March 1966 Erhard began a 'peace initiative'. Diplomatic notes were sent to 115 states, including those of Western Europe, proposing a reduction in nuclear weapons; an agreement to prevent the transfer of nuclear weapons to non-nuclear powers; and a declaration of the renunciation of the use of force between the states of Eastern and Western Europe in international disputes. The aim was to increase mutual trust by tackling the less important causes of tension first and then the larger ones. Erhard still insisted, however, on the recognition of the borders of 31 December 1937. The Soviet reaction was that this was an increased degree of FRG revanchism. In April 1966 the Soviet Union made a number of security suggestions on a European basis which excluded the USA.

In December 1966 the Grand Coalition (CDU/CSU and SPD (Social Democratic Party)), under the Chancellorship of Kurt Kiesinger and with Willy Brandt as Foreign Minister, announced a 'new Ostpolitik' – normalisation of relations was to be no longer considered as a consequence but as a pre-condition for lasting détente. However, the FRG believed that the Soviet Union was still the main stumbling block in achieving the reduction of tension and also the CDU had strong reservations about negotiating with East Berlin. This meant that the FRG started with the 'easier' states such as Romania and Yugoslavia, circumventing the GDR and Moscow, and advocating a policy of 'small steps'. The Federal Republic established diplomatic relations with Romania (January 1967) and Yugoslavia (January 1968).

The Soviet intervention in Czechoslovakia showed how risky such a policy was; one reason for Moscow's action was ostensibly that after Yugoslavia and Romania, Bonn was now turning its attention to Prague. It became clear that anyone seeking fundamental changes in Eastern Europe would have to go through Moscow first.

In 1969 the SPD/FDP (Free Democratic Party) coalition government was formed with Brandt as Chancellor and Walter Scheel as Foreign Minister. The new government accorded reunification the place in their concept of Ostpolitik which they felt reflected reality, i.e. reunification still remained an aim but its realisation was without any prospect in the immediate future. The present aim, therefore, was to work towards a *modus vivendi* which would prevent the further drifting apart of the divided German people and keep the way open for a fair solution to the problem of the divided nation in a future European peace settlement. The emphasis was to be shifted from reunification to the easing of human problems (*menschliche Erleichterungen*) and to overcoming the border with the GDR by recognising it. Brandt took the view that although the existence of the two German states should be acknowledged, the FRG could never accept the GDR as a foreign nation. He put forward the theory of two states within the single German nation (*zwei Staaten deutscher Nation*) who therefore should have a special relationship.

The two main elements of the Federal Republic's Ostpolitik were the renunciation of the use of force towards the Soviet Union and the East European states coupled with the agreement of a *modus vivendi* for disputes which were at that time unsolvable, especially those relating to the European borders. Its starting point was the *de facto* recognition (but not in terms of international law) of the status quo. Brandt took the view that the existing facts must be taken as the starting point if they were to be changed. He felt that only uncontested borders might one day become permeable and only regimes whose sovereignty was unchallenged might become capable of extending co-operation. His policy was one of change through *rapprochement* (Egon Bahr's *Wandel durch Annäherung*). At the same time Brandt took care to stress his commitment to and integration with the West.

The FRG realised that Moscow was the key to relations with Eastern Europe and with East Germany and therefore to its main aim of reconciliation with East Germany. Negotiations were therefore begun with the Soviet Union which resulted in the signature on 12 August 1970 of the Treaty between the Federal Republic of Germany and the Union of Soviet Socialist Republics (Moscow Treaty).

Ratification of the treaty was made dependent by the FRG on a satisfactory Berlin agreement being reached, and in September 1971 the Four Powers concluded the Quadripartite Agreement on Berlin which, though it stated that West Berlin was not a constituent part of the FRG, confirmed West Berlin's ties to the Federal Republic and guaranteed Western access rights to West Berlin. It also provided the right, withheld since 1961, for West Berliners to visit East Berlin and the GDR. Details of the Agreement, for example those concerning transit traffic etc., were left to negotiations between the FRG and the GDR governments and the West Berlin Senate and the GDR government.

On 21 December 1972 the Treaty on the Basis of Relations between the Federal Republic of Germany and the German Democratic Republic (Basic Treaty) was signed. In the agreement both states proceeded on the assumption that neither could represent the other internationally or act in its name (thus abandoning a position which the FRG had held since Adenauer), though a letter of interpretation from the Federal government was sent to the German Democratic government stating that the Treaty did not conflict with the political aim of the FRG to work for a state of peace in Europe in which the German nation could regain its unity through free self-determination. For its part, although it continued to maintain it was one, the GDR gave up its insistence on being explicitly recognised as a foreign state in international law. The exchange of permanent representatives, rather than ambassadors, was provided for in one of the appendices.

Treaties normalising relations were signed with Poland (7 December 1970), Czechoslovakia (11 December 1973), and on 21 December 1973 agreements were signed establishing diplomatic relations with Bulgaria and Hungary.

The Moscow Treaty thus laid a solid foundation for the development of relations between the FRG and the USSR and for détente in Europe. It paved the way for a regulation of the FRG's relations with the GDR and the other East European countries. It constituted one of the pre-conditions for the conclusion of the Quadripartite Agreement on Berlin which regulated the most troublesome questions connected with the city. Ultimately it also helped pave the way for the Conference on Security and Co-operation in Europe in Helsinki in 1975.

On 16 May 1974 Schmidt became Chancellor at the head of the SPD/FDP coalition with Hans-Dietrich Genscher as Foreign Minister. The preceding Brandt period had been both dramatic and fast-moving. It was characterised by a certain amount of euphoria and high expectations of détente on the West German side – feelings which were also shared by the Soviets and Americans.[1] Leading FRG politicians and commentators saw the conclusion of the Ostpolitik treaties as the opening of a new chapter or turning point which justified great hopes for a fundamental improvement in atmosphere and co-operation.[2]

However, already in 1973 difficulties and disappointments had begun to appear. Problems arose, for example, over the implementation of the Quadripartite Agreement; the GDR embarked on its policy of *Abgrenzung* or de-limitation whereby contacts between East and West German citizens were discouraged – in November 1973 the GDR government, fully supported by the USSR, suddenly doubled the minimum exchange rate for Western visitors to the GDR and East Berlin, which represented a violation of the Basic Treaty. Furthermore, by the time Schmidt took office in 1974 he was faced with pressing problems caused by the world economic crisis, thus influencing the FRG's political priorities. References to a 'stagnation' in Ostpolitik and a 'cooling-off' of Soviet German relations began to appear in the West German press.[3] Moreover, as early as the autumn of 1973, the beginnings of the process of disillusionment in détente on the American and Soviet sides had started to emerge,[4] gradually leading during the middle seventies to an overall climate less conducive to the FRG's Ostpolitik than that of the Brandt period.

Nevertheless, Chancellor Brandt constructed the framework for future German–Soviet relations and his successor, Chancellor Schmidt, saw his role as one of concretely filling out this framework through detailed spadework.[5] As the government official, Paul Frank, said of the FRG's relations with the USSR,

> The Federal Republic of Germany cannot do without striving for good relations with the Soviet Union. A country in the middle of Europe with more neighbours than any other European country, is

dependent on being friendly with its neighbours on all sides. In this way she helps to create a balance of good relations which in hard times can have a steadfast and in favourable constellations an accelerating effect. It should also be borne in mind with regard to relations with the Soviet Union, that the Soviet Union is de facto the determinative force in Eastern Europe.[6]

2   Ethnic Germans

Humanitarian considerations have always been of great importance in the FRG's Ostpolitik in general, the process of normalisation of relations with the East and in its relations with the Soviet Union in particular. The state of German–Soviet relations, apart from playing a key role in humanitarian improvements in FRG–GDR relations and the West Berlin situation, also affected a specific bilateral problem between the FRG and the USSR – that of emigration rights for Germans living in the Soviet Union. This was true as long ago as 1955 when the establishment of diplomatic relations between the FRG and the Soviet Union made the solving of humanitarian problems easier. During his visit to Moscow, as well as securing the release of German prisoners of war held in the Soviet Union, Chancellor Adenauer was also able to obtain agreement in principle to return some 130,000 civilians of German origin who had applied to the Federal authorities for repatriation.

Family reunification and emigration rights for ethnic Germans living in the Soviet Union is an issue to which the Federal Republic attaches great importance and one which is given a high priority. Indeed, emigration rights for ethnic Germans living in Eastern Europe in general was part of the FRG's price for détente with the USSR. However, the numbers of ethnic Germans allowed to leave the Soviet Union have in the past been small proportional to their overall population size, with a marked decline between 1977 and 1983. There were several underlying reasons for this but the Soviet response must also be seen against the background of Soviet nationality problems in general and the implications of what was at stake for that country (see pp. 27–31).

In geographical area the third largest state in the world, with a population of more than 262 million,[1] the Soviet Union is not, however, a homogeneous national unit. The Soviet state is made up of well over 100 larger and smaller ethnic groups.

Russians, although numerically the largest ethnic group, amount to only about a half of the total population. According to the 1979 census, after the Russians there come twenty-one other major ethnic groups with more than a million members, the largest of these being the Ukrainians (42.3 million members) and the Uzbeks (12.5 million members). The other ethnic groups are listed as totalling 9.8 million;[2] some of these are tribal fragments numbering only a few thousand. The range of nationalities and languages is tremendous and all these groups have their own distinct ethnic cultures and traditions, often linking them to ethnic groups and nationalities outside the Soviet Union. Many of the ethnic groups have their own territorial units, the largest being the Russian Soviet Federal Socialist Republic. Fourteen of the other large ethnic minorities also have their own union republics. Lesser national territorial units are the autonomous republics (of which there are twenty), autonomous regions (of which there are eight), and autonomous national areas (of which there are ten).

The official Soviet position on nationality policy until recently was that for a temporary period of transition ethnic languages and cultures were to be maintained by the formula 'national in form, socialist in content', whereby the ultimate, long-term aim was the emergence of a homogeneous single communist Soviet nation, free of nationalist and ethnic characteristics. Officially this also applied to the dominant Russian ethnic group. However, in practice over the years Soviet nationality policy has not been consistent: on the one hand there have been phases, particularly in the 1920s, of toleration and even encouragement of national independence through the allowing of linguistic and cultural autonomy, and on the other hand there have been restrictive periods where the notion of the gradual formation of a homogeneous Soviet nation was energetically pursued. There have been repeated waves of russification of the ethnic minorities including one which began in the late 1970s and still persisted in 1982. This was expressed above all in the educational system. For example, obligatory teaching of Russian was introduced at the kindergarten level and attempts were made to replace national native languages with Russian as the teaching language in colleges and universities.

There are several different broad types of nationalist dissent in the Soviet Union. One is nationalism within the Baltic, Georgian, Armenian and Ukrainian Union Republics expressed in the past mainly through protests against the denationising effects of the Soviet policy of a merging of nationalities which they feared would lead in practice to russification. Demands have been made since the 1950s for greater linguistic, cultural, religious, economic and sometimes political autonomy, wherein the Catholic Lithuanians, Georgians and the Ukrainians are the strongest and most activist. The Soviet authorities have taken a very serious view of Georgian and Ukrainian nationalist dissent and some of the radical political dissidents have been executed – the only political dissidents to suffer that fate in the post-Stalin period. Another form of dissent is by Russian nationalists who have become a considerable force since the late 1960s. Yet another group are the Crimean Tartars. Since the late 1950s they have pressed for the right to return to their homeland on the Crimea from where they were deported during the Second World War. The ethnic Germans and the Jews present a different kind of problem to the Soviet authorities: their demands are to unite with their fellow countrymen outside the Soviet Union.

One potentially very grave problem for the Soviet authorities is that posed by the Muslims of Central Asia. It would seem that there is quite strong, though mainly hidden, dissent among the Muslims; also resentment felt by them towards the large and rising numbers of immigrants from the European parts of the Soviet Union. However, the real threat lies in the future: in general the Muslims are not well assimilated and their birth rate is very high (it is expected that by the year 2000 every second child born in the Soviet Union will be of Muslim origin).[3] Coupled with the recent religious revival and developments in Iran and Afghanistan, the 'Muslim problem' has serious implications.

Western scholarly opinion has differed on the actual extent and depth of nationalist feeling and tension and the threat the ethnic groups pose to the Soviet Union.[4] However, the *potential* for these problems to present a serious threat to, or even the break up of, the Soviet Union is obviously there, thus making the issue of ethnic minorities an extremely sensitive one to the Soviet authorities and one where much is at stake. Mikhail Suslov singled out ethnic antagonism as one of the three major conflicts standing in the way of the building of communism in the Soviet Union.[5] In 1972 a CPSU Central Committee resolution recognised the national problem as being 'one of the critical sectors in the struggle between socialism and capitalism'.[6] And in his report to the 26th Congress of the CPSU in 1981, Brezhnev said, 'The unity of Soviet nations is now closer than ever. This does not mean, of course, that all questions of nationality relations have been solved already. The degree of development of such a large multinational state as ours gives rise to many problems which demand the Party's close attention.'[7]

As far as emigration was concerned, the Soviet Union, then, was for most of the postwar period in a reverse position to that of the FRG: the FRG was a national unit but one which had for various reasons, such as the Second World War and its aftermath, parts of it so to speak 'missing', whereas the Soviet Union was not a national unit but a state which was made up of a number of national units. The Soviet Union will, we can assume, seek to limit centrifugal nationalist tendencies. Soviet reluctance to grant generous emigration rights to the ethnic Germans stemmed, therefore, not just from Moscow's objections in principle to the idea of free movement for Soviet citizens nor from the fear that official acknowledgement and recognition of demands for emigration could be construed as official admission of the failure of the socialist system. It also stemmed very much from internal reasons and the price it feared it could have to pay for such a policy. Maintaining its coalition of minorities had to be a prime objective for the Soviet Union. Special treatment for the Germans over emigration would presumably have had to mean special treatment of the Jews. Privileges for these two groups of minorities would have meant demands for privileges (if of another kind) from other ethnic groups. At the least it could have undermined the credibility of the policy of the emergence of a homo-geneous single Soviet nation and at worst the risks could have been incalculable.

Ethnic Germans

Numbering over 2 million, the ethnic Germans living in the Soviet Union in 1982 made up the largest German ethnic group in the Eastern Bloc. Despite this, they were the least well known of all the ethnic groups to the German public. The Germans in Poland (over 1 million), Czechoslovakia (about 55,000), Hungary (220,000) and par-ticularly those in Romania (about 350,000)[8] were in every respect better known and more in the public eye. Historically, the lot of the ethnic Germans in the Soviet Union was harder than that of Germans living in other East European countries and in comparison they had the least opportunity to preserve their German identity.

The Germans in the Soviet Union are made up of several different groups. By far the numerically largest group are the old-established settlers (*altansässige Russlanddeutsche*), mainly descendants of German immigrants from the 1764–1842 period – the so-called Catherine

Germans (*Katharinendeutsche*) who had settled in different areas of Russia with concentrations in the Ukraine, the Crimean Peninsula, the Black Sea and the middle Volga. The outbreak of war with Germany in 1941 led to these Germans being forcibly removed by the Soviet authorities to the interior of the Soviet Union. Some managed to avoid this and remained in the areas of the Soviet Union that were occupied by the German armed forces and some of these were granted German nationality through collective naturalisation (Ukraine Decree). Before the retreat of the German troops in 1943, many of these ethnic Germans had resettled in what was then Warthegau and had become naturalised through individual granting of German citizenship. Neither type of naturalisation was recognised by the Soviet Union after the end of the war. These groups of ethnic Germans are termed administrative resettlers (*Administrativumsiedler*). Further groups are German nationals (*Reichsdeutsche*) from Northern East Prussia, Memel Germans (after the war the Soviet Union acquired both Northern East Prussia and Memelland from Germany) and also the treaty resettlers (*Vertragsumsiedler*) – those Germans from Estonia, Latvia, Lithuania, Galicia, Volhynia, Bessarabia and Northern Bukovinia who resettled in Germany in the years 1939–41 under German–Soviet agreements, became naturalised as German nationals but through the war and its aftermath ended up in the Soviet Union.

After the ending of the Second World War, the Soviet Union took the view that anyone who was born on state territory belonging to the Soviet Union was to be regarded as a Soviet citizen and must return to his native country. This meant that not only the administrative resettlers but also the treaty resettlers and the Memel Germans were brought into the Soviet Union from the Soviet occupied zone of Germany and interned there against their will. To some extent after the end of the war this 'repatriation' was carried out in the Western occupied zones with the help of Soviet repatriation commissions and in some cases even in countries of Western Europe. These forcible measures meant that a great many families were cruelly separated. The whole operation caused much distress and suffering.

The situation of the ethnic Germans living in the Soviet Union since the Second World War appears generally not to have been good: on the whole they have lived under a repressive regime.[9] Arraigned as spies by Stalin, they were driven from their Autonomous Soviet Republic on the Volga during the war and deported to Siberia and Central Asia. Ethnic Germans living in other parts of the Soviet Union received the same treatment. Their Autonomous Republic was dissolved

Table 1. *Ethnic Germans living in the Union Republics RSFSR,
Kazakhstan, Kirgizia and Tadzhikistan, 1979*

Union Republic	Total population	Ethnic Germans
RSFSR	137,409,921	790,762
Kazakhstan	14,684,283	900,207
Kirgizia	3,522,832	101,057
Tadzhikistan	3,806,220	38,853

Source: Oschlies, *Sowjetunion 1982/3*, p. 104.

and they have never been allowed to return there. (The Autonomous
Soviet Socialist Republic of the Volga Germans had been established in
1924.) Although an 'amnesty' was brought into force on 17 September
1955 by the lifting of restrictions in their legal status, it was not until
1964 that the Soviet leadership admitted that the deportations had
been based on random accusations made during the personality cult of
Stalin.

The main body of ethnic Germans live in the Union Republics
RSFSR, Kazakhstan, Kirgizia and Tadzhikistan. According to the 1979
census, almost half were concentrated in Central Asiatic exile in
Kazakhstan. The rest lived scattered over the Soviet Union. Very few
lived in the capital Moscow.

Although in 1981 an ethnic German made it for the first time to the
post of Soviet minister – at the important ministry for the machine tool
industry, in fact – ethnic Germans have been as a rule excluded from
leading positions. The presence of ethnic Germans in central institutions of the Soviet Union has been extremely small. It was only in 1970
that two Germans were elected to the Supreme Soviet and in 1982
there were only two German deputies in the Soviet parliament. The
ethnic Germans were also poorly represented at the level of the Soviet
republics, though more strongly and in rising numbers at regional and
municipal level.

Shut out, as a rule, from leading positions, discriminated against in
education (it has happened that they were refused university places
for holding the wrong nationality) and poorly represented at central
and republic level, many ethnic Germans wanted to return to their
ancestral land, Germany. This lack of opportunity for integration and
identity with the system may have been reflected in the past low level
of actual commitment in the Communist Party. Estimates put it in 1982

at 15 party members per 1,000 members of the German ethnic group. This was an extremely low ratio, probably only undercut by that of the Poles in White Russia (5 per 1,000).[10]

Andreas Lorenz, who visited the ethnic Germans in Kazakhstan and published his report in *Der Spiegel* in 1982, found that many ethnic Germans were motivated less by material or family reasons to move to the West than out of fear of otherwise losing their German identity.[11] The German minority have indeed lacked sufficient opportunity to cultivate their language and culture in the way they had been able to in the German Autonomous Volga Republic up until 1941. Since the amnesty of 1955 the ethnic Germans formally have had all the constitutional minority rights, including the right of tuition in the mother-tongue, German. However, in practice this has been for several reasons available only in extremely restricted form. For one thing, whether by design or accident, native-speaking teachers of German and German books have not generally ended up in the German settlements. Such teachers have had to teach German as a foreign language in Russian schools and, although a modest amount of teaching material, textbooks and reading books have been available, German books have been most easily obtainable where hardly anyone could read them. In many schools where German was once taught as the mother-tongue, German has since only been taught as a foreign language. In fact in January 1982, the Landsmannschaft der Deutschen aus Russland (the organisation for ethnic Germans from the Soviet Union in West Germany) claimed that at that time there was not one German school for the 2 million Germans.[12] The Autonomous Soviet Socialist Republic of the Volga Germans by contrast had its own system of education with 400 schools and 5 establishments of higher education.

Very few German children are fluent in their mother-tongue, and adults, especially those without contact with their fellow Germans, speak mostly only Russian. The German language is gradually dying out. Wolf Oschlies, in his report in *Sowjetunion 82/83*, gave an estimate based on official Soviet figures for four Union Republics that in the 1980s the number of those not speaking German would rise to more than 50 per cent.[13] The German language has in the past been discriminated against in public. For example, the German language weekly *Neues Leben*, published in the Soviet Union for the German minority, stated in 1982 that German was almost never used in public and complained of the psychological effect this had on ethnic German children.[14]

Although some provision was, in fact, made to cater for the German minority – a few German newspapers, radio programmes – it was far from adequate. Ethnic German works of literature were published in Moscow but this was very small and books from the GDR could be obtained in small amounts. One German theatre existed in Kazakhstan but its opportunities to put on performances for all Germans in the Soviet Union were pretty limited. The religious groups of registered and non-registered congregations have had a big influence on the preservation of a national and national cultural identity. Since the early 1970s, these groups have enjoyed increasing state tolerance: registered congregations may erect churches, though registration has, however, sometimes been attached to conditions, for example, no public processions, and members of the congregation had to give an undertaking not to leave the Soviet Union. Apart from the churches, however, the Soviet German cultural 'supply' has been shockingly poor.

It seems, however, that the German identity will not be lost, despite the difficulties encountered (the national cultural opportunities are even scarcer in the towns than in the country communities) and the poor German language situation. A revival of national consciousness has been brought about by the ending of legal discrimination in 1955 and the rise of the emigration movement. Furthermore, recent research shows that the ethnic German identity is now founded on the commonly perceived lack of freedom, efficiency (*Tüchtigkeit*), and certain moral values (*Anständigkeit* – respectability) which ethnic Germans do not see as characteristic to the same extent of other Soviet nationalities.[15] This perception cannot be reduced by linguistic loss but rather enormously strengthened by access to education and social advancement.

According to the 1979 official Soviet census, there were 1,936,000 ethnic Germans living in the Soviet Union, 90,000 more than at the last census in 1970 when the figure was 1,846,000.[16] This figure, however, did not take into account the 20,000 ethnic Germans living in the Baltic republics who did not appear in the official statistics. Furthermore, official Soviet figures represented the minimum number of ethnic Germans. Whereas the nationality entry in a passport remained unchanged for life, at each census a citizen could opt for the nationality to which he or she subjectively felt that they belonged. As a result of decades of discrimination against the Germans as 'fascist' etc., the number of 'passport Germans' was probably still higher than the number of 'census Germans', though the discrepancy was certainly not as large as with earlier censuses with the rise in national conscious-

Table 2. *Ethnic Germans wishing to leave the Soviet Union, 1974–1982*

	Requests to leave
1974	53,422
1975	60,002
1976	61,978
1977	67,963
1978	72,370
1979	82,396
1980	88,179
1981	87,462
1982	87,065

ness in the interim. Out of a total of roughly 2 million ethnic Germans, one source at the end of the 1970s put the total, according to Western estimates, of those who wanted to leave at 200,000;[17] another in 1982 put the figure at about 100,000.[18] The German Red Cross gave the author the following table of people wishing to leave, pointing out that the table covered those requests to leave which had been made known to the German Red Cross either by those wishing to leave or by their relatives in a period of five years before the fixed day of 31 December of each year.[19]

Emigration

Since 1955 the Federal Government has made intensive efforts on behalf of those ethnic Germans who wish to leave the Soviet Union. Despite the agreement in principle that Adenauer obtained in Moscow that some 130,000 would be allowed to emigrate, the Soviet Union continued to be obstructive in the question of repatriation of German civilians. As was to be done later in 1970 with the treaty with Poland, the Federal Republic therefore linked concessions on their part to humanitarian questions. The realisation of a trade agreement, an agreement on economic-technical co-operation and an agreement on consular rights was made dependent on a satisfactory solution to the repatriation question. After almost ten months of tough negotiations this resulted in the German–Soviet agreement of 8 April 1958 on the repatriation of Germans. It was a verbal agreement as the Soviets refused treaty form. Only those who had possessed German nationality at the outbreak of the German–Soviet war on 21 June 1941 were entitled to repatriation. They were, in the main, German nationals from Northern East Prussia, the Memel Germans and the treaty resettlers. Special mention of the Memel Germans was made because in 1945 the Memel area had fallen to the Russians and the Memel Germans had been declared Soviet citizens. From the start of the negotiations, however, there were differing views between the two sides which had long-term consequences because the Soviet side introduced the problem of family reunification.

There was a marked increase in the numbers of ethnic Germans leaving the Soviet Union for the next three years but in the following ten years from 1961 to 1970 the number of resettlers was very small, often involving only a few hundred a year. There were only two years, 1966 and 1967, when the numbers were over 1,000. These were the result of the October 1965 Red Cross Conference held in Vienna which passed resolution No. 19 concerning family reunification which enabled the German Red Cross to make renewed efforts on behalf of the ethnic Germans.

The Treaty of Moscow between the Federal Republic of Germany and the USSR of 12 August 1970 led to a new and very obvious increase in the number of resettlers. During his October 1974 visit to Moscow, Chancellor Schmidt was informed by Brezhnev that the Soviet Union would keep to the then quota of 3,500–4,000 exit permits a year. In fact, in the years 1975–7 alone almost 25,000 ethnic Germans were able to leave the Soviet Union. Indeed, the Federal government's more 'reserved' policy on the issue of human rights (as opposed to President Carter's human rights campaign supported by the CDU/CSU) paid off in the seventies – reflected in the number of exit permits granted. With more than 40,000 exits for the period 1970–7 the ethnic Germans made up the largest emigration contingent from the Soviet Union after the Jews.

The emigration figures for ethnic Germans leaving the Soviet Union during the Social–Liberal coalition were much higher after CSCE than during the period before: between January 1970 and July 1975, 21,000 exit permits were issued by the Soviet authorities as opposed to 45,000 between the signing of the Final Act and April 1981.[20] Before Helsinki the problem of family contacts and family reunification had been mainly a bilateral issue. CSCE meant that for the first time it was addressed on a multilateral level. At Helsinki the West succeeded in getting the East European states to agree to the adoption of certain standards of conduct i.e., the declaration of their readiness to deal positively with the applications of persons for travel to visit members of their families and for family reunification. This had an important impact as it meant that any signatory state could refer to these principles and use them to assess the conduct of any other country. Any state could therefore censure governments for not having implemented the Final Act. The Federal Republic thus gained leverage. Furthermore, the Soviet Union now faced international pressure to be seen to fulfil its commitment to family reunification.

After record figures for the year 1974, the number of ethnic Germans leaving the Soviet Union in 1975 sank to under 6,000. In the autumn of 1975, in fact, the Soviet Union ignored most of the provisions of The Final Act. In the long term, however, this would have destroyed the credibility of the East's CSCE policy at the Belgrade follow-up conference. Brezhnev therefore laid down a new line on 9 December at the VII Party Congress of the Polish Communist Party – the concrete points of the CSCE document were to be 'resolutely filled with life' and the whole document in all its elements was to be translated into reality. Another reason for this change in policy was that given the interest of the Western public in the implementation of Basket III, the Soviet Union had an interest in being seen to be keeping to the principles of Helsinki. Furthermore, the Western position of making implementation of the Baskets I and II resolutions dependent on certain progress in the humanitarian area was not without influence. Although it did not accept this linkage of the three baskets, the Soviet Union had a very strong interest in obtaining Western economic and technological co-operation and in credit concessions.

Applications for family reunification from ethnic Germans were, from February 1976, granted more frequently. The largest numbers of ethnic Germans ever allowed up until that time to leave the Soviet Union occurred in 1976, the year after the signing of the CSCE Final Act. The numbers reached a new record level of 9,700 and this despite a general stagnating in the relations of the Soviet Union with the FRG and some discord and friction (particularly with regard to differences on the Berlin question).[21] The reason for this unprecedently high figure was not purely the result of CSCE, however, but the partial granting of concessions by the Soviet Union for political purposes in its bilateral relations with the FRG, i.e. it was also a gesture of support for the SPD. As in 1972, when almost 2,000 ethnic Germans were granted exit visas before the West German national elections, 1976 was also an election year. There may, too, have been an additional reason. It is possible that the 1976 positive development in family reunification was one of certain goodwill gestures made by the Soviet Union indicating increased interest in improving its relations with the FRG in view of the growing deterioration in Soviet–American relations.

In its co-operation in the humanitarian area, the Soviet Union partially modified its practice with regard to family reunification. Exit permits were granted more frequently than before, exit charges were reduced but remained higher than the average rate of two months' earnings. Refusals to applications for exit visas continued to be issued – even in cases of extreme hardship. Occasionally an applicant suffered loss of status – something which was in contravention of CSCE terms. According to the report on family reunification in *Sowjetunion 76/77*[22] difficulties experienced by ethnic Germans occurred above all to those living in Kirgizia and Kazakhstan: in many cases these applicants (whose status mostly did not become known to the FRG) were rejected or even penalised. The Soviet Union applied differing interpretations of the term 'family'. In applications by Jews for family reunification in Israel, only parents and children were considered. With regard to ethnic Germans, however, a wider interpretation was applied and family reunification with sisters and brothers living in the FRG was considered perfectly acceptable. For visits to relatives in the FRG, application procedures were such as to discourage applicants. For example, applicants were required to produce a testimony of positive performance at work, signed by the party organisation secretary and the union representative at their place of work. Such procedures were difficult to reconcile with the Helsinki resolutions to assist family contacts.

In the course of the 1970s, the combined effect of the FRG's Ostpolitik and the signing of the Final Act of Helsinki caused a significant growth in the demand for exit permits. Already by 1972 it had become a mass movement. The ethnic Germans demonstrated for their right of freedom of movement in letters, resolutions and petitions and occasionally in public. Since about 1972 there has existed a Vereinigung der in der Sowjetunion lebenden Deutschen (Association for Germans living in the Soviet Union) whose main aim is the compilation of lists of those wishing to leave the Soviet Union, and the drawing up of petitions. As with the dissidents in the Soviet Union, CSCE gave the ethnic Germans something they could refer to, something they could base their claim on – the internationally recognised right to legally leave the Soviet Union. At the beginning of March 1977 ten ethnic Germans demonstrated on Red Square in Moscow. They carried banners, referring to the CSCE Final Act, demanding permission to leave the Soviet Union.

In 1977 the number of ethnic Germans leaving the Soviet Union was also very high at 9,274 – just under the 1976 record of 9,704. After 1977, although the numbers of applications to leave not only remained high but continued to rise, a new downward trend in the figures for ethnic Germans leaving the Soviet Union appeared which was to accelerate sharply after 1980.

The 1978 Brezhnev visit to Bonn led to an improvement in bilateral relations, though this was not reflected in any positive upsurge in the 1978 figure for ethnic Germans leaving the Soviet Union. The figure was down to 8,455. Family reunification has always been given a high priority by the FRG and the Federal Government wanted written mention made of this issue at the 1978 visit. This was met by reluctance on the Soviet side. Although in the communiqué published after Brezhnev's visit both sides declared their readiness to continue to find positive solutions to humanitarian questions in the future,[23] family reunification was not taken up into the agreed Joint Declaration.[24] Family reunification was one of the topics addressed by President Walter Scheel in his speech given at the reception at Schloss August-burg during Brezhnev's visit to Bonn. The President noted with satis-faction the steps taken by the Soviet government and expressed his hope that the Soviet Union would continue this policy.[25] This was one of the parts of his speech which was reproduced in the Soviet news-papers only in abridged form.

In 1979 the downward trend in family reunification figures for ethnic Germans continued. The FRG foreign office report for 1979 stated that this was despite 'persistent efforts' by the Federal Govern-ment.[26] In 1980 the figure declined again from 7,226 in 1979 to 6,954. In 1981, however, it fell as far as 3,773 despite Soviet declarations of goodwill.[27] The FRG foreign office report for 1981 listed the downward trend since 1977 in the number of exit permits issued to ethnic Germans and the sharp drop since 1980 as adding further strain on bilateral relations whose development was already hampered by the strains on East–West relations, in particular the continuing Soviet occupation of Afghanistan and the developments in Poland.[28]

At the meeting between Foreign Ministers Genscher and Gromyko in Moscow at the beginning of April 1981, international rather than bilateral problems were at the centre of discussion. The importance of family reunification to the FRG, however, meant that Genscher demanded that the Soviet Union cease obstructing those ethnic Germans who wished to leave. The response by Gromyko tended toward the evasive.[29]

The problem of family reunification was brought up anew during Brezhnev's visit to Bonn in November 1981. The Federal government impressed on the Soviet side, as they had repeatedly done in the past, the great political significance which it attached to a prompt and unbureaucratic granting of exit visas to those ethnic Germans wishing to leave the Soviet Union. Despite insistence by Chancellor Schmidt, the Soviet Union refused to make any precise commitments.

Already in the spring of 1982 the Federal government described the throttling of the numbers as 'giving cause for concern'[30] and by the end of that year the figure came only to 2,071 – below the annual quota of 3,500–4,000 for which Brezhnev had given Schmidt his support during the Chancellor's visit to Moscow in 1974.

In 1982 the trend which had begun in the late seventies to put difficulties in the way of those ethnic Germans wishing to leave the Soviet Union reached a record level. This development led to isolated acts of desperation. At the beginning of November 1982, for example, three ethnic Germans hijacked a Soviet passenger plane to Turkey. A greater number tried to draw the attention of the Western world to their plight. In September 1982, for example, there was a demonstration on Red Square by ethnic Germans bearing placards with the slogan 'SOS – we want to go to our homeland'.[31]

The Soviet authorities employed three ways to choke off emigration.[32] The procedures for application and granting of permission to leave were made frustrating and unpleasant. The mere application generally meant the loss of job or place of study. Answers on application forms had to be typed (hardly any ethnic Germans owned typewriters), documents that were difficult to obtain had to be attached, for example, death certificates of deceased where earlier registers etc. had been destroyed. The application had to pass through numerous official channels and they all delayed it as long as possible. High charges were imposed. Applicants had to wait up to ten months for answers, and refusals – the norm rather than the exception – were only given verbally and without giving grounds.[33]

The second channel of control was measures aimed at preventing an ethnic German from submitting an application. Ethnic Germans married to non-Germans could only obtain permission to leave with especial difficulty. Mostly they were unable to leave at all as the Soviet authorities refused such applications on the grounds that the majority of the family lived in the Soviet Union. German men between the ages of eighteen and forty-five were drafted into the army and given the sort of posting, for example Afghanistan, which made their families 'bearers of secrets' and barred them from leaving. It was forbidden for ethnic Germans to move to cities with diplomatic missions (Moscow and Leningrad among others). They were also banned from moving to the Baltic provinces or to Moldavia – until the middle seventies a 'spring-board' to the West.[34]

The third method of control was crude propaganda. The Federal Republic was depicted in newspaper articles and books, the latter occasionally even in the German language, as a warmongering, misanthropic country where living conditions bordered on slavery and where ethnic Germans were singled out as objects of general hatred so that all they wanted was to return as soon as possible to the 'homeland', the Soviet Union.[35]

In addition to the above three methods of repression, would-be emigrants could also be subjected to personal threats and slander, house searches, arbitrary arrest, assault and other similar measures.[36]

Applications for visitors' visas were controlled in almost the same way. Although the number of those entering the Federal Republic as visitors from the Soviet Union rose in the last years of the Schmidt period – 1980: 17,882; 1981: 20,555; January to October 1982: 17,829 – most of these were visits for business purposes.[37] Visits to close relatives in the Federal Republic were made difficult even in those cases where illness or similar serious reasons made the visit plainly of a humanitarian nature.[38]

Reasons for the decline in ethnic German emigration

The West German Government tried to raise the figures up to 10,000 resettlers a year but 9,704 in 1976 was the highest figure achieved. With so many ethnic Germans living in the Soviet Union, on the issue of human rights the Federal Republic concentrated on emigration i.e., the human right of movement. The constant decline since 1977 and the sharp decrease after 1980 in the number of ethnic Germans allowed to leave, therefore, was a source of considerable concern and disappointment for the FRG in its relations with the Soviet Union. This decline in permits issued by the Soviet Union had several underlying reasons.

One of the problems for the soviet Union was that ethnic German emigration caused a loss of skilled workers which could not be replaced overnight by the domestic labour force. It is said that during a discussion in 1965 with a Volga German delegation, Mikoyan turned down the restoration of their Autonomous Republic for the reason that

Table 3. *Ethnic German resettlers leaving the Soviet Union, 1950–1982*

1950	
1951	1,721
1952	63
1953	
1954	18
1955	154
1956	1,016
1957	923
1958	4,122
1959	5,563
1960	3,272
1961	345
1962	894
1963	209
1964	234
1965	366
1966	1,245
1967	1,092
1968	598
1969	316
1970	342
1971	1,145
1972	3,420
1973	4,493
1974	6,541
1975	5,985
1976	9,704
1977	9,274
1978	8,455
1979	7,226
1980	6,954
1981	3,773
1982	2,071

Source: Figures for 1950–81 from *Betrifft: Eingliederung der Vertriebenen, Flüchtlinge und Kriegsgeschädigten in der Bundesrepublik Deutschland.* Bonn: Der Bundesminister des Innern, 1982, p. 107. Figures for 1982 from *Auswärtiges Amt. Sonderdruck aus dem Jahresbericht der Bundesregierung.* Bonn: Auswärtiges Amt, Referat für Öffentlichkeitsarbeit, p. 37.

it would be 'impossible to manage without the Germans in the virgin territories'.[39] What is certainly fact, is a comment made by the then party head of Kazakhstan, Kunaev, after the signing of the Final Act of Helsinki, 'If I were to let all the Germans leave I could no longer take the responsibility for agriculture in Kazakhstan.'[40] There was, in fact, hardly a sector of the Soviet economy in which there were no ethnic Germans employed and their role in the economic life of Siberia and Kazakhstan and some of the Central Asian Republics was of extreme importance. Indeed, it is significant that in the period 1976 to 1977, at a time when emigration figures for ethnic Germans were at their highest, that when difficulties did occur they were experienced above all by those Germans living in Kirgizia and Kazakhstan (see p. 24). The ethnic German group was slowly developing in the direction of a 'normal' social structure where there were established and new generations of intellectuals. At that time skilled workers predominated. Andreas Lorenz in his report on the ethnic Germans in *Der Spiegel* found that the ethnic German worker was valued throughout the Soviet Union as reliable and hard-working.

One reason for the decline in numbers of ethnic Germans allowed to leave the Soviet Union since 1976/7 was quite simply that the Soviets had originally felt that if they let a lot out then the numbers of applications should go down. Wolf Oschlies in his report in *Sowjetunion 1982/83* also puts forward this reason. He writes that in the early seventies the Soviet Union was of the opinion that the German ethnic group could be 'pacified' if certain 'ringleaders' were allowed to emigrate. The door to the West was therefore opened a little wider to accommodate this. An increase in applications for exit permits of avalanche proportions – the Red Cross speaks of 100,000 – proved this calculation wrong and the Soviet authorities henceforth resorted to repression.[41]

Another reason was that in 1976, quite soon after the signing of the CSCE Final Act, there was a hardening of the Soviet government's internal attitude in order to stop negative effects in their own country, for example, hard action was taken against the dissidents. For the same internal reasons the Soviets did not want to allow a general emigration of ethnic German citizens. Indeed, the Soviet Union in the 1970s was in a difficult position. The massive growth in demand by ethnic Germans to leave the Soviet Union meant that in order to prevent the problem of family reunification from becoming a serious strain on relations between the Federal and Soviet governments, Moscow should grant a generous number of exit permits. However, most of the ethnic

Germans came to Russia under Catherine II and Alexander I and to give in to such an old-established group would have undermined the Soviet nationality policy which aimed at bringing autonomous trends into line and at linguistic and cultural assimilation. The possible consequences of this were potentially very serious (see pp. 13–16). Andreas Lorenz writes in *Der Spiegel* that the inflexible attitude adopted in the later Schmidt years towards German emigration was because the Kremlin feared that other groups with relatives abroad such as the Armenians or the Ukrainians might make stronger demands for family reunification. He quotes a Moscow official as saying, *Wir wollen anderen kein Beispiel geben.* [We don't want to set an example for others to follow].[42] And in fairness to the Soviet position it should be pointed out that there is, in fact, a certain peculiarity attached to the FRG's claim on Petrine and Catherinian Germans: a person descended from British settlers 200 years ago in Patagonia, for example, would not be entitled to British citizenship merely by that fact. Even the indigenous Falklanders, despite the reclamation of the islands as sovereign territory, are only 'Overseas British Citizens' with no automatic entitlement to settle in the United Kingdom.

The repatriation figures for ethnic Germans may be said to have followed a curve like that of the state of East–West relations in several senses. It may be that Soviet reluctance to respond to West German appeals to increase the number of exit permits was due to the general deterioration of détente and also to Soviet disappointment in material benefits (economic) expected from the FRG–Soviet relations. The Soviets may well have decided that they were not getting very much out of détente and therefore they would not give very much. The repatriation figures also followed the curve of East–West relations in another sense. At the time of the May 1978 Brezhnev visit to Bonn, the two sides had undertaken to examine favourably in future the solution to humanitarian problems, but the deterioration of the general climate of international relations in the last years slowed this movement. At a time of East–West tension, i.e. during a period of instability in their external relations, the Soviet Union was especially less inclined than usual to grant concessions in such a sensitive area and so open up the way to the contagion of the idea of national identity purely on the basis of ethno-culture – something greatly feared by the Soviet government.

The problem of family reunification only became acute in the last few years of the Schmidt period. According to an FRG government official,[43] the sharp decrease since 1980 in the number of exit permits granted by the Soviet authorities to ethnic Germans wishing to emigrate to the Federal Republic was a Soviet response to the NATO double-track decision and to the FRG not doing in foreign policy security questions what the Soviets wanted. It was, in a sense, a kind of sanction. In fact, the emigration figures for ethnic Germans since 1970 followed a curve like that of the state of East–West relations in a way which specifically linked to the USA: if the Soviet Union felt that the FRG was following USA policy too closely when superpower relations were poor then it applied moral pressure, and emigration, an issue which was very important to the Federal Republic, was one of the areas where this was applied.

3 Berlin

It is undoubtedly one of the achievements of détente that the international situation of Berlin became one of calm and that the city was no longer the barometer of East–West relations. As a result of the 1971 Quadripartite Agreement on Berlin the situation of the city was stabilised and the city removed from the world's present-day crisis register. Postwar developments have clearly shown how changes in the East–West relationship were reflected in Berlin, the most sensitive spot in Central Europe. East–West tension in Africa since the middle seventies, the worsening of East–West relations since the NATO double-track decision and Soviet intervention in Afghanistan in 1979, the crisis in Poland – the city reflected none of these. The Four Power Agreement held, Berlin remained calm, to all intents and purposes an island of détente. Once the situation in and around Berlin had become stabilised, the city was no longer a 'disturbance factor' for international security. Tension was reduced round this potential trouble spot in the centre of Europe and this helped to bring about a decisive improvement in the political climate of Central Europe.

However, although there were no great crises in and around Berlin after 1972 and the Four Power Agreement regulated the most troublesome questions and brought great practical improvements, the conflict between East and West over Berlin had not so much been overcome as undergone a change. The legal and political problems carried on after 1971 but it was not so clearly perceptible from the outside as there were no crises. Each side interpreted the Agreement differently, which in practice repeatedly led to tension and controversy even though the scale and intensity of the conflict had changed. For the Federal Republic this meant that Berlin despite the Four Power Agreement remained a problem in its bilateral relations with the Soviet Union. The expectation that the Four Power Agreement would bring an end to the dispute over the character and development of the ties between Berlin and the Federal Republic and so remove one of the stumbling blocks in the process of changing confrontation to co-operation in West Germany's relations with the Warsaw Pact countries was not realised. The dispute continued to have a detrimental effect on the Federal Republic's relations with the Soviet Union generating an atmosphere of mistrust and growing tension. In fact, until 1978 and the summit meeting between Brezhnev and Chancellor Schmidt, Berlin was a major stumbling block in FRG–Soviet relations.

The Four Power Agreement

The Quadripartite Agreement on Berlin comprised the preamble and two sections. Part I dealt with general provisions and contained declarations concerning détente, renunciation of the use of force and mutual respect of rights 'in the relevant area'. Part II dealt with provisions relating to the Western sectors of Berlin and included declarations on transit traffic, the ties between Berlin and the Federal Republic, visiting rights for West Berliners and the representation abroad of West Berlin. Four annexes concerning these agreements on the Western sectors of Berlin were attached. The details of this main framework agreement were then filled out by executive agreements between the German Democratic Republic and the Federal Republic and between the government of the German Democratic Republic and the Senate.[1]

The Quadripartite Agreement did not create a new status for Berlin nor did it provide a final settlement of the Berlin question. The status of Berlin, the Quadripartite rights and responsibilities for Berlin as a whole and the Three Power rights and responsibilities for West Berlin remained unaffected. As agreement between the Soviet Union and the Western allies on the differing legal positions could not be achieved, the agreement was meant to achieve a *modus vivendi*. The aim was, through practical regulations of problems which had caused difficulties in the past, to reduce tension in the Berlin situation and to make life easier for the Berliners.

The Berlin agreements dealt with three main issues: ties between West Berlin and the Federal Republic of Germany, access to West Berlin, improvements for residents of West Berlin.

Ties between West Berlin and the FRG

The Quadripartite Agreement provided that the Western sectors of Berlin were not a 'constituent part' of the Federal Republic and were not to be governed by it. It prohibited 'constitutional or official' acts in West Berlin by the Federal President, the Federal Government, the Bundesversammlung, the Bundesrat and the Bundestag, including their Committees and Fraktionen, as well as other state bodies of the Federal Republic of Germany which would contradict this. Existing ties between West Berlin and the FRG might be 'maintained and developed'. Provided that matters of 'security and status' were not affected the following were permitted: the FRG might perform consular services for permanent residents of the Western Sectors of Berlin; the FRG might represent the interests of the Western Sectors of Berlin in international organisations and international conferences; permanent residents of the Western Sectors of Berlin might participate jointly with participants from the Federal Republic of Germany in international exchanges and exhibitions; meetings of international organisations and international conferences as well as exhibitions with international participation might be held in the Western Sectors of Berlin and invitations were to be issued by the Senate or jointly by the Federal Republic of Germany and the Senate; international agreements and arrangements entered into by the FRG might be extended to the Western Sectors of Berlin provided that the extension of such agreements and arrangements was specified in each case.

Access to West Berlin

Civilian access to West Berlin was guaranteed in the Berlin agreements. The Soviet Union took responsibility for unimpeded free access. Traffic clearance was to be effected as simply and as quickly as possible. Goods could be transported in sealed vehicles without a clearance of the inside of the vehicle. Persons using trains or buses were not to be subjected to any formalities other than proof of identification. Persons travelling in cars were to be given immediate clearance and were not to be subjected to search, detention or exclusion except in certain specified cases where there was sufficient reason to suspect misuse.

Improvements for West Berliners

The agreements entitled West Berliners to travel to and visit East Berlin and the GDR for visits totalling thirty days a year for compassionate, family, religious and cultural reasons and for touring visits. Before the Berlin agreements West Berliners were only able to visit East Berlin for urgent family reasons. Telephone links were established between East and West Berlin. Access to enclaves belonging to West Berlin were made more secure by the exchange of territory.

Evaluation of the Quadripartite Agreement on Berlin

Overall, the Berlin agreements brought in practice a great improvement over the hitherto existing situation. Nowhere was this more evident than in the very important transit agreements. For the first time the Soviet Union took responsibility for free access for civilian traffic on the roads, rail and waterways. Before the Quadripartite Agreement the GDR had claimed full sovereignty over access and it was subject to arbitrary acts by the GDR authorities. Civilian free access was without any legal basis in the past and had been the cause of various Berlin crises. It was now regulated on a legal basis and civilian traffic henceforth ran virtually without hindrance. The processing of civilian traffic was made much simpler. Access to Berlin became secure. Passenger and freight movements to and from West Berlin thus greatly benefited, and the vital traffic links between West Berlin and the FRG were secured. There was increased freedom of movement between West Berlin and East Berlin and the GDR. The Western side achieved its major objective.

The Berlin agreements brought major improvements to various aspects of life in West Berlin. They facilitated communications between East and West Germany and improved German–German contacts. Freedom of movement of West Berliners was increased. Within the framework of the Quadripartite Agreement representatives of the Federal Republic and the Senate continued to conduct negotiations aimed at various improvements for the city and its population. The viability of West Berlin was improved, making the city more attractive for business and industry.

On the whole the Berlin agreements guaranteed the political status quo of West Berlin. The isolated geographic situation of West Berlin and the lack of legal basis had enabled the East in the past to threaten the status quo by the various Berlin crises and by claims that West

Berlin was situated on the territory of the GDR. The situation in and around Berlin was stabilised and the Berlin agreements brought a relative calm in and around the city. The Berlin agreements lessened the danger of escalation of conflicts over Berlin, not only because troublesome questions were now legally regulated, but also because the Four Powers kept to the provision of the Quadripartite Agreement in which it was laid down that the four governments would strive to promote the elimination of tensions and the prevention of complications and that differences were to be settled only through peaceful means. This was aimed at, and largely achieved, the ending of the former situation whereby actions on the part of the Western side, which were considered inadmissible by the Eastern side, were met with boycotts and retaliatory measures, and even retaliation on the transit routes, and which were met, in turn, by Western protests and counter-measures.

In the question of ties between West Berlin and the FRG, a watertight regulation was not reached in the Berlin agreements. However, considerable improvements were achieved in that for the first time the ties between West Berlin and the Federal Republic were legally recognised by the East, and for the first time, representation abroad of West Berlin by the Federal Republic was recognised under an agreement.

The Eastern and Western sides had been unable to reach agreement on a common legal position on Berlin and this question was therefore left out. This left the Quadripartite Agreement open to criticism. Furthermore, the Agreement has been criticised for ambiguous language in some of its formulations,[2] for equivocal stipulations and for the fact that certain provisions were not laid down in detail. However, Chancellor Schmidt and Egon Bahr have defended the Berlin agreements against such criticism by stating that those who complained that the Berlin problem had not been solved had not understood the nature of the Berlin agreements.

> From the start the Federal Government warned against excessive optimism with regard to Ostpolitik. Disappointment, therefore, could only have occurred and can only occur in those who did not correctly grasp Ostpolitik. The treaties and agreements could not and were not meant to do away with the differing interests and the differing legal positions but rather to form a basis for a long-term process of normalisation. The Quadripartite Agreement is a good example of this fundamental objective of opening up new areas of co-operation. (Chancellor Schmidt)[3]

Egon Bahr, who along with US Ambassador Rush and the USSR Ambassador Falin took part in the so-called 'back-channel' negotiations in the Berlin talks,[4] has said that in his view the Four Power Agreement was 'wisely negotiated between the Four Powers in that it represented a framework agreement which did not make the attempt, doomed to failure, of trying to settle every single question'.[5] He went on to say that 'The differing legal views were retained. A uniform legal view could not be found but rather regulations were found and the framework laid out for practical questions of great importance.'[6]

Furthermore, the formal negotiations between the four ambassadors (the British, French and American ambassadors in Bonn and the Soviet representative in East Berlin) proved to be exceedingly difficult and no less than thirty-three discussion sessions were needed before a draft agreement could be put forward.[7] Agreement on some points could only be reached by deliberately resorting to ambiguous language.

The Quadripartite Agreement has also been criticised for not being comprehensive enough in that it regulated only those questions which had given trouble in the past. As Egon Bahr said in 1975,

> It would have needed an impossible stretch of the imagination to answer in advance all the questions which have arisen in the last four years. It cannot be ruled out that this will also prove to be the case in the future. We did not expect that the Quadripartite Agreement would be able once and for all to remove all friction. No agreement provides a guarantee that there will be no more dispute. He who wishes to shut out all dispute must shut out politics.[8]

It may be, then, that the Quadripartite Agreement with all its positive and negative aspects was the best that could be achieved under the circumstances. As Martin J. Hillenbrand, a former American official in Berlin, Bonn and Washington put it:

> few will dispute that the Agreement represents a considerable net gain for the city. Within its framework, representatives of the Federal Republic and the Berlin Senate have conducted and are conducting negotiations with the GDR aimed at various improvements for the city and its population. These will undoubtedly continue as new needs arise. No one is proposing, however, any discussion which would in any fundamental way affect the underlying legal situation, for to do this would raise issues of immediate political significance affecting the security of the city. While one might regret that everything is not tied up more neatly, here is one area where the best could well be the enemy of the good.[9]

The real test of the Quadripartite Agreement, the criterion by which it should be judged, according to Egon Bahr, was not the absence of problems since 1972 but rather that: 'We were of the opinion that as long as a policy of détente remained, the danger of a crisis-type of escalation round Berlin, which has occurred in the past and which went as far as endangering peace, would be excluded. This positive expectation has been fulfilled to this day.'[10]

Nevertheless, whether avoidable or not, justifiable or not, the fact that the differing legal positions were retained, the ambiguity and lack of detail in some of the provisions, the problem of unanticipated trouble arising in previously trouble free areas not specifically covered by the Berlin agreements (for example, membership of the EEC) all gave rise to differences of interpretation between the Soviet Union and the Western side and corresponding actions which repeatedly led to protests.

No agreement could be reached on the territory actually covered by the Quadripartite Agreement and this was one of the points on which a compromise, using omission and deliberately vague language, had to be brought in to achieve an acceptable text which each side could claim as either meeting their position or not running counter to it. Thus the final official document is headed only with the words 'Quadripartite Agreement' and the territory is referred to simply as 'the relevant area'. This meant that while the Soviets viewed the document as an agreement on West Berlin, the Western Allies insisted on the Four Power Status of Greater Berlin. The Soviet Union and the GDR increasingly used the Quadripartite Agreement as the basis for all rights in Berlin, operating as if the status of the Western sectors, including Western rights in Berlin, were established and regulated for the first time in the Agreement.

The Quadripartite Agreement provided that the 'ties' between West Berlin and the Federal Republic might be 'maintained and developed' but did not state in what way these ties could be developed. Although the Quadripartite Agreement then went on to state: 'Detailed arrangements concerning the relationship between the Western Sectors of Berlin and the Federal Republic of Germany are set forth in Annex II', in fact the arrangements in Annex II were not detailed. A smaller matter, but one that was perhaps a harbinger of troubles to come, concerned questions of translations and wordings as between the FRG, GDR and Soviet versions of the Quadripartite Agreement. The West Germans translated 'ties' as 'Bindungen' whereas the East Germans, despite prior discussion and agreement, published their text using 'Verbindungen' – a weaker word implying 'connections'. The 'svyazi' of the Soviet version was possibly also weaker than the English 'ties'.[11]

The Quadripartite Agreement provided that West Berlin might ('may') be included in international agreements signed by the Federal Republic provided that this extension was specified in each case. The Federal Republic and the Western Powers interpreted this as *de facto* Soviet acceptance of the 'Berlin clause' (i.e., the extension of a treaty to West Berlin, which in the past had blocked treaties between the FRG and the Warsaw Pact states, except Romania) and also of the fact that the inclusion of West Berlin in treaties signed by the Federal Republic should be automatic provided that matters of security and status were not affected and the extension was specified as required by 2(b) of Annex IV. The Soviets refused to accept this, their position being that the legitimising legal basis for the inclusion of West Berlin in treaties signed by the FRG was the Quadripartite Agreement and that such an extension could only take place by virtue of an exceptional ruling having been made in the Quadripartite Agreement, i.e. the Soviet Union took the view that West Berlin was a separate political entity and might therefore only be included in treaties signed by the Federal Republic because of this exceptional ruling. The word 'may' was interpreted by the West German side in the sense that there was no doubt about the possibility, i.e. the possibility to include West Berlin in treaties was clear and it was up to the FRG to use it. The Soviet side interpreted the term 'may' as meaning that the whole question was totally open, i.e. in principle West Berlin could be included but in individual cases the Soviet Union and the GDR can decide.

Difficulties arose over the representation of West Berlin abroad by Bonn, the question being whether legal assistance could be given only to individuals from West Berlin or whether it could be given also to institutions in West Berlin – something which was not unequivocally enough laid down in the agreements.

For the first time, the Soviet Union began to contest West Berlin's links with the EEC. This was a matter which had not come into question before and the West therefore had not had specific mention made of it in the Agreement. The Quadripartite Agreement provided that the 'existing situation in the relevant area' was to be taken into account. West Berlin had been treated as an integral part of the Community since it came into being on 1 January 1958 by virtue of the specific action taken by the Federal Republic at the time of signing the Treaty of Rome to ensure its inclusion. Owing to more than fifteen years of uncontested practice, the Western side believed that 'the existing situation' would apply to West Berlin's links with the European Community as long as questions of security and status were not involved. The Soviets took this position: since the goal of the European Community was political integration, this must raise questions of security and status. This was incompatible with the status of the Western Sectors of Berlin, particularly as laid down in the Quadripartite Agreement. The Quadripartite Agreement, therefore, could not have sanctioned West Berlin's incorporation into the European Community.

The differing positions on Berlin

The three Western Powers on the one hand and the Soviet Union on the other had differing political and legal positions on Berlin. The Western side's position was that they were doing nothing more than repeating long-standing doctrine by defining the status of the Western Sectors of Berlin as not being a constituent part of the Federal Republic of Germany and therefore not to be governed by it. The Western view was that on the grounds of original occupation rights in West Berlin, the three Western states alone held the determination over West Berlin. The Soviet Union might only make demands over certain restrictions which the Western Powers agreed to in the Quadripartite Agreement. Apart from this, the three Western Powers were entirely free to allow ties between West Berlin and the FRG according to their discretion. The Western view was that the word 'maintained' in the provision in the Quadripartite Agreement dealing with ties meant that the Federal presence (i.e. Federal institutions, officials etc.) could remain and that the word 'developed' meant that an increase in this presence was permissible. The incorporation of the Western Sectors of Berlin into the West German state and constitutional system was only impermissible where this would clash with the maintenance of the Western occupation or where this would be in contradiction of the explicitly laid down restrictions in the Quadripartite Agreement.

The Federal Republic frequently stressed the importance of Berlin in its foreign policy. For example, the foreign office report for 1979 stated: 'Berlin remains a main issue in our policy and a barometer for détente.'[12] The Federal Republic made it clear to the Soviets again and again how important a positive solution to the problems connected with Berlin would be for bilateral co-operation and so for détente in general.

The Federal Republic's view on Berlin's legal position was generally similar to that of the Western Powers but there were some differences of interpretation and emphasis.

The West German interpretation was that West Berlin was really an integral part of the Federal Republic. In 1949 this was laid down in the Basic Law and in 1950 in the Constitution of West Berlin but the clauses were immediately suspended by the Western Powers. The Federal Constitutional Court a number of times declared that the city was a Federal Land. The view taken, therefore, was that West Berlin was actually, i.e. by German law, an integral part of the West German state and was only prevented by contrary circumstances, i.e. superimposed Allied Occupation authority, from fully realising this. FRG acceptance at the time of the Quadripartite Agreement that constitutional or official acts by state bodies might no longer be performed in West Berlin was seen as a relatively painless, tactical, and in the matter of principle, meaningless concession – i.e. a reduction in the merely demonstrative presence of the Federal Republic in West Berlin which obtained what was most important to the Federal Republic: Soviet official acceptance of the ties between West Berlin and the FRG. In the matter of emphasis, the prime concern of the Allies was to maintain the purity of their legal position but they were also prepared to combine this with flexibility in practice where questions of principle were not involved. The Federal Republic's interest lay in achieving maximum legal and practical unity between the Federal Republic and West Berlin so long as this did not jeopardise basic security. In its daily practice the FRG tried to illustrate the ties between West Berlin and the Federal Republic and the right to the representation abroad of West Berlin by the FRG. With regard to representation abroad, for example, the FRG did this by including Berlin in all the treaties the FRG signed.

Chancellor Schmidt and Foreign Minister Genscher had different approaches to the Berlin problem. Schmidt was a pragmatist. For him the Quadripartite Agreement was an instrument for the management of the here and now. He was more for practical solutions in a global sense. Genscher's approach was much more committed. He was more Europe-orientated. He thought in terms of continuity and he was for keeping to the Ostpolitik agreements in the strictest sense. Added to this was the fact that Foreign Minister Genscher was head of the FDP in an SPD/FDP coalition and in coalitions there is a natural tendency for each party to try to achieve a 'profile'. In particular, at the start of his period as foreign minister he insisted that West Berlin should take part in co-operation with Eastern Europe under the roof of the FRG. He was strongly against the separate political entity concept. He was determinedly consistent which made it difficult, in fact, to include Berlin in co-operation with Eastern Europe. Genscher felt that there should be a 'dynamic development of the ties' (*dynamische Entwicklung der Bindungen*) between the Federal Republic and West Berlin. He was also associated with a policy of trying to test the 'stressing capacity' (*Erprobung der Belastbarkeit*) of the Quadripartite Agreement. During an interview Schmidt was asked whether he believed that it was wise and right policy to pursue an extensive interpretation of the Berlin Agreement and so in practice test its stressing capacity. His reply was:

> Formulae such as that of the 'extensive interpretation' of the Quadripartite Agreement should be rejected. That also goes for the formula which crops up now and again of 'testing the stressing capacity'. Rather, it should be a matter of closest co-ordination with our Western Allies France, Great Britain and the USA as signatory powers of the Agreement who, as you know, adhere to the concept of the strict observance and full implementation of the Quadripartite Agreement, that is, therefore, that the Agreement is carried out according to the spirit and the letter.[13]

In contrast to the Western position that the Quadripartite Agreement was only repeating long-standing doctrine, the fact that the Agreement stated that the Western Sectors of Berlin were not a constituent part of the Federal Republic and not to be governed by it was counted by the Soviet Union as a victory and as useful ammunition in its objective of separating the city from the Federal Republic. Their position was that West Berlin was a separate entity, an independent political unit. The ties laid down in the Agreement should be of an economic, cultural etc. nature with no state-political affiliation whatsoever and therefore the reservation over security and status was applied to all political and state matters. The restrictions over the ties in the Quadripartite Agreement proved their fundamental inadmissibility – only as an exception to the general ruling might ties be allowed in some instances. The Soviet justification for their interpretation was that the status of West Berlin and its relationship with the FRG was first established in the Quadripartite Agreement between the Soviet Union and the Western Powers. Therefore only that which was explicitly agreed to by the Soviet side in the agreement, and since then had been recognised by it as conforming with the Agreement, might be considered legal. The Soviet Union had the right to object to any ties which were not permissible according to its interpretation. With regard to the Federal presence in West Berlin, the USSR fundamentally denied this right. Furthermore, in the Soviet view, the passage in the Quadripartite Agreement 'Taking into account the existing situation' did not mean that everything involving the Federal Republic in West Berlin before the agreement not objected to in those days was now legally acceptable. This meant that the Soviets objected to practices long established.

At the time of the negotiations for the Quadripartite Agreement the Federal Republic and the Western Powers made the ratification of the Moscow Treaty and the holding of the CSCE dependent on a satisfactory Berlin settlement. Moscow also feared that Kissinger's Peking visit might mean a danger of an anti-Soviet alignment between the USA and China. Therefore, the Soviet Union was strongly motivated towards making concessions. From the start they looked for possibilities of interpretation in order to restrict as much as possible the practical consequences of the concessions made and also to work against the Western interpretation of the ties as a close special relationship and interwovenness.

In the communiqué issued at the end of the Brezhnev visit to Bonn in May 1973, both sides stated that they regarded 'the strict observance and full implementation' (*strikte Einhaltung und volle Anwendung*) of the Quadripartite Agreement as a precondition for the maintenance of détente in the centre of Europe and for an improvement in bilateral relations.[14] Afterwards the Soviet Union tended to stress the 'strict observance' side. In fact, in political statements in the GDR and other East European states the Soviet Union often dropped the 'full implementation' part of the phrase and retained only 'strict observance'. Bonn always insisted that the entire phrase retained full validity – something to which Schmidt had to draw Brezhnev's attention during his visit to Moscow in October 1974. In his opening speech at the start of the visit, Brezhnev spoke only of strict adherence and Schmidt therefore had to quickly add a passage to his prepared answer reminding Brezhnev of his agreement in 1973 of the need for both.[15]

There was genuine Soviet mistrust and sense of upset over what they felt to be the FRG's intentions towards West Berlin. Shortly after the conclusion of the Quadripartite Agreement a new Federal Environmental Agency was set up in West Berlin on the instigation of the then Interior Minister Genscher (although they defended the FRG's decision, the Western Allies were not convinced that it was necessary or advisable). The Soviets saw this as a serious blow against the status quo. In the following years they formed the impression that the Federal Government was trying by small steps to develop their position in West Berlin. In addition to this the governing mayors of West Berlin, above all Stobbe, advocated a national function for West Berlin, not only as the 'Window of the West' but as the symbol of a future reunified Germany. The Soviets felt that the FRG was not showing much appreciation of the concessions which the Soviet Union had made in the Berlin question. Their view was that the Federal Republic was taking all the advantages of the agreement, above all the smooth-running access to the city, for granted and in return had greatly increased its activities in the city and was trying, against the spirit and letter of the agreement, to incorporate the Western Sectors bit by bit into the Federal Republic.

The FRG tried to strengthen West Berlin's ties with the Federal Republic and Moscow tried to prevent this. Given the fact that it was always likely that the differing interpretations would come into practice in those cases where the applicability of a procedure or a provision was not unambiguous or where there was a lack of detail, conflict and controversy was bound to emerge.

The conflict over Berlin

The conflict over the recognition of West Berlin's ties to the Federal Republic

Eastern objections first surfaced over the use of the term 'Land Berlin' (Federal State of Berlin) for West Berlin. Objections were raised on the grounds that this term was incompatible with the Quadripartite Agreement which stated that the Western Sectors were not a constituent part of the Federal Republic and might not be governed by it. On the basis of this the Soviet Union and the GDR objected to the extension of numerous West German treaties to the 'Land Berlin'.[16]

The Soviet Union and the GDR tried in various ways to press West Berlin into demonstrating its quasi-state independence. For example, special importance was attached to the displaying of flags. When West Germans and West Berliners jointly participated in events on East German or Soviet territory, they demanded that the West Berlin flag must be flown next to the Federal Republic's flag. At international events or on important occasions held in West Berlin the Soviet and East German representatives insisted that the West Berlin flag must not be flown next to the Federal flag for the reason that West German political presence might not be demonstrated on West Berlin territory. The aim was to stylise the West Berlin flag as the independent national flag. It was with great difficulty that a compromise was found for the flag dispute. Gradually the procedure was established whereby West Berlin was entered neither with its own flag nor as an independent state. In return, however, the West Berliners had to display a small pennant and a sign with the passage from the Quadripartite Agreement allowing their inclusion in West German delegations and events. This procedure accommodated both sides' interpretations: West Berlin could be regarded equally as an area incorporated, with certain reservations, into the Federal Republic or as a territory which happened to be putting in a joint appearance with the West German state. This compromise procedure did not resolve the differing positions, however, and the conflict therefore continued to break out from time to time.

The inclusion of West Berlin in treaties entered into by the Federal Republic

After the Quadripartite Agreement the Western side thought that the Soviet Union and its allies would no longer try to block representation abroad of the Western Sectors of Berlin by the FRG in so far as the Western Powers had transferred representation to the Federal Republic in the Agreement. Very early on, however, it became apparent that the Soviet Union was not prepared to generally concede such representation.

In the middle of 1972 at the negotiations over the West German–Soviet Trade Agreement, Moscow objected to the adoption of the customary Berlin clause declaring the extension of the treaty to West Berlin. The result of diplomatic discussion on this was an altered form for the inclusion of West Berlin which was named the Frank–Falin Formula after the chief negotiators (Paul Frank was the then State Secretary at the Bonn Foreign Office and later State Secretary at the President's Office and Valentin Falin was the Soviet Ambassador in Bonn): 'In accordance with the Four Power Agreement of 3 December 1971 this agreement is extended to Berlin (West) in keeping with the procedures laid down.' The trade agreement was concluded on 5 July 1972, adopting this formula.

The problem with replacing the Berlin clause (which was still used for treaties outside Eastern Europe) with the Frank–Falin Formula was that the Soviet side attached the interpretation to the formula that the representation abroad of West Berlin through Federal state organs had its legal basis in the Quadripartite Agreement, that is, in a decision which had been made with the participation of the Soviet Union. According to the Soviet view the Quadripartite Agreement laid down under international law that West Berlin was a separate entity which did not belong to the Federal Republic and was not under its control.

Accordingly the status of West Berlin was regarded as the result of the jointly laid down determination of the Four Powers and the political determination of what was legally allowable in the Western Sectors of Berlin did not, therefore, originate from previously acquired original rights of the three Western Powers but from a joint ruling by the Four Powers. This was at variance with the Western legal conception, whereby the authorisation of the Federal Republic by the three Western Occupying Powers in West Berlin had been previously established and to which mere reference was made in the Quadripartite Agreement and thus authorisation had come about through the Western Powers alone and not jointly with the Soviet Union.

In the following period the Soviet side maintained in reference to the Frank–Falin Formula that West Berlin might and should only be included in any agreement in so far as it was according to the Soviet view in line with the procedure laid down on 3 September 1971. The Frank–Falin Formula was not, therefore, as West Germany had hoped, automatically accepted by the Soviet Union with every treaty. It may be that two considerations could have been contributory factors in the Soviet position.[17] One was that an automatic and unquestioning acceptance of the Federal Republic's representation abroad of West Berlin could have been construed as recognition by established right of a relationship of firm and extensive ties between West Berlin and the Federal Republic. The other was that Moscow may have regarded it as an advantage when the Federal Republic was obliged to negotiate anew and 'purchase' the inclusion of West Berlin in bilateral treaties.

The Soviet Union generally used two arguments when it tried to restrict West Germany's representation abroad of West Berlin. One was that the nature of the agreement must, in addition to being strictly allowed by the Quadripartite Agreement, also be of direct practical value to West Berlin. Only such practical necessity could justify the inclusion of West Berlin. This was in complete contrast to the Federal Constitutional Court ruling of 31 July 1973 which stated that the Federal Government in concluding treaties with the GDR must insist on the inclusion of Berlin when the contents of the agreement made it possible to apply it in Berlin.[18] The two views were bound to come into conflict. Furthermore, in addition to the above two arguments the reservations in Annex IV regarding security and status had to be very broadly defined.

Matters of peace were related to security and specifically political settlements came within the field of state sovereignty which according to the status laid down in the Quadripartite Agreement did not concern the Federal Republic.[19] The security argument was used as the reason for Soviet and East German objections to the extension of the status of the International Atomic Energy Agency (IAEA) and the Agreement over the Non-Proliferation of Nuclear Weapons to West Berlin.[20] The Western counter-argument was that these treaties contained very important elements for West Berlin, i.e. the pledges of the nuclear powers to promote the peaceful use of nuclear energy. Status was used as the basis for Eastern objections to the Federal Republic extending the International Convention over Civilian and Political Rights to West Berlin.[21]

The Federal Republic did, however, sign many agreements with the Warsaw Pact states on the basis of the Frank–Falin Formula. Whether an agreement was extended to West Berlin always depended on the extent of the Eastern interest in the agreement and on the extent, according to the Soviet view, of its compatibility with a non-political relationship between West Berlin and the Federal Republic. Such agreements were as a rule of a commercial or other narrowly specialised nature outside 'high politics', for example co-operation in transport and communication or tourism. Due to the Quadripartite Agreement, West Berlin participated more strongly than before in West Germany's relations with Eastern Europe – most strongly in economic relations with Eastern Europe where there had been hardly any practical difficulties before, and least strongly in more politically accentuated relations which had previously been completely blocked.

Consular services

A fundamental disagreement developed over the provision in the Quadripartite Agreement which allowed the Federal Republic of Germany to perform consular services for permanent residents of the Western Sectors of Berlin. This provision went further than that which the Soviet Union and its allies had accepted and allowed on their territory before the Agreement, and the Soviet Union afterwards applied a restriction to its concession. From the summer of 1973 the Soviet Union's allies only accepted consular services for individuals. Consular services for institutions in West Berlin were not accepted. West Germany, however, believed that 'permanent residents of the Western Sectors of Berlin' was meant to include institutions and that it had the right to give official and legal assistance to West Berlin authorities and courts through its missions. Eventually compromises were reached whereby private juristic persons from West Berlin were to be represented in consular matters in the Warsaw Pact countries by the West German missions, and legal assistance between these states and the FRG as well as Berlin was to be conducted directly between the courts without going through the missions.

At the beginning of 1973 the Soviet foreign ministry, in an attempt to demonstrate the Soviet view of West Berlin's separate state entity, insisted that the governing mayor of West Berlin, in a planned visit to the USSR, could not use the services of the West German Embassy for his programme. The mayor, Klaus Schütz, cancelled his visit. The Soviet Union and its allies did not allow the Federal Embassies to provide consular services for official visiting groups from the Federal Republic where West Berliners were present.

The increasing conflict

Initially, the Soviet Union and the GDR accepted the temporary presence in West Berlin of officials and constitutional organs of the Federal Republic without comment. However, the situation changed when, at the turn of the year 1972/3, the President of the Bundestag, Renger, started a public discussion on the adaptation of voting rights of the West Berlin members of parliament to those of the West German members of parliament. The Soviet Embassy in East Berlin and the East German government protested and declared that mere discussion of such a step was not compatible with the Quadripartite Agreement which stated that the Western Sectors of Berlin were not part of the FRG and were not to be governed by it.[22] After this, the Eastern side displayed more suspicion of any activities carried out by officials and constitutional organs of the Federal Republic in West Berlin. During the spring of 1973, the GDR repeatedly expressed its displeasure through the official medium of the ADN on such occasions. A meeting of the legal committee of the Bundesrat was criticised at the end of March 1973 by both the central organ of the SED and the Soviet government newspaper *Isvestia*.[23]

In the spring of 1973 controversy emerged over the permanent presence of the Federal Republic in West Berlin. When a two-year executive programme for the West German–Soviet Cultural Agreement was to be drawn up, the Eastern side questioned the legality of existing Federal institutions in West Berlin and refused to include them in the proposed co-operation.

Also in the spring of 1973 the conclusion of an agreement between the Sender Freies Berlin (SFB) – a West Berlin broadcasting station –

and the Soviet broadcasting and television committee broke down over the Soviet demand that the SFB as a West Berlin institution must sever its ties with the West German 'Arbeitsgemeinschaft der öffentlich-rechtlichen Rundfunkanstalten der Bundesrepublik Deutschland' (Association of the Broadcasting Organisations under Public Law in the FRG). From then on the Soviet Union shut out the SFB from all contacts.[24] At the end of June 1973 the usual communiqué had to be omitted at the end of a visit to the Soviet Union by West German journalists because the hosts would not drop their demand that the West Berlin participants must be listed as a separate delegation. Visiting Soviet groups repeatedly broke off their visits to the Federal Republic early in order to avoid the scheduled visit to West Berlin.[25]

The Soviet Union and the GDR began to take exception to what they viewed as a far too extensive inclusion of West Berlin in the legal and constitutional system of the Federal Republic. In the summer of 1973, they issued detailed diplomatic protests[26] against the extension by the Bundestag and the Bundesrat of the new introductory law to the penal code to West Berlin. The reason given was that some of the provisions brought the Western Sectors of Berlin into the jurisdiction of the Basic Law and West German government organs; for example, where reference was made to the Federal Constitutional Court Law which could not claim authority in West Berlin. The GDR and the USSR claimed that, contrary to the Quadripartite Agreement, questions of security were being dealt with in the various provisions that made it a punishable offence in the Western Sectors for acts to be carried out against the security and basic order of the Federal Republic or which dealt with violations of or threats to public order.

Eastern objections escalated further when the Federal Constitutional Court on 31 July 1973, in its judgement on the Basic Treaty, explicitly declared West Berlin to be a 'Land' of the Federal Republic.[27] This ruling was met with sharp Soviet and East German protests.[28] The establishment of a Federal environmental protection agency in West Berlin brought a sharp reaction from the USSR and the GDR. They maintained that this was in contradiction to the agreement reached in the Quadripartite Agreement that the Western Sectors of Berlin did not belong to the Federal Republic, that the Federal presence in West Berlin must be restricted and that there would be no unilateral changes in the area covered by the Four Power Agreement.[29] Apparently Eastern distrust of the Federal Republic's intentions in West Berlin increased and it seems that this had a negative influence on their assessment of customarily practised ties. In September 1973, the USSR and the GDR objected for the first time in official, diplomatic form against the professional activity of a West German constitutional organ in West Berlin. They took the view that the meeting of the Bundestag interior committee in West Berlin scheduled for 1 October would, contrary to the Quadripartite Agreement, be dealing with questions of security which therefore amounted to treating the Western Sectors as a 'Land' of the Federal Republic and to the explicitly disallowed usurpation of powers by the West German state. This represented a 'gross violation' of the Quadripartite Agreement and the meeting was therefore 'illegal' and 'provocative'.[30]

The conflict over the establishment of the Federal Environmental Protection Agency in West Berlin issued in a new phase. Already in the autumn of 1973 the Soviet Union and the GDR had vigorously protested against such an intention. Their view was that the planned step was contrary to the agreement reached in the Quadripartite Agreement over the restriction of the Federal presence in West Berlin.[31] The Federal Government, however, felt that according to the provisions in the Quadripartite Agreement which stated that the ties between West Berlin and the FRG were to be maintained and developed, the establishment of the Federal Environmental Agency was legitimate.[32] In its view the wording gave it the right to add new Federal institutions to those already existing there. Furthermore, the Agency had no governmental powers in West Berlin; legislation was to go first through Bonn, undergo adoption by the Berlin Senate and finally be approved by the three Western Allies. The project had been proposed under Brandt in order to strengthen and underline the ties between West Berlin and the Federal Republic – it was felt that it was important to show that détente did not mean that Bonn intended them to be weakened. The Federal Environmental Agency was one of the first issues with which Schmidt was faced when he took over as Chancellor after Brandt's resignation. Foreign Minister Genscher was strongly in favour of it and argued that the Soviet Union would accept it in the interests of overall East–West détente, that it would cause no complications and that it was not contrary to the Quadripartite Agreement. Schmidt, however, had misgivings and would have liked to cancel the project in West Berlin but was compelled by internal political reasons to go along with the proposal.[33] What added considerably to the problem was that Foreign Minister Genscher, whilst in his former post of Minister of the Interior, had been unable to resist stating in public that the establishment of the Federal Environmental Agency was intended as a political act.[34] Thus the Eastern side was bound to see the move as provocative.

On 19 June 1974, the West German Bundestag decided that the Federal Environmental Agency would be established in West Berlin. The Soviet Union and the GDR responded with sharp diplomatic and journalistic protest and with heavy threats. The GDR began to harass traffic on the West Berlin Autobahn, subjecting travellers to searches and strict controls. The East German government issued a transit ban for all employees of the Agency and enforced it on 29 July against the head of the central department of the Agency. Things had reached the verge of crisis. As a result of sharp Western and above all American pressure these actions were never repeated. The harassment of traffic was stopped. For the Western Allies and the Federal Republic the central point of the Quadripartite Agreement, the one by which it stood or fell, was the Eastern side's abandonment of harassment of West Berlin traffic as a means of objecting to the ties between the FRG and West Berlin. In Western eyes such action against transit traffic called the whole treaty into question. Their view was that even if the West had been acting illegally – and they believed it had not – the signatories to the Quadripartite Agreement and to the intra-German follow-up agreements had undertaken to promote the prevention of complications in the area, not to use or threaten the use of force, to settle disputes by solely peaceful means and not unilaterally to change the existing situation in the area. Any differences were to be settled through Four Power consultations and in the intra-German transit commission.

The Western Powers emphasised to the Soviet Union that in their view the entire Quadripartite Agreement was endangered and that this could have unforeseen consequences for the détente process. For its part, the Soviet Union also had no interest in allowing the acute conflict of the summer of 1974 to develop into a major or lasting confrontation – the more so since it was hoping for good results from the negotiations over CSCE. And it may also be that Moscow felt that the Eastern side had made its point and that in future the West would be more cautious in their policy towards West Berlin and refrain from similar projects:[35] in fact, a plan, first proposed by Brandt, to set up a foundation in West Berlin to collect documentation about the German nation east and west was indeed abandoned as a result of the Eastern action.[36]

The conflict of summer 1974 had long-term implications. The Soviet suspicion which had already arisen during the Four Power negotiations in 1970/1 that the Western side wanted to systematically incorporate West Berlin into the Federal Republic found new nourishment. The result was that after that the smallest proceeding was suspiciously scrutinised for possible implications concerning the theory that the city was a 'Land' of the Federal Republic. The Eastern position on the ties between West Berlin and the Federal Republic hardened after the conflict. Since then, the line – first formulated in statements against the establishment of the Environmental Agency – that the Quadripartite Agreement provided that the Federal agencies should be reduced in West Berlin was generally applied by the Soviet Union and the GDR. From the late autumn of 1973 the line was emphasised that strictly speaking according to the Quadripartite Agreement all Federal Agencies had no right to be in West Berlin. Only non-political ties, especially those in the fields of trade and culture, could be developed.

Between 28 and 31 October 1974, Schmidt and Genscher visited Moscow. The Berlin problem and the Federal Environmental Agency figured prominently in the talks which they held with General Secretary Brezhnev and Foreign Minister Gromyko. No long-term progress was made, however, on the defusing of the conflict over the interpretation of the Quadripartite Agreement nor on three agreements on scientific and technological co-operation, cultural exchange and legal aid which had become deadlocked over the question of the inclusion of West Berlin.[37] The Norddeutsche Rundfunk (North German Radio) which was among the German journalistic presence in Moscow spoke of a 'profound and genuine Soviet irritation over the siting of the Federal Environmental Agency in Berlin ... The resulting mistrust (is) [sic] now the main obstacle for progress in the Berlin question.'[38] The Berlin problem remained one of the main topics of subsequent talks with the Soviet leadership in the following years.[39] In 1975, for example, during the bilateral talks held in Helsinki at the summit of the Conference on Security and Co-operation in Europe, there was a strong exchange between Schmidt and Gromyko over Berlin.[40]

Eastern hostility was directed first and foremost towards Federal institutions in West Berlin. The Soviet Union, the GDR and their allies steadfastly refused to include these agencies in any co-operation with the Federal Republic. From the beginning of 1975 the Soviet Union and East Germany continually protested against the Federal government being represented where necessary by representatives of her West Berlin agencies in international specialised organisations. For example, the USSR and the GDR protested in letters to the United Nations General Secretary Waldheim against a representative of the Bundeskartellamt (Federal Cartel Agency), which was situated in West Berlin, participating as a member of the West German delegation in a United Nations working group. The Federal Cartel Agency's presence in West Berlin was described as illegal even though it had existed in West Berlin, and with the consent of the Western Powers, long before the Quadripartite Agreement was concluded.[41]

The Soviet Union's and East Germany's restrictive position on the activities of constitutional organs and officials of the Federal Republic in West Berlin hardened from the summer of 1974. The view taken seemed to be that what was not explicitly allowed in the Quadripartite Agreement must be inadmissible.[42] For example, meetings of the Ältestenrat and Präsidium of the Bundestag in West Berlin were objected to on the grounds that the Quadripartite Agreement did not provide for this possibility.[43] The Eastern side frequently protested against meetings of Bundestag committees, ministerial conferences and against working visits by Federal German politicians in West Berlin. For example, Moscow's ambassador in East Berlin, Piotr Abrasimov, objected in May 1975 when Foreign Minister Genscher accompanied Dr Kissinger on his visit to address the West Berlin City Parliament, claiming that Genscher had breached the Quadripartite Agreement by illegally exercising his role as Foreign Minister in West Berlin where the FRG was not sovereign;[44] exception was taken to Genscher accompanying first the French Foreign Minister and then the newly elected US Vice-President Walter Mondale to West Berlin in 1977.[45] The Soviet Union protested to the Western Powers over Genscher accompanying Mondale to West Berlin.[46]

The Eastern side repeatedly objected to the presence in West Berlin of the Federal President or members of the Federal government. Objections were repeatedly raised over visits by state guests of the Federal Republic to West Berlin, above all when they were accompanied by high-ranking personages from Bonn. The hardening of the Eastern position over state visits was justified by interpreting the provision in the Quadripartite Agreement that state representatives of the Federal Republic might not perform constitutional or official acts in West Berlin where this would make the city into a constituent part of the Federal Republic and governed by it, as meaning that all official acts by Federal German office-holders were forbidden.

In May 1975, *The Times*, spoke of 'disturbing developments in Berlin in recent months arising from Soviet pinpricks' and reported that there had been an alarming increase in recent months in difficulties over the inclusion of West Berlin in West German trade delegations, exhibitions and cultural events, and the extension to West Berlin of trade agreements signed by West Germany with countries of Eastern Europe.[47]

The Soviet Union and the GDR attempted in various ways to emphasise their theory that West Berlin was a separate state. For example, in a number of cases consular missions substituted the nationality entry 'German' in Western Berliners' visa applications with 'Persons with permanent residence in the Western Sectors of Berlin'. From February 1976, diplomatic passes issued by the Federal government to West Berlin members of the Bundestag were no longer recognised.

In January 1976 the Soviet Ambassador to the Federal Republic excluded the West Berlin participants from the closing reception of a symposium between representatives of the West German Bundestag and the Supreme Soviet. The Eastern side repeatedly declined invitations issued by both the Senate and the Federal Government to international events in West Berlin.

The inclusion of West Berlin in the legal system of the Federal Republic came under increasingly severe attack by the USSR and the GDR. The extension of Federal laws to West Berlin was increasingly frequently claimed to be illegal by being in contradiction to the security and status reservation in the Quadripartite Agreement.

On 14 January 1976 the Soviet Union protested over an amendment to the electoral law which, with the reservation regarding direct elections, was extended to West Berlin in the usual way. The Soviet Union claimed that the Federal aim was to give the impression that West Berlin was a 'Land' of the Federal Republic and that its representatives could be represented in the Bundestag.[48]

With the aim of forcing the status of a separate state entity on West Berlin, attempts were made to establish inter-governmental relations with the Senate of West Berlin. West Berlin was dependent on co-operation with East Germany on a number of practical questions. Agreements, on which West Berlin was very keen, were blocked by the East German demand that the Senate should drop the concept of 'intercity agreements' by which it had been able to negotiate with the GDR government without appearing to operate as the government of a state – a demand which, even if the Senate had been prepared to agree to it, would never have been allowed by the three Western Occupying Powers and was therefore impossible.

By June 1976, about a hundred Soviet protests to the Allies had been counted since the Quadripartite Agreement with scores of less formal Soviet and East German complaints ranging from protests against a meeting of the German Chimney-sweep Association to protests against a visit of Schleswig-Holstein parliamentarians.[49] On 13 August 1976, a group of young Christian Democrats were barred from crossing East Germany to West Berlin to hold a commemoration of the fifteenth anniversary of the building of the Berlin Wall. A protest by the United States, Britain and France alleging that East Germany had violated the right of access to West Berlin was rejected by the Soviet Union. A Soviet Embassy spokesman in Berlin said that the East Germans had been completely justified.[50]

From 1974 the intensity of Soviet government criticism of West Berlin's membership of the European Community began to increase. The Soviet Union repeatedly disputed that the jurisdiction of the Treaties of Rome of 1957 included West Berlin and in this respect did not even accept the existing situation before the Quadripartite Agreement. From the second half of 1974 the Soviet Union and the GDR objected to meetings of European bodies in West Berlin, maintaining that such demonstrations were an attempt by the Federal Republic to undermine the fundamental stipulation of the Quadripartite Agreement that West Berlin did not belong to the West German state.[51] On 20 January 1975 the EEC Council of Ministers decided to establish a European Centre for Vocational Training in West Berlin. For reasons of national interest the FRG and West Berlin wanted the Centre established in West Berlin rather than the Federal Republic and the Soviet Union took a similar view to the one they had taken over the Federal Environmental Agency, that is, they felt it implied incorporation of West Berlin into the FRG. Already on 6 February 1975 the Soviet Embassy in the GDR protested with a memorandum to the USA mission in Berlin.[52]

In July 1976 the European Summit decided to move towards direct elections to the European Parliament. On 3 August 1976 the Soviet Foreign Ministry protested for the first time in due form to the ambassadors of the three Western Powers in Moscow against the inclusion of West Berlin in the direct elections, even though it had been provided that the West Berlin deputies would not be elected directly but through the Berlin Abgeordnetenhaus (chamber of deputies).[53] The participation of West Berlin representatives in the European parliament, something previously not objected to, was described as a gross violation of the Quadripartite Agreement which would lead to complications.[54] Soviet diplomats frequently tried to get representatives of Western states to adopt the Soviet position on this – for example, Foreign Minister Gromyko during his visit to Brussels in October

1976.[55] Soviet protests continued through 1977. In August 1977, for example, Ambassador Abrasimov said that if West Berlin took part in the elections it would entitle the USSR to a revision of the Quadripartite Agreement.[56] And in November 1977, Soviet military patrols obstructed the motor cavalcade of the President of the European Parliament, Emilio Colombo, when he visited West Berlin.[57]

Up till the end of 1976 the Eastern side had confined itself to the verbal expression of the position that the Quadripartite Agreement applied to West Berlin only. However, at the beginning of 1977 the GDR took a number of concrete steps to abolish the visible distinctions between East Germany and East Berlin and to emphasise the isolation of West Berlin. From January, Western visitors to East Berlin were required to obtain visas instead of permits for day visits and a road toll for trips between West and East Berlin was introduced. The control post on the city boundary between East Berlin and the GDR was removed and the discontinuation of the publication of the government gazette promulgating GDR legislation in East Berlin was announced. The Soviet ambassador in the GDR stated that Allied rights and responsibilities applied only to West Berlin and that the Eastern section of Berlin was the capital of the GDR. The Western response was unusually forceful. The heads of state and government of the three Western Powers, Presidents Carter and Giscard d'Estaing and Prime Minister Callaghan, and Chancellor Schmidt met in London to discuss the developments – the first such discussion of Berlin since the 1975 Helsinki Conference. On 9 May they issued a joint declaration rejecting any unilateral attempt to alter the special status of Berlin as a whole. The Soviet response was to support the GDR.[58]

From the second half of 1976 to the end of spring 1977, relations between the Soviet Union and the Federal Republic stagnated. The differences over West Berlin continued, and with increasing tendency, to be an important stumbling block which hindered the development of political relations, and of the agreement side of relations between the two states. The Berlin problem had become acute and was at the centre of the bilateral conflicts during this period. It burdened relations between the two states and generated an atmosphere of distrust and growing tension.

The *Frankfurter Allgemeine Zeitung* reports on a steep increase in the number of West Berliners turned back at border crossings to East Berlin: on 29 January 1977 the news agency dpa reported from West Berlin that in January more than 150 West Berliners had been turned back; and according to a spokesman for the Berlin Senate the GDR authorities from the beginning of January till the end of June 1977 turned back 954 West Berliners – during the same period in 1976 the GDR had only refused entry to 143 West Berliners.[59]

With regard to the agreement side of relations between the Soviet Union and the Federal Republic, the agreement over scientific and technological co-operation was still unsigned and the Agreement on Cultural Exchange which had been signed in 1973 remained a 'dead letter' (both sides were unable to agree on a two-year implementation programme) due to disagreements on the practical inclusion of West Berlin and the appellation of its authorities and institutions. Already in 1975, Egon Bahr had said, 'the solution of practical questions in connection with Berlin (West) has become the most effective obstacle against the further development of our relations.'[60] He went on to express his disappointment that 'a number of agreements between the Federal Republic of Germany and the Soviet Union, which are necessary in order to overcome the impairment in the further development of our relations, are still outstanding with regard to Berlin (West).'[61]

Despite signs after the spring of 1977 that the Soviet Union was trying to inject new life into the stagnating relations between the two states, friction over the Berlin question continued undiminished through 1977 and the first months of 1978. On 9 March 1978, Chancellor Schmidt in his 'Erklärung der Bundesregierung zur Lage der Nation' (Statement of the Federal Government on the Divided Nation) to the Bundestag said this about Berlin: 'We are concerned about the Soviet Union's and the GDR's protests and polemics against the institutions, events and visits in Berlin, which after all in accordance with the provisions of the Quadripartite Agreement – not just in our opinion but also in that of the three Western Powers – cannot in any way provide grounds for critical protests.'[62]

The 1978 Brezhnev visit to Bonn

From 4 to 7 May 1978 Brezhnev visited Bonn and Hamburg at the head of a delegation of seventy. In the talks which Brezhnev and his delegation held with the Federal President, the Chancellor, members of the Federal government and of the opposition, arms control and disarmament questions and economic and technological co-operation figured particularly largely. The Berlin problem was, so to speak, dealt with only on the edge of the talks, but in fact figured largely in the talks held between Chancellor Schmidt and General Secretary Brezhnev and between Foreign Ministers Genscher and

Gromyko. A very significant discussion was held in Hamburg between Schmidt and Brezhnev over ways to reduce friction in the Berlin question, and it was during this discussion that Schmidt told Brezhnev that the Federal Republic would not increase its presence in West Berlin, nor would it, however, take anything away from Bonn's already existing presence – in Soviet eyes all FRG presence was illegal. The German side assured the Soviets that they would not test the treaty to its limits. They made it clear to the Soviets that they had no intention whatsoever to alter the status of West Berlin or to expand the existing ties. The existing ties, however, would be maintained. The Soviets were told that they could keep their legal position, i.e. that the FRG did not expect them to give it up, but that they should be more flexible in their practical policy.[63]

The Petersberger Formula of 1973[64] was included in the Gemeinsame Deklaration (joint declaration) of the visit and in such a way that 'the strict observance and full implementation of the Quadripartite Agreement of 3 September 1971' was to be considered as an 'essential requirement for lasting détente in the centre of Europe and for an improvement in the relations between ... the Federal Republic of Germany and the Soviet Union.'[65] West Berlin was included under the Frank–Falin Formula in the very important 'Agreement on Developing and Deepening the Long-term Co-operation between the Federal Republic of Germany and the Union of Soviet Socialist Republics in the Economic and Industrial Fields' (see appendices A and B).

In his speech to the Bundestag on 11 May 1978 in which he reported on the Brezhnev state visit, Schmidt said this about the Berlin problem:

> No-one who is in a position to assess the Berlin situation expected that it could have been made possible during this German–Soviet meeting for the fundamental differences of opinion in the Berlin question to be removed and for a solution to the various concrete problems which are connected with this to be found. We have, however, talked about both – the fundamental questions and the repeated friction resulting from them in practice – in great detail ... I believe that there is reason to assume that the Soviet interlocutors understand our Berlin policy better now, that some misunderstandings were cleared up and that at least part of the mutual distrust has really been removed.[66]

The FRG foreign office report for 1978 also stated:

> Although the fundamental differences of opinion in the Berlin question could not be removed during the visit to the Federal Republic of Brezhnev, General Secretary of the Central Committee of the CPSU,

in May 1978, the Federal Government has reason to assume that, through the development of mutual understanding and trust, the preconditions can be created for a long-term defusing of the confrontation over the Berlin question and to make outstanding Berlin problems solvable.[67]

After the Brezhnev visit there were also signs of relaxation in German–German relations (see chapter 4). The subsequent intra-German negotiations on the building of a motorway from Hamburg to Berlin and the restoration and opening of the (for the southern districts of West Berlin very important) Teltow Canal led relatively quickly to agreement (November 1978). It would seem that the conclusion of these German–German traffic negotiations apparently occurred with Soviet approval and was in a sense a consequence of the meeting with Brezhnev and his foreign minister in Bonn, and Gromyko's visit to East Berlin in May 1978.

West German claims after the Brezhnev visit that the Soviet attitude towards the Berlin problem had changed positively were borne out by a marked calming down, expressed in a deliberately exercised restraint by the Soviets. The acute irritation on both sides over the existing differences on the Berlin question was eased. A year later, in his speech to the Bundestag on the State of the Divided Nation (*Lage der Nation*) on 17 May 1979, Chancellor Schmidt said,

> In my talks with the Soviet General Secretary Brezhnev last May I gained the impression that the Soviet leadership today sees the Berlin situation more realistically and sees, just as we do, its importance for détente in Europe and for German–Soviet relations. The fact is that the political situation of the city has become quieter since the middle of last year. The friction with the Eastern side has been reduced.[68]

This situation was to outlast the strains of the post-Afghanistan international climate and East–West tension over Poland. The quietening down of the Berlin question in 1978 was one of the successes of FRG–Soviet relations under Chancellor Schmidt.

The 1978 talks on Berlin brought about a calming of the conflict over West Berlin but should not be regarded so much as being the result of a sudden alteration in the FRG's policy towards Berlin but rather as a 'breakthrough' achieved at a summit meeting in convincing the Soviets of the FRG's intentions towards Berlin. Schmidt had been unintentionally drawn into the conflict through Genscher's Berlin 'zeal', and the problems caused by the establishment of the Federal Environmental Agency in Berlin made him feel that he must try to find ways to 'deconfront' without giving up the Federal Republic's position on Berlin. When Schmidt came into office, therefore, the Federal government increasingly tried to counteract Soviet fears of over-strong ties between West Berlin and the Federal Republic as far as this was possible without surrendering the Western legal position. For example, the exhaustion of all, according to the Western view, allowable possibilities was refrained from and a painstakingly exact observance of all the restrictions resulting from the Quadripartite Agreement was signalled to the Soviet side. During these years, however, there had been no summit meeting.

Schmidt had always felt that the Federal Republic had two principal problems in its foreign policy which distinguished it from all other states – the divided German nation and divided Berlin – and he believed that they must always be taken into account in West Germany's foreign policy. He also saw very clearly that nothing should be done which could hurt the people in the GDR and Berlin. He felt that it was not a wise policy to increase the Federal Republic's presence and to go beyond the Quadripartite Agreement and risk sharp reaction by the Soviet Union. A strict adherence to the Quadripartite Agreement would avoid giving the Soviet Union a pretext to hurt the FRG. Any reaction by the Soviet Union would not be good for West Berlin not only out of reasons of security of West Berlin and consideration for the West Berliners but also for the reason that West Berlin needed peace and stability for its economy. In his speech to the Bundestag on 11 May 1978 he said:

> The idea that the security and vitality of Berlin really can be strengthened through merely demonstrative activities and initiatives which are of no actual benefit to anyone must be parted with. In the interest of Berlin, a responsible Berlin policy must focus on the possibilities and limits set by the Quadripartite Agreement.[69]

Berlin after the 1978 visit

The 1978 breakthrough over the Berlin question did not mean that after 1978 the Soviets never again expressed criticism – for example they sharply criticised Carter's and Reagan's visits to Berlin – or that there were no further difficulties – for example, at the beginning of January 1979 there was an open quarrel over the way in which the West Berliners were to be included in the Federal German team in the 1980 Olympics in Moscow. This could not be the case because the differences of opinion over the correct interpretation of the provisions of the Quadripartite Agreement continued. What it did mean was that there was a considerable decrease in Soviet warnings, protests, etc. The regularity and intensity of criticism decreased. From the second half of July 1978 the Soviet Union kept to the course of mutual restraint and respect. Visits of Western politicians and members of the armed forces in West Berlin were met merely with the requisite protests to maintain its legal position. When the mayor of West Berlin took his turn as chairman in the Bundesrat in the autumn of 1978, Moscow did not carry out earlier implied threats. Soviet protests in the run up to the European elections were relatively restrained.[70] Although announcement of Soviet approval of direct elections in June 1979 to the GDR Volkskammer of East Berlin representatives was probably meant as a riposte,[71] there was no specific Soviet reaction, despite a warning to the contrary,[72] when West Berlin representatives participated in July 1979 in the first session of the European parliament. In fact it seems that none was anticipated by the West German side. Berlin and the direct European elections had been discussed at the 1978 Brezhnev visit and apparently 'some more noise' – according to an adviser to the Chancellor – was expected but 'no grave upsets'.[73] All this signified a calming down of the situation.

Both sides took the view that the Quadripartite Agreement should not be subjected to any unnecessary tests and that their respective positions should only be expressed with due consideration of the sensitivities of the other side. Critical boundaries were in particular the free and unhindered transit traffic for the West and for the East, any formal step implying incorporation of West Berlin into the state system of the Federal Republic.

Although the Soviets did not give up the expression of their legal position on Berlin, they did not do anything that would cause more difficulties and they gave more leeway. For example, they allowed the GDR to continue to enter into agreements with the Federal Republic that in the final effect made things easier for West Berlin and the West Berliners. The new motorway, for example, between Hamburg and Berlin was originally intended to have a new crossing in north Berlin. There were enormous difficulties, however, in West Berlin as this would have involved getting rid of woods and the people of West Berlin took the matter to court. In order to avoid this problem, the GDR was asked to strengthen an existing road which they did in the summer of 1984 and which was to be allowed to stay until 1987. A concession was needed for this from the Soviet Union, which was not a simple matter. The fact that this concession was made shows that since

1978 the Soviets did not only not make difficulties but that they were ready for improvements for West Berlin. A second example was the agreement over the new telecommunication connections signed in 1985 between the GDR and the FRG which meant improved telephone links.

Evidence of the change is traceable through a number of sources. The change showed up in dramatic clarity in the protocols of the talks held between the British, French and American ambassadors in Bonn and their colleagues in East Berlin. Before the 1978 visit, 80 per cent of these talks consisted of Soviet complaints relating to Berlin and 20 per cent was devoted to other, including international, topics. In the years following the visit, exactly the reverse was the case.[74] The development may also be traced through press coverage of Berlin. The Berlin press files held at the International Institute for Strategic Studies, London contain the following number of articles for the years preceding the visit: 1974 (76), 1975 (31), 1976 (43), 1977 (30).[75] After 1977, there is a sudden and sustained drop: 1978 (11), 1979 (11), 1980 (6), 1981 (43), 1982 (15)*. Die Internationale Politik 1977/78, the yearbook of the Deutsche Gesellschaft für Auswärtige Politik, Bonn, also reports that from mid-1978 a change in Soviet behaviour appeared and a calming down of the conflict over the status of Berlin occurred.[76]

On the negative side, many agreements between the FRG and the USSR remained unsigned because of Berlin. For example, the agreement on scientific and technological co-operation was not signed until some years later and it was even longer before the cultural skeleton agreement signed in 1973 was implemented by a concrete exchange programme. The inclusion of the Berlin clause as such was not the problem for any of these agreements but rather the practical realisation of these treaties. The Frank–Falin formula had been shown in practice to be not enough and what the FRG wanted to ensure was the real inclusion of West Berlin's Federal institutes, agencies and universities in these agreements – something to which the Soviets were not prepared to agree.[77]

---

* The high figure for 1981 is due to press coverage of elections in West Berlin and the party political problems caused by them for Schmidt and the SPD; only six of the articles are devoted to the Berlin problem. Of the fifteen articles for 1982, twelve concern the Berlin problem; three deal with the internal problem of rioting which occurred that year.

4 The Federal Republic of Germany's relations with the German Democratic Republic

The triangle FRG–USSR–GDR

Government and party officials were, when interviewed, generally reluctant to discuss the FRG's relations with the GDR in the context of FRG–Soviet relations, one party official stating to the author that it was a difficult and discreet question on which only the Chancellor could decide whether to release information. In answer to the question as to whether the FRG was able to put a lot of pressure on the GDR through Moscow, one government official's response was that apart from one exception over the raising and extension of the minimum daily exchange rate for visitors to the GDR in 1980, the FRG never did this for the reason that they would not like to have seen the Soviet Union put pressure on the GDR, because the more the Soviet Union did this, the more it would have weakened East Germany. It would have encouraged the Soviet Union in the installation of itself as a hegemonial power and the FRG did not want the Soviet Union to use even benevolent influence. The only time the Soviet Union was used was for practical issues such as the exchange of spies. Another government official agreed with this view and said that the Federal Republic could not achieve better relations with the GDR behind the back of the Soviet Union but equally could not play alone with the Soviets and ask them to put pressure on the GDR. However, one West German researcher into East–West relations tended towards the view, when interviewed, that for the FRG, Soviet hegemony in Eastern Europe was a fact of life and that it would only have been realistic for the FRG to have made use of this. And Josef Joffe, a member of the editorial staff of *Die Zeit* has written in an article in the journal *Foreign Policy*,

> Bonn remains locked in a silent but stubborn contest with the GDR over the future of Germany ('two states in one nation', according to Bonn, vs. 'two nation states', according to East Berlin) and the rules of

coexistence (interaction vs. insulation). Especially where Berlin is concerned, this is a contest where marginal leverage is frequently provided by Soviet goodwill translated into pressure on East Germany.[1]

Without access to classified documentary evidence of talks held, and in view of the reluctance of those interviewed to impart more than a minimum of information, it is, of course, impossible to state where the truth of the matter lies – both views of FRG policy being equally plausible. What was certainly true, as Gerhard Wettig has written, was that 'Because of her interest in relaxation of the East German policy of 'delimitation', the Federal Republic is … dependent on co-operation with the USSR, that is on her approval of relevant relations with the GDR.'[2] (See pp. 66–7 for the GDR's policy of *Abgrenzung*.)

Gerhard Wettig, researcher at the Bundesinstitut für ostwissen-schaftliche und internationale Studien in Cologne (Federal Institute for Eastern and International Studies), who has written extensively in the past on Berlin questions, also has asserted that:

> The three West Berlin protecting powers have delegated the responsibility for the viability of the city to the West German state. If this charge is to be fulfilled, then more than a passive tolerance of West Berlin is required from the Eastern side. It requires, even though the extent can only be limited, a co-operation with the GDR and the USSR in order to solve various questions. Moscow can, without violating the peace obligation arising from the Four Power Agreement, put obstacles affecting its existence into the City's path through refusals to co-operate and through appropriate suggestions to the GDR. It can, on the other hand, by allowing and furthering co-operation between the two German states also decisively ease West Berlin's situation.[3]

It is significant that after the 1978 Brezhnev visit to Bonn there was new movement in FRG–GDR relations (see p. 90), and that after this visit the Soviets allowed the GDR to continue to enter into agreements with the Federal Republic that made things easier for West Berlin and the West Berliners (see chapter 3) and that after several attempts came to nothing, the Honecker–Schmidt summit meeting went ahead after the 1981 Brezhnev visit to Bonn.

At least since the Soviet intervention in Afghanistan and the NATO double-track decision, the FRG has tried to persuade the GDR to put pressure on the USSR to alter Soviet behaviour: Klaus Bölling, who was the Federal Republic's Permanent Representative in the GDR, wrote in connection with Schmidt's December 1981 visit to the GDR:

At the latest after his meeting with the General Secretary in Belgrade, the Chancellor knew that Erich Honecker, despite all his loyalty towards his most important ally, had realised that a solution in Geneva was not possible without co-operation from his Soviet friends. Schmidt had no illusions that the GDR man could speak to his main ally with the same openness with which he himself had done to two American presidents and which had resulted in him having to put up with an increasingly bad press. All the same, he constantly tried anew to motivate the Saarländer to actively use his nevertheless considerable influence to make it clear to the men in the Kremlin that a return to the policy of confrontation would mean first of all a heavy burden for the two German states. The grey zone of strategic weapons not covered by SALT II must be removed with the utmost expedition said Schmidt. 'We are assisting in this. And my urgent wish is, Mr. General Secretary, that you do the same. We have signed the treaty on the non-proliferation of nuclear weapons, you have and we have. The world powers have a duty towards us. We must put pressure on the Superpowers.'[4]

The Chancellor once more made a great effort to win over the General Secretary of the SED and most important ally of the USSR for a positive complicity to prevent the re-armament.[5]

Obviously the Soviet Union was aware of Bonn's interest in good relations with the GDR. Apparently, every time the West German side spoke to the Soviets, they made it very clear to them that human contacts with the GDR were very important, that if the Soviet Union put pressure on the GDR to adversely affect these then they would regard this as a very unfriendly act, and they told the Soviet Union that they would have to take Bonn's interest into account in being friendly with the GDR. The Soviet Union tried to make use of Bonn's interest in promoting FRG–GDR relations (see pp. 88–9 and ch. 5). One party official told the author that the Soviets, knowing how much the FRG insisted on humanitarian improvements, used to tell the West German side that when the FRG adopted a 'correct' position on security and the international situation, then relations between the GDR and the FRG could be expanded. According to the party official, the FRG had to take this into account but without being dependent. The same party official also put it this way: if you want to engage in politics with the GDR then you can never leave the Soviet Union 'draussen vor der Tür' (i.e. leave the Soviet Union out), Honecker has only the room for manoeuvre that Moscow gives him and that is dependent on the Moscow–Bonn relationship and Schmidt saw this very clearly.

The Soviet Union had an underlying fear of a too close German–

German *rapprochement*. On the economic side (the GDR was, in fact, partly competing with the Soviet Union for Federal financial help and economic co-operation),[6] for example, the Soviets were always on the alert to see that the GDR did not become too dependent on the FRG. They feared that the FRG was pursuing a policy which could remove the GDR from the Eastern bloc. Schmidt knew this and showed consideration for Soviet fears. Indeed, government officials told the author that one of the successes of the Schmidt period was the relax-ation of the FRG's relations with the GDR. The Soviets felt that they could lean back. Schmidt convinced them that the FRG was not a dangerous enemy. This was not the result of any specific talks at which Schmidt convinced the Soviets that it was safe for them to let FRG–GDR relations develop, but was rather the general posture of the Schmidt government over a longer period of time and the growing consolidation of the GDR system which made the Soviets more relaxed with regard to the intensification of FRG–GDR relations. The posture of the Schmidt government was to leave the reunification issue aside and deal instead more with day-to-day issues of a practical nature (see p. 74).

Normalisation of relations between the two German states entailed increased personal contacts between the Germans of both countries, the consequences of which the GDR felt to be incalculable and potentially politically destabilising. The GDR therefore responded from the start with a policy of *Abgrenzung* (Delimitation) intended to limit and counter the damage, and in which it was generally backed by the Soviet Union (an example of this was the increase in 1980 of the minimum daily exchange rate for visitors to the GDR, see pp. 84–8). The GDR leadership declared that in a period of peaceful co-existence the ideological battle between two states with differing social and political systems necessarily had to intensify and that peaceful co-existence was nothing but another form of class warfare.[7] After the September 1970 meetings in Erfurt and Kassel and shortly before the beginning of the negotiations on the Basic Treaty, Hermann Axen, a member of the SED Politburo and responsible for international liaison, stated that the GDR was under an obligation to 'continue to delimit itself in all areas from the imperialist Federal Republic'.[8] Premier Willi Stoph described delimitation as 'an objective process that is inevitable in view of the contradictions between the two sociopolitical systems'.[9] What this meant in practice was that the GDR government actively discouraged contacts between East and West Germans in order to insulate its citizens from potential Western and West German influences. Normalisation was to be kept to governmental level. Of all the East European countries, East Germany had the greatest legitimacy problem. The existence of the FRG and the declared aim of the FRG to preserve the sense of the nation and to work towards reunification through self-determination meant that not only her socialist structure might be challenged but also her national identity. General Secretary Honecker repeatedly declared that the German question was no longer open, i.e. it had been determined in the form of two national states.

Nevertheless, the author was told more than once during interviews that the GDR gained in weight and confidence in later years. This appeared also to apply personally to Honecker. Internationally, since signing the Basic Treaty in 1972 and entering the United Nations in 1973, the GDR greatly gained in importance. It more than quadrupled the number of states with which diplomatic relations were exchanged. Foreign policy activities were extended to the Third World, supporting politically, militarily and economically Soviet aims in this area. Indeed, in some parts of Africa the GDR was competing directly with West Germany for economic and political influence. At the time of Schmidt's 1981 visit to the GDR *The Times* published an article in which it was stated that observers in East Berlin believed that Honecker wanted to become Eastern Europe's most important contact man with the West after President Brezhnev.[10] At home, in view of relatively favourable economic development and the fact that, since 1953, unlike Czecho-slovakia, Romania, the Soviet Union and Poland, it had had to face no domestic crisis either economic or political, self-confidence had grown to the extent that an independent peace movement was tolerated (i.e. it was less suppressed than would have been the case ten years before) and a 'national inheritance' policy was embarked on – for example, Martin Luther's five hundredth anniversary was celebrated in the GDR.

The 1975 twenty-five year Treaty of Friendship, Co-operation and Mutual Assistance signed between the Soviet Union and the GDR tied the two states closer together than before. It was not only the case that the GDR needed the Soviet Union. The Soviet Union also needed the GDR and the stronger the GDR became politically, economically and militarily, the more important it became to Moscow. One FRG govern-ment official expressed to the author the view that the Soviet Union was much more conscious of the value of the GDR, both within the Eastern bloc and internationally, than formerly and it has happened that it took the decision not to override the interests of the GDR. The

Kaliningrad nuclear power plant project was a good example of this. The project for the West German firm Kraftwerk Union to build a nuclear power plant near Kaliningrad in the Soviet Union had first been discussed by Brandt and Brezhnev. The idea was that, in return for Federal German financial and technical support in the construction, Moscow would supply electricity to the FRG. As the power line would have to go through Poland and the GDR, Brezhnev himself had apparently discussed the plan in Warsaw and East Berlin and the Federal Republic was informed that Poland and the GDR had in principle given their approval.[11] The idea was then put forward to supply West Berlin as well with the electricity. West Berlin was not connected to the Federal Republic's power supply system. Coal for power stations had to be brought into the city and the need for energy for industry was growing. The GDR had reservations about this: at first it would only consent to a power line running through the GDR some distance from West Berlin with a branch line under East German control running to West Berlin. Bonn could not agree to this.[12] Moscow apparently understood the FRG's position.[13] During Schmidt's 1975 visit to Moscow, agreement was reached that the power line would run through Poland and the GDR to the border of West Berlin where the direct current would be changed into a three-phase current and about half would go to West Berlin industry and half to the Federal Republic. East Berlin would have to provide the ground for the pylons but apart from that would play no part in the project because the power line from Kaliningrad to the GDR–FRG border would be in Soviet hands. If the GDR wanted the power supply interrupted it could only be done via Moscow and if the power supply did fail the Federal Republic could send power from West Germany to West Berlin. Kosygin gave Schmidt the impression that it would not be difficult to obtain East German agreement to the project.[14] However, the project came to nothing. Apparently the Soviet side put forward complicated financial calculations which raised the prospect of unexpectedly high, economically unjustifiable prices and also tried to persuade the Federal Republic to commit itself to pre-financing amounting to milliards of DMs, and to the large-scale installation of the newest reactor technology. On 30 March 1976 it was announced in Moscow at the end of the sixth conference of the German–Soviet Economic Commission that for reasons of costs the project would not be pursued any further.[15]

In reality it is very likely that the project broke down due to East German opposition. The Federal Republic would only pursue the project if West Berlin was fully included. Both the Soviet Union and the GDR wanted to prevent close ties between West Berlin and the

Federal Republic and connecting West Berlin to the West German power supply would have meant a departure from their restrictive interpretation of the Four Power Agreement. However, the Soviets were more interested in this instance in acquiring a nuclear power station while East Berlin on the other hand was against the project for several reasons. It objected to West Berlin being supplied with energy from the outside and having a direct power line from West Berlin to the Federal Republic;[16] East Berlin itself would have liked to sell electricity to West Berlin in order to make West Berlin more dependent on the GDR;[17] East Berlin was also bidding for a West German nuclear power plant.[18] One Soviet source offered this as an explanation as to why Moscow had dropped a project advantageous to itself: 'Just as America sometimes has to show consideration to the Federal Republic, we sometimes have to show consideration to the GDR.'[19]

FRG–GDR relations not only could not be divorced from GDR–USSR and FRG–USSR relations, they were also affected by and dependent on the superpower relationship and the overall East–West climate. This could have both a positive and a negative effect. Initially, during 1970–3 when FRG–GDR relations were being established, the positive climate of détente obviously had a conducive effect. Conversely, progress in FRG–GDR relations was much more difficult to achieve during a period of worsening superpower relations and international tension. As Chancellor Schmidt said in 1978, 'Détente is not just a bilateral matter. We cannot expect everything between the two German states to be all sweetness and light when all around the overall climate is unfriendly.'[20] In a speech in 1981 on the state of the nation, Schmidt also put it this way,

> Many years ago the notion of rapprochement between East Berlin and Bonn, between both German states, frequently aroused the suspicion of third parties: the German question appeared to disturb the status quo; it appeared to endanger the peace in Europe. Today the reverse is more the case: unrest and fear in the world and in Europe endanger the German–German co-operation that has since been achieved. The increase and extension of the minimum exchange rate for tourist traffic ordered by the GDR Government under this world state of affairs is an example of this. It dealt the relations between both German states a considerable setback.[21]

The FRG's policy towards the GDR

The declared aim of the Federal Republic's German policy was to 'work for a state of peace in Europe, in which the German nation will regain its unity through free self-determination' (see, for example, the Federal Minister for Foreign Affairs in his speech to the 32nd General Assembly of the United Nations in New York on 29 September 1977 and the State Secretary of the Foreign Office in the opening statement at the follow-up conference of the Conference on Security and Co-operation in Europe on 5 November 1977, cited in the foreign office report in Jahresbericht der Bundesregierung 1977).[22] This aim was also declared in the Letter on German Unity[23] handed over by the Federal Government in the Soviet Foreign Ministry on the occasion of the signing of the Treaty between the FRG and the USSR (Moscow Treaty) on 12 August 1970 and again in the letter on German Unity from the Government of the Federal Republic of Germany to the Government of the German Democratic Republic[24] at the time of the signing of the Basic Treaty on 21 December 1972. In the meantime, the Federal Government tried to preserve the sense of nationhood for the duration of the separation, to prevent further drifting apart of the German people, to alleviate the consequences of the division and to establish better relations between the two states.[25]

The Basic Treaty between the Federal Republic and the German Democratic Republic did not and could not alter the special situation of Germany as a whole as there had been no peace treaty and the rights of the Four Powers remained. It aimed instead, despite the different positions of the two German states on the national question, to create a common basis for the further development of relations, to exchange the policy of confrontation for one of co-operation. In the years after 1972 substantial improvements were achieved in transit and tourist traffic, environmental protection and cultural exchange. Talks by officials and political leaders of both sides were conducted on a regular basis. Contact between the Germans on both sides was improved. In 1979, for example, a total of 3.6 million West Germans travelled to the GDR. In the same year 1.4 million (in round figures) East Germans of retirement age visited Federal territory (including West Berlin).[26] Trips for urgent family reasons from the GDR to the Federal Republic by persons not yet of retirement age rose from 11,421 in 1972 to 45,709 in 1982.[27] Telephone calls from the Federal Republic and West Berlin to the GDR and East Berlin rose from 0.7 million in 1970 to 23 million in 1982.[28] East Germans, although unable to travel freely to the FRG, were able to watch West German television and were thus well informed of events in the Federal Republic. The improved contacts between both parts of Germany maintained the substance of the nation, the feeling in both German states of belonging to one nation. Scientifically based polls showed that there had been no lessening of the sense of national unity among Germans.[29]

On the negative side, there were also setbacks and disappointments, particularly that of East Germany's policy of *Abgrenzung*, heightened since the late 1970s. The 'convergence' of the two systems that was once talked about (i.e. Egon Bahr's *Wandel durch Annäherung* or 'change through *rapprochement*') did not happen. As Dr Wilhelm Bruns wrote in his book on German–German relations published in 1984, 'the state of German–German relations has become much better since the Basic Treaty.[30] Better does not mean, however, good and normal!'[31] Chancellor Schmidt in an after-dinner speech during his visit to East Germany in December 1981 declared that good neighbourly relations were still a long way off, that relations were, in fact, still not even reasonably neighbourly.[32]

Demotion of German–German relations during the Schmidt period?

During the Chancellor Schmidt period there was a view held in Bonn that, unlike Willy Brandt, Schmidt was not particularly interested in the GDR, had no emotional relationship with it and therefore just allowed FRG–GDR relations to drag along. Günter Gaus, head of the West German Permanent Mission in East Berlin that took the place of a West German Embassy in the GDR, held the suspicion that Chancellor Schmidt was more or less treating German policy as a *quantité négligeable*[33] – a suspicion which was also held by a small circle of GDR citizens. In intellectual and artistic circles especially, but also in Protestant Church circles, Schmidt was seen as a chancellor who, unlike Brandt, did not want to acknowledge the great historical and moral challenge inherent in the existence of two German states. They felt that Schmidt, a trained economist, was governed only by cost-benefit criteria and besides this, viewed relations with the insignificant GDR functionary, and apparently indecisive man at the top, as a waste of time. These groups were also very sure that Schmidt did not have an emotional relationship with the other part of Germany.[34] One party researcher into German–German relations expressed the view during an interview that for a long time the GDR did not play a big role with Schmidt – his attitude towards Honecker was condescending, feeling that Honecker was beneath him, preferring to talk only with what he felt were the top people such as the American and Soviet leaders, Jim Callaghan in England, or Mitterand in France, but that this changed, however, at the end of his time in office. Frank R. Pfetsch writing on foreign policy under Schmidt–Genscher in his book *Die Aussenpolitik der BRD 1949–1980* wrote that the policy of small steps towards the GDR 'has been continued with still smaller steps; the pace has become slower in the second half of the seventies',[35] and William G. Hyland wrote of USSR–FRG relations in the seventies that 'German unity ... seems to be a dormant if not politically dead issue ... the process of post-treaty normalisation between Bonn and Moscow continues, but appears to be largely an end in itself rather than a bridge to a larger settlement. In West Germany, only a pale reflection of the original illusion survives.'[36]

What certainly does seem to be the case is that to begin with Schmidt judged Honecker as an 'extremely cautious and inhibited man',[37] and that until his second meeting with him, at Marshal Tito's funeral at Belgrade in 1980, (the first had been at Helsinki in 1975) he could not envisage Honecker as being of any use as a partner for meaningful political agreements.[38] At Tito's funeral Schmidt noticed for the first time that Honecker had more political weight than could be judged from his immediate appearance.[39] By this time also Schmidt had got to know Honecker better through occasional telephone conversations.[40] It was certainly not until very late in his office as Chancellor that Schmidt felt the time had come for an open and concrete meeting with the East German leader rather than side-line talks, and by this time Honecker was, astoundingly, almost the only communist leader with whom he had not had a proper meeting.

One government official said during interview that Schmidt placed special emphasis on disarmament and security. He thought balance and arms control were of particular importance. Therefore, for Schmidt, obviously the main place to talk to was Moscow and therefore he was not really bothered with the GDR. By the time of his 1981 visit to Werbellinsee, East Germany, Schmidt did think it was important to have good relations with the GDR. He was quite impressed with Honecker at that visit and had the longest talk with him that he had ever had with a foreign politician.

Furthermore, the adoption of a new policy towards the East and the signing of the Ostpolitik treaties led to greater room for manoeuvre in foreign policy. The time had come to move off in new directions and to move into the mainstream of 'big' issues – those deriving from American–Soviet relations – and for the FRG to act to influence the superpowers where they were able in the same way that the British and French did, for example. The time was past when one could say that Bonn's foreign policy started and finished with East Germany. (See, e.g. Schmidt's June/July 1980 visit to Moscow, p. 125.) Schmidt also most probably felt that if the wider, 'bigger' international issues came right then the GDR issue would come right. This is borne out by Hans Georg Lehmann, private archivist to Helmut Schmidt, in his book *Öffnung nach Osten: Die Ostreisen Helmut Schmidts und die Entstehung der Ost- und Entspannungspolitik* who has written that Schmidt was already thinking along these lines as far back as 1966:

> At the 1966 Dortmund Party Congress deputy parliamentary leader Helmut Schmidt set out, to applause by the delegates, the concept of an active East and détente policy, which he carefully tried *for the first time* [emphasis by Lehmann] to uncouple from the German policy. With Brandt and Bahr they were mainly a function of the reunification policy, and therefore dependent on it, whereas with Schmidt they were largely independent, hitherto blocked opportunities for the Federal Republic having 'come of age' to sound out new room for movement and action under the signs of 'changing world political conditions' (Dortmund keynote speech by Schmidt of 3 June 1966).[41]

Moreover, at the start of Schmidt's term of office, policy with respect to the GDR did not have such a high priority because Schmidt took office in 1974 when there were other pressing problems such as the state of the Western alliance, the EEC and the world economic crisis. The economic pressures in the 1970s affected the Federal Republic as they did the rest of the world, and influenced the Federal Republic's political priorities. Klaus Bölling writes, 'although the impatience of some GDR Protestants with the Bonn "immobility" did not escape Schmidt's notice, he was generally only able in the years of world-wide recession caused by two oil-price increases to concentrate his activities on German–German affairs when conflict occurred between Bonn and East Berlin'.[42]

Another factor which hampered Schmidt, according to inside information, was that in the middle seventies Foreign Minister Genscher could not be persuaded to adopt a policy which would break down the 'taboos' between Bonn and East Berlin.[43] Furthermore, the 1976 general elections returned Schmidt and Genscher with a much reduced majority, leaving them with limited room for manoeuvre and Schmidt was also increasingly faced with signs of weakness in the SPD–FDP coalition. He therefore lacked the political strength to push through any radical changes.

An answer to William G. Hyland's contention, that German unity seemed to have become a dormant if not politically dead issue with the process of post-treaty normalisation between Bonn and Moscow appearing to be largely an end in itself rather than a bridge to a larger settlement and that only a pale reflection of the original illusion had survived, is that at the time of the signing of the Ostpolitik treaties the reunification aim had always been intended to be long-term, something which would be part of a larger European settlement. Although one of the major reasons for signing the Moscow Treaty was to establish relations with the GDR, the treaty had also been signed for its own sake, i.e. to have a good relationship with Moscow. How to get on with its Russian neighbour has always been an issue for Germany, whether reunified or not.

According to Klaus Bölling, Schmidt's position on the divided nation question was never a defeatist one. Rather, it was the case that he distanced himself from self-deceiving reunification rhetoric.[44] Moreover, he believed that the pre-conditions both in the GDR, and the FRG for a great leap forward in German–German relations were lacking.[45] The grand concepts in Ostpolitik of the Brandt period had disappeared under Schmidt and Schmidt's approach was much more pragmatic. Klaus Bölling also writes;

> It is true that Helmut Schmidt did not want to join in speculation as to how with the help of a new concept the German policy could be qualitatively changed. Where were, he asked those party colleagues who were pressing for initiatives during the eight and a half years of his chancellorship, the not only intellectually stimulating but also politically translatable plans that Honecker could really respond to? Convincing answers were not given to him.[46]

And Schmidt, himself, has said during interview:

> It is not so much due to the formula of 'change through rapprochement' but rather it is far more due to concrete steps actually carried out in the direction of the Warsaw Pact states that the encrustation in Europe and in Germany, which arose during the time of the Cold War, has been reduced during successive years. It is not a matter of formulae but rather that we really do negotiate and achieve something.[47]

FRG–GDR relations

The second half of the seventies was marked by a slowing up of the pace of German–German relations. In the summer of 1974, there was a temporary worsening of the climate of FRG–GDR relations due to the East German hindrance of transit traffic on the West Berlin

Autobahn in protest at the establishment of the Federal Environmental Agency in Berlin, a project which both the GDR and the Soviet Union were bitterly opposed. Although the GDR was not a partner to the Quadripartite Agreement and therefore also not immediately entitled to protest against any violation of that agreement, the Soviet Union in many individual cases left it to the GDR to adopt a sharper conduct towards the Federal Republic. In this way the Soviet Union was able to avoid making direct advances and attacks against the three Western Powers without however foregoing comments and measures aimed at its own objectives.[48] However, the GDR was obviously more interested in damage limitation in FRG–GDR relations than in a fundamental crisis. Already in August both sides indicated at secret sounding talks that they were even interested in an expansion of German–German negotiations. Furthermore, despite the political tension during this period, only a few of the commissions involved in the follow-up negotiations to the Basic Treaty were affected by a short 'work break' and others continued as normal. The border commission, for example, reached important agreements on 29 June and 3 July.[49]

In the summer of 1975 Schmidt met Honecker at the CSCE Conference at Helsinki. It was the first time that the two German leaders had met. It seems that Honecker appeared constrained, even intimidated, and Schmidt could not or would not conceal from him that he did not consider Honecker's ability to influence German–German relations to be exactly high.[50] Schmidt expressed his annoyance over the Guillaume affair but also let it be known that he had not thought it a particularly brilliant idea to set up the Federal Office for Ecology in West Berlin.[51] Apparently both leaders did feel that they had grown closer to one another as a result of the meeting.[52]

Leading Social Democratic party members felt that Schmidt's task for the May 1978 Brezhnev visit to Bonn should be to point out Bonn's keen interest in a stable East Germany which would then have the confidence and bargaining room to develop German–German relations further without becoming a security risk to Moscow. They felt that if Schmidt could convince Brezhnev that Bonn regarded the division of Germany as the consequence of losing the war and not as an outrage committed by the Russians which must be revised as soon as possible, then the Brezhnev visit might give new impulses not only to German–Soviet but also to German–German relations.[53] In fact, German policy, in comparison with arms control and economic and technological co-operation, played only a minor role at the 1978 Bonn talks. The Soviets insisted that the German question should not be

taken on to the agenda of the German–Soviet talks.[54] The Federal
President publicly and unequivocally referred to the German question
in his speech at the reception at Schloss Augustusburg, 'It remains our
aim – and we made that clear at the treaty negotiations – to work
towards a condition of peace in Europe, in which the German people
can regain their unity through free self-determination.' He stated that
this was only possible through a lengthy process which required
mutual trust. The present policy of the Federal Government was
directed at creating more contact between the people despite the
barriers.[55] Brezhnev completely ignored these references.[56] The Soviet
Union scrupulously avoided giving in to the Federal German aim of
mentioning German–German relations in documents agreed upon at
the visit.[57] However, in his autobiography, Chancellor Schmidt does
list FRG–GDR relations, along with another discussion of troop reduction in Europe (MBFR) and a very detailed discussion of China, as
being one of the topics that the Soviet guests wished to discuss on the
last day of the trip during Brezhnev's private visit to Langenhorn,
Hamburg.[58]

Nevertheless, with regard to the FRG's relations with the GDR,
although details were not necessarily discussed at the 1978 talks, it
seems that the FRG emphasised its interest in the Soviet Union supporting its efforts to normalise German–German relations and after the
Brezhnev visit there was new movement in these relations.[59] Less than
a week after the Soviet state visit to Bonn, Soviet Foreign Minister
Gromyko visited East Berlin. How close the connection was between
the Brezhnev visit to the Federal Republic and Foreign Minister Gromyko's talks in East Berlin may be gathered from the composition of
the Soviet delegation which met from 11 to 12 May with Honecker,
Central Committee Secretary Axen and Foreign Minister Fischer and
his State Secretary Nier; of the five Soviet delegation members who
met the SED leadership, at least three had previously accompanied
Brezhnev to Bonn – Politburo member and Foreign Minister Gromyko,
his deputy A. P. Kovalev and the head of the third European Department, A. P. Bondarenko.[60]

Before Gromyko's East Berlin visit, Honecker had greeted Brezhnev's state visit to the FRG simply with 'satisfaction'. At the end of the
visit by the Soviet Foreign Minister, Honecker now expressed his 'full
satisfaction over the successful results of this visit'.[61] The SED General
Secretary assured the Soviet interlocutors that the SED was ready on
its part 'to further normalise relations between the GDR and the
Federal Republic of Germany on the basis of the concluded treaties, in

accordance with the principles of international law'.[62] The Politburo report to the 8th congress of the Central Committee of the SED at the end of May evaluated the conduct of the Soviet delegation as having been of great importance 'under certain circumstances for the normalisation of relations between the GDR and the Federal Republic' thus establishing a connection, even if a limited one, between the German–Soviet and intra-German dialogue.[63] Honecker blamed Bonn alone for the 'bad climate' in relations between the GDR and the FRG, however he gave his assurance that the SED was ready 'to help remove obstacles from the path which have not been put there by us'.[64]

Whatever was said during the talks, or whether Soviet pressure was put on the GDR or not – or even needed or not – what is certain is that Honecker was acting with Soviet approval when he adopted steps to inject a new impetus into German–German relations. One month after Gromyko's visit to East Berlin, Honecker invited West Germany's Permanent Representative, Gaus, to a new meeting in order to discuss the construction of a motorway from Hamburg to Berlin. A visit by Chancellor Schmidt to the GDR was also discussed at this meeting but both sides felt that at present the climate had 'not yet warmed up enough'.[65] Following negotiations on the building of the motorway, the restoration and opening of the – for the southern districts of West Berlin very important – Teltow Canal and on the non-commercial transfers of credit led relatively quickly to agreement (16 November 1978). The agreements were the most extensive negotiated since the conclusion of the Basic Treaty.

An important achievement of the 1978 negotiations was that for the first time since the Four Power Agreement was concluded, a new traffic connection between the Federal Republic and West Berlin was to be built and that it would be fully covered by the Four Power Agreement and the Transit Agreement. It was also the largest joint project undertaken by the FRG and the GDR since the concluding of the Basic Treaty. The two new border crossings, one south-west of Schwerin and the other to the north of West Berlin, were to be opened up not only for transit traffic but also for tourist and visitor traffic and for lorries travelling in both directions. Entrances and exits were to make visits to the northern districts of the GDR easier and would mean that the motorway was much more than just a through road to West Berlin.

Since the end of the war, the opening of the Teltow Canal from the West was repeatedly brought up in Allied and German–German negotiations, in order to save the inland shipping travelling to the West

Berlin ports on the Teltow Canal a time-consuming detour over the Spree and East Berlin City, but the topic was even dropped from the Four Power Discussions because the obstacles appeared insurmountable. For one thing, the legal positions of the three Allies and the Berlin Senate on the one hand and the GDR and the Soviet Union on the other were too opposing. Another problem was caused by the fact that the closed section of the Canal wound back and forth between East and West thus making the political geography, in addition to questions of legal status, a complicated affair. The successful outcome of the Teltow Canal negotiations in 1978, therefore, was a real breakthrough, not least because the GDR, which had previously stubbornly tried to enforce its theory of the independent political entity of West Berlin, now accepted during the negotiations, for the first time, that the Federal Republic could act for West Berlin interests.

The improvement achieved in the November 1978 agreement on non-commercial currency transfers was necessary in order to solve the problems which had made the transfer of credit, already negotiated in 1974, of pensioners and the younger needy from the GDR to the Federal Republic difficult. The 1974 agreement had stipulated that transfers from the one state could not be higher than transfers from the other, and in addition there was a ceiling of 30 million DM or DDR Marks in either direction. It very quickly became clear that far more applications were being made to transfer money from accounts in the GDR to the Federal Republic than vice versa and since 1976, therefore, no more applications could be accepted by the Federal Republic. In the November 1978 agreement the GDR agreed to pay 50 million DM yearly to the German Federal Bank, for five years starting in 1979, in order to cope with the backlog.

The traffic and financial agreements were important not only for their practical benefits but also for their political significance with regard to the normalisation of German–German relations. Through various time stipulations and the long-term nature of their effects the agreements brought an element of stability into German–German relations.[66] The GDR not only agreed that it would, in 1980, enter into negotiations over the construction of a branch in a southerly direction into the Lower Saxony district of Leuchow-Dannenberg from the motorway between Berlin and Hamburg due to be finished in 1983, but it was also firmly agreed that in 1980 negotiations over further traffic improvements would begin – the creation of a continuous motorway between Eisenach and Bad Hersfeld, improvements in railway traffic between the Federal Republic and West Berlin and possibly further development for the transit waterways were proposed. The Federal Government already firmly informed the GDR that it planned a 500 DM share of the costs for the – still to be agreed in detail – building projects on the assumption that the building projects would extend over a period of five years beginning from 1981. Regular intra-German dialogue was extremely valuable in itself and the firm agreement to negotiate definite topics to a definite time schedule meant that this dialogue would continue at least until 1985, even if the world political climate worsened, and that the Soviet Union would have to go as far as forcing the GDR to commit 'breach of contract' if it wanted at any point to put a stop to the dialogue.

In spring 1979 there was a temporary cooling of FRG–GDR relations as a result of, among other things, changes in conditions of work for West German journalists in the GDR. In April 1979 the GDR issued new regulations according to which, for example, interviews had to be approved. The Federal Government strongly protested to the German Democratic Government and tried, also together with other Western states, to get the restrictions on journalistic work in the GDR removed.[67] Officially, the FRG Government took the view that this was not an intra-German dispute but was a measure which affected not only West German journalists but also the admittedly small number of other Western correspondents.[68] However, it is possible that another interpretation could be placed on the East German action:[69] in ministerial bureaucratic circles the suspicion was that the GDR leadership, in view of Western speculation about all-German developmental possibilities, wanted to destroy highflown hopes in its own population and in the Federal Republic and to disperse analogous fears abroad in both East and West. In the winter of 1978–9 a revival of the discussion which had taken place in the early days of Ostpolitik about long-term perspectives for the FRG's German policy had occurred in the FRG.[70] The aim of the revival had been merely to counteract the criticism that the social–liberal coalition treaty policy was cementing the division of Germany, but its effect outside the FRG on both East and West had tended to be a disturbing one. For example, the Social Democrat Herbert Wehner was clearly made aware of this during his visit to Poland at the beginning of April 1979. In view of the Soviet Union's perception of any tendencies towards a change in the status quo of the Western border of the Eastern bloc as being a threat to her security, it may be assumed that Moscow was particularly concerned. At the same time Moscow was also obviously concerned to keep Bonn's interest alive in détente through privileged treatment. Thus, without endangering its own relationship with the FRG, Moscow could use GDR–FRG relations to designate the limits of FRG German policy, all the more so since the GDR, for its part, would presumably be concerned itself to nip in the bud any all-German political illusions. The measures restricting the activities of journalists were chosen because the West German media – in particular, television which was received in the GDR – created a kind of all-German general public.

In the autumn of 1979, during the conflict over the impending NATO double-track decision, the GDR adopted a kind of double strategy which 'faithfully' mirror-imaged Soviet policy.[71] On 6 October 1979, Brezhnev had announced the following line in East Berlin: readiness on the one hand for arms control negotiations coupled with the announcement to unilaterally withdraw 20,000 Soviet soldiers and 1,000 tanks from the GDR; and threats on the other hand of Soviet countermeasures if American medium-range (INF) weapons were stationed in Europe, whereby particularly dire threats were directed at the FRG (for example, that stationing on German soil would in the event of war greatly increase the chance of a counter-blow against the FRG).

The GDR translated this line into the context of German–German relations. On 1 November 1979, in a speech in Sofia, Honecker predicted negative consequences for GDR–FRG relations if the NATO double-track decision was taken. He urged Chancellor Schmidt in a letter to reject such a decision. According to SED Politburo member Hager it was a question of either the continuation of détente or re-armament with all its negative effects on relations between the two German states. In fact, in the last months of 1979 numerous dramatically formulated announcements that a NATO decision to re-arm would have repercussions on intra-German relations were made by SED Politburo members Hager, Axen and Verner.[72]

At the same time the GDR enticed Bonn with the expansion of existing ties and relations. For example, interest was shown in the conclusion of a long-term German–German treaty on economic co-operation. Suggestions were made with reference to Article 5 of the Basic Treaty (which dealt with the promotion of peaceful relations and co-operation in Europe and support for disarmament and arms limitation) to begin co-operation in the question of disarmament.[73] Various negotiations between Bonn and East Berlin which had been broken off in spring and summer, ostensibly due to difficulties over dates, were resumed. On 31 October, agreements were signed on the facilitation of passenger car and lorry traffic and on the same day the GDR declared its readiness to expand the local cross-border traffic.[74]

In 1979 the world political background conditions to German–German relations changed. On 12 December 1979, in answer to the Soviet SS20s, NATO decided to go ahead with the construction and stationing of new American intermediate range nuclear weapons in Western Europe. On 26 December 1979, the Soviet military intervention in Afghanistan began. These events led to a hardening of Soviet–American relations and a worsening international climate. At the same speed that East–West relations went down, the FRG and the GDR tried to keep up German–German relations. Both sides tried to limit the damage to their relations. The report of the Federal Ministry for Intra-German Relations for 1980 stated:

> In view of the political situation at the beginning of the year 1980 which was overshadowed by international burdens and strains in East–West relations (problems of military security, Afghanistan crisis, Olympic boycott, also developments inside the Eastern Bloc), the Federal Government strove to prevent the relations between the two German states from causing additional problems but rather through talks at different levels to carefully continue to develop the improvement in co-operation.[75]

And Honecker said in an interview: 'I think that the most important contribution which the Federal Germans and the GDR Germans can make to peace is the further normalisation of relations between both German states ...'[76]

For both German states their expectations of the benefits of détente had been largely fulfilled and therefore both states wished to continue to conduct their relations as before – though for the GDR, of course, this had always meant a dual policy of hindering inter-personal contacts coupled with a policy of treaty based relations, willingness to engage in dialogue and a desire for co-operation. There were strong economic reasons for the GDR's interest in continuing good relations with the Federal Republic. West Germany's position that although there were two states there continued to be one nation meant that she pursued a special economic relationship with the GDR. Trade with the GDR was treated as domestic trade not just by the FRG but also according to the terms of the 1957 Treaty of Rome (i.e. Protocol on German Internal Trade and Connected Problems of 25 March 1957) and thus the GDR was able to export her goods to the European market at Common Market terms. The GDR obtained consumer goods and raw materials from West Germany. There were other considerable financial benefits to the GDR. In 1980 income (from for example transit fees, the minimum exchange rate, the buying free of prisoners and family reunification, compensation for services in post and tele-communications, the removal of refuse and sewage from Berlin), benefits such as the interest free credit 'swing' and direct payments (e.g. for the construction of the Berlin–Hamburg motorway, the development of the transit waterways) all came to about 2,000 million DM.[77]

Despite her threats to the contrary, the GDR did not effect any negative repercussions on intra-German relations following the NATO double-track decision, indeed quite the reverse was the case. One day after the NATO decision of 12 December, Honecker announced, in his keynote speech at the eleventh plenum of the Central Committee of the SED, that it had been decided over the telephone that Schmidt would visit the GDR in the near future and that a return visit on his part was planned.[78] When Honecker, in response it seems to Moscow's reservations,[79] was obliged immediately after the Soviet intervention in Afghanistan to cancel Schmidt's scheduled visit to the GDR, both leaders consulted beforehand on the manner in which they would announce the cancellation. East Germany did so in terms which left little doubt of its reluctance and the importance it attached to the continuation of good relations with Bonn.[80] From the middle of December, after the NATO decision, Bonn was the object of sharp attacks in the Soviet press, whereby it was portrayed as being either the more or less voluntary victim of the American policy of adventurism, or as following its own hegemonial and aggressive aims in the shadow of the USA. The GDR press avoided direct attacks on the Federal Republic by merely reprinting, as a rule, Soviet contributions. Even its treatment of the FRG decision to boycott the Olympics was mainly through Federal Republic and foreign comment.[81]

German–German relations flourished throughout the autumn and winter of 1979–80. In the area of trade, for example, Honecker predicted that the 'sound barrier' would be broken through and the volume of 10 billion marks would be exceeded.[82] The treaty policy continued and agreements were reached.[83] In exploratory talks with Permanent Representative Gaus, the GDR outlined a new and extensive offer of co-operation involving the electrification of railway lines between the Federal Republic and West Berlin and the construction of a coal-fired power station in Leipzig or Magdeburg. As in the 1978 agreements, West German currency was to be exchanged for improvements in transit traffic and in this case, energy supplies.[84]

In May 1980 Schmidt met Honecker at Tito's funeral in Belgrade. As stated earlier (p. 72), on this occasion Schmidt realised for the first time that Honecker had more political weight than his outward

appearance indicated.[85] By this time they had had occasional telephone conversations which, although they did not lead to decisive
operative agreements, promoted better acquaintanceship with one
another's way of thinking. Honecker began to realise that Schmidt did
not want to exclude him from his maxim that talks with responsible
politicians during critical times were worthwhile in themselves.[86] At
their talk in Belgrade, Honecker acted as advocate for Brezhnev's
concern about the stationing of Pershing II and cruise missiles and
complained about American blackening of the Soviet Union. He
warned against a boycott of the Olympic Games by the Federal
Republic and described what would be in his opinion the serious
psychological effect on the Russians if precisely a *German* team stayed
away.[87] Honecker urged that Schmidt should keep to his visit to
Moscow despite the harsh international climate and despite the bitter-
ness that the Soviets felt over the boycott of the Olympic Games. Both
German states should try to distance themselves from the negative
effects of the Afghanistan crisis, or at least to keep them in check.[88]

Schmidt did not content himself simply with justifying the decision
of the Federal Government to boycott the Olympic Games with the
Soviet intervention in Afghanistan. He also indicated to Honecker that
Bonn was by no means always convinced of the wisdom of Jimmy
Carter's policy and that he felt that détente policy should be continued
despite all setbacks. Schmidt did not hold back on criticism of the
Soviet high level armament policy but Honecker was also able to
report to Moscow later that Schmidt still viewed Brezhnev as basically
being a politician committed to peace and that Schmidt had little
inclination to go along with the new American philosophy of 'punishing' the Soviet Union.[89]

In June/July 1980 Chancellor Schmidt visited Moscow. In his statement to the Federal Government on his talks in Moscow Schmidt said:

> In addition to this detailed exchange of thoughts about international
> problems we also spoke of course with the Soviet side about the
> development of bilateral relations ... I stressed our interest in a
> further development of relations with the German Democratic
> Republic. I also pointed out that a facilitation and expansion of tourist
> traffic from the GDR to the Federal Republic would benefit détente
> between West and East.[90]

However, as opposed to Brandt's visit to the Soviet Union in 1970
where bilateral questions, including the state and development of
German–German relations, were in the foreground of German–Soviet
talks, and only three lines of the joint communiqué were devoted to

exchange of views on international questions, during Schmidt's 1980 visit world political topics were in the foreground of discussions reflecting the bilateral development which had occurred since then in FRG–Soviet relations and also the altered, strengthened weight of the Federal Republic.[91]

It seems that the GDR was able to maintain its policy of insulating German–German relations from the worsening US–Soviet relations without interference or objection by Moscow until the outbreak of the Polish crisis in July and August 1980. In October, however, the GDR sharply increased its *Abgrenzung* policy by drastically raising the minimum daily exchange rate for visitors to the GDR and East Berlin, and, on 13 October, by making a number of unacceptable old legal demands to the Bonn Government. The prompt condoning by the Soviet media of this anti-national SED policy burdened the German–Soviet relationship.[92]

On 13 October Honecker gave a speech in Gera in which he made demands towards the FRG that would place German–German relations on a different basis to that agreed in the Basic Treaty: recognition of GDR state citizenship, the permanent missions to be changed into embassies and the exchange of ambassadors which would be 'in accordance with international law'; the dissolution of the Central Registration Office of the Justice Ministers of the Federal States in Salzgitter; and the speedy settlement of the border along the Elbe. Honecker made the fulfilment of these demands the inalienable precondition for further normalisation steps in German–German relations.

The demand that the permanent missions should be changed into embassies went totally against Article 8 of the Basic Treaty signed by the GDR, thus giving the impression that the GDR no longer accepted the Basic Treaty as the basis of German–German relations. The FRG could not comply with the recognition of GDR state citizenship nor the transformation of the permanent missions into embassies as this would have amounted to a recognition in international law of the GDR as a foreign country. The FRG took the view that even though two states in Germany existed, they could not be foreign countries to one another and their relationship could only be a special one. The fact that the rights and responsibilities of the Four Powers continued to exist and that there had been no final settlement of the results of the Second World War and the division of Germany meant that the German question remained open.

In its Letter on German Unity which belonged to the Treaty of

Moscow of 1970 and to the Basic Treaty set of agreements of 1972, the Federal Republic declared its aims on national unity to the GDR. Furthermore, Articles 16 and 116 of the Grundgesetz (Basic Law or Constitution) and the judgement by the Federal Constitutional Court both stipulated that the Federal Republic must adhere to a uniform German nationality. German nationality according to the 1913 Reichs- und Staatsangehörigkeitsgesetz (1913 Nationality Act) still in force included all Federal citizens, West Berliners and citizens of the GDR. The East German demand for Federal Republic recognition of GDR citizenship would have implied a separate citizenship of the Federal Republic which West Berliners could not receive because of reserved Allied rights. West Berlin would have to have had its own nationality which would then have made it an independent political entity or state, something which would have been completely unacceptable to the FRG but would have been in accordance with the GDR and Soviet position on Berlin (see chapter 3).

The increase in the compulsory minimum daily exchange rate came into effect on 13 October. The new regulations meant that the daily exchange rate was increased from 13 DM to 25 DM, the special rate for day visits to East Berlin of 6.50 DM was also increased to 25 DM and the exemption of old-age pensioners and children was abolished though children were not charged the full rate of 25 DM but rather 7.50 DM. This meant that for many families, trips to the GDR became very difficult to afford. Furthermore, the fact that the Intershops took only foreign currency meant that visitors to the GDR had little opportunity to spend the money in the poorly stocked East German shops. The number of visitors from the Federal Republic to the GDR dropped sharply (2,923,212 in 1979, 2,088,213 in 1981).[93] Visits across the border by West Berliners on the basis of the visiting arrangements under the Quadripartite Agreement declined by almost 50 per cent (3,036,711 in 1979, 1,728,584 in 1981).[94] The GDR also introduced customs fees between 10 and 40 per cent of the value for gifts brought by Western visitors, thus adding further expense for visits as the value was based on the mostly very high East German prices. Furthermore, the increase in the compulsory exchange rate was not accompanied by any lower- ing of the 50 million DM paid by the FRG for use of East German roads despite the fact that the real usage had fallen sharply.

There was no formal agreement between the Federal Government and the GDR on the level of the compulsory minimum exchange rate so the increase for West Germans was legal in terms of international law, but it did violate the spirit of the Basic Treaty. With regard to the situation for West Berliners, the GDR had made a unilateral declaration on travel and visitors in which the original exchange requirements were laid down and in which it was also laid down that pensioners and children were exempted.[95] This declaration belonged to the context of the agreement of 20 December 1971 between the Senate and the GDR Government on the facilitation and improvement on travel and visitor traffic which in turn was part of the complex of the Quadripartite Agreement on Berlin.[96] The increase for West Berliners was, therefore, in an indirect way a violation of the Quadripartite Agreement and not just according to the Western position – Soviet sources, too, said that all the documents published in connection with the Quadripartite Agreement on Berlin were 'equally important' and applied 'as a complex, i.e. parallel'.[97]

The Federal Republic took a very serious view of the East German increases because they struck at the very heart of the Federal Republic's German–German treaty policy, i.e. to achieve through negotiation arrangements which would help ease life for the Germans on both sides of the division, prevent the two German peoples from growing apart, reduce tension and improve relations between the two states. The new measures affected the alleviation and improvements that had been achieved since the Basic Treaty. The 1980 report by the Federal Ministry for Intra-German Relations stated:

> This action represents a heavy setback for the efforts to improve co-operation as the modalities for tourist traffic belong to the political basis for business of the relations between the two German states. The action, moreover, is inconsistent with the provisions of the Final Acts of Helsinki which were also signed by the GDR.[98]

The Federal Government stated that the East German action was

> a massive intervention into the human contacts which have arisen in the course of the treaty policy. With this action the GDR has offended against the aim of the treaties to improve co-operation and intensify contacts.[99]

It was a prime objective of the Federal Republic to reverse the GDR's action or at least to obtain what they felt would be a 'substantial correction': they intimated several times to the East Berlin leadership that they should at least consider a 'social component'. For a state of 'Workers and Farmers' it would look particularly good if the minimum exchange rate for pensioners and juveniles were lowered or abolished.[100] However, such suggestions did not meet with a positive response for several years (on 27 September 1983 young people up to

14 years were exempted from the exchange requirements altogether). From October 1980 the demand for the removal or correction of the increase in the minimum exchange rate became one of the ritual declarations of West German politicians. The Federal Government did not give in to opposition demands to undertake counter-measures. In his Regierungserklärung (Policy Statement of the Government) of 25 November 1980, Schmidt said:

> This is a heavy setback for all Germans. The Federal Government will not resign itself to it. It will persist in its aim of easing the situation of the Germans through improvements in our relations with the GDR. In reality there is no other course. We offer, also for the future, co-operation and development of relations with the GDR. We have no intention of replying to acts of demarcation with acts of demarcation on our part: for this would deepen the trenches between Germans and Germans. We put co-operation in the face of delimitation.[101]

One government official said during interview in 1984 that this was the only time that the FRG had specifically complained to Moscow about GDR behaviour in order that Moscow should put pressure on the GDR. They put it to Moscow that this was no way to carry on relations with the GDR, that it prevented them from developing ties with the GDR and that it stopped poor people of West Berlin from visiting East Berlin. The Russian reply was that they could not do anything about it as it was the GDR's affair, i.e. it was a sovereign matter.

The East German government gave as the official reason for its action that the increased buying power of the East Mark in the face of the inflationary Deutschmark was forcing it to set this new level. However, as Genscher pointed out, 'The motives of the GDR leadership in taking this step are obviously of a political and not of a fiscal nature. The political propaganda accompanying music of maximum political demands made at the same time also speaks for this.[102] (See Gera speech, p. 84.) The real immediate aim appears to have been the reduction of the number of visitors, viewed by the leadership as a potential source of unrest. The events in Poland alarmed the East German leadership and precautions were taken in the form of intensified military training, extension of military legislation, the effective closure of the border with Poland, increased activity on the part of the security organs and, of course, the increase in the minimum exchange rate. One German researcher into East–West relations also put the GDR action this way during interview: there were about 100,000 Polish workers in Rostock, East Germany and Honecker felt threatened by events in Poland. The border between Poland and the GDR had been opened in 1972, the first case of a border being opened in the socialist bloc. This had to be reversed in 1980. In order to balance this decision and explain it to his population, Honecker introduced restrictions in traffic with West Germany.

Peter Jochen Winters, among other sources,[103] puts forward the view that the decision to change GDR policy towards Bonn was not solely made by the GDR. Rather, the main reason for the abrupt change was to be found in Soviet pressure on the GDR and on Honecker himself to end its special détente policy with Germany and fall back into the ranks of the socialist camp because the Soviet Union – in view of the change of president in the United States and the events in Poland – did not want to run any risk with intra-German special relationships.[104]

From October 1980 the Soviet Union began to use the FRG's interest in good German–German relations in its attempts to undermine the FRG's support of the NATO rearmament (see chapter 5). It used the GDR as a channel for this with the GDR holding up better prospects in German–German relations for Bonn's 'good behaviour' and also issuing threats that at least further development would be blocked if Bonn took part in rearmament steps in the event of a failure of the Geneva INF negotiations. For example during his October 1980 Gera speech Honecker said,

> For us it goes without saying that our treaty policy with the FRG is a part of the co-ordinated policy of our alliance of Warsaw Treaty states of safeguarding peace. Making this clear once again coincides with the requirements of our time. After all no one should seriously believe that he can actively support Western Alliance policy, boycott the Olympic Games in Moscow out of solidarity with the USA, act as the inventor and party-whip of the Brussels missile decision and at the same time act as if they only need to speak to the GDR about 'travel facilitations'.[105]

In his report to the X. SED Congress Honecker said:

> We were always ready to constructively promote the development of normal, what is more, good neighbourly relations between the GDR and the FRG. That will continue to be the case. However the relations between both German states cannot be uncoupled from the international situation. Whoever spurs on NATO rearmament, whoever interferes with the military-strategic balance in Europe through new

nuclear missiles will create a state of affairs which will work against further normalisation and jeopardise that which has already been achieved.[106]

and at their talks held during Schmidt's visit to East Germany in December 1981, Honecker said to Schmidt that effects on German–German relations were to be feared in the event of a stationing of the new American missiles.[107] The GDR apparently also played a considerable role in the Soviet attempts to stir up the West German public against deployment. In particular, this was promoted through the Western department of the SED and its control over and support of the West German Communist Party and West German front organisations.[108]

However, the increase in the minimum exchange rate and the Gera speech did not, in fact, subsequently prove to be the break in German–German relations it appeared to signify: the GDR gradually withdrew itself from the position whereby Honecker's demands were a precondition for further normalisation in German–German relations; at the Leipzig Spring Fair Honecker declared that difficult East–West politics must not affect German–German relations, and West German visitors to the Fair were unanimous in reporting that the SED leadership was interested in improved relations with the Federal Republic;[109] in December 1981, despite the Polish crisis, Honecker met Chancellor Schmidt at Werbellinsee in the GDR.

Given the GDR's need for Western currency and financial credit, the Federal Republic obviously did possess means of influencing GDR policy, without enlisting Soviet pressure. At the end of July 1981, the Federal Government announced that it was prepared to guarantee a loan of 950 million Marks to the GDR granted by a consortium of West German banks. Although the GDR emphasised that there was no connection, it was announced at the same time that the GDR had agreed to several measures to improve travel. These included increased travel opportunities for GDR pensioners, increased duration of stay for visitors to the GDR, simplification of some bureaucratic procedures, and most importantly, a lowering of the minimum daily exchange requirement for pensioners visiting the GDR, i.e. a small retraction of the October 1980 decision showing a certain compliance with the FRG's aim of reversal or substantial improvement of that decision.

A visit by Schmidt to the GDR scheduled for December 1979 had been called off by the GDR and rescheduled for February 1980, but this had also been cancelled by Honecker immediately after his return from Moscow. Presumably both cancellations were due to Soviet reservations about German–German contacts in view of their intervention in Afghanistan and the ensuing world-wide criticism. A new date had been set for a working meeting at the end of August 1980 but this, too, had been cancelled, this time by the Federal Republic, because of the danger of troops being sent into Poland.[110] At the time of cancellation the Federal Government stated that it continued to consider a meeting between the Federal Chancellor and the Chairman of the Council of State necessary in the interests of the further development of relations.[111]

Since March 1981 the Federal Government had been considering a Soviet request for an invitation for Brezhnev to visit the Federal Republic for the third time. Apparently, at first, Schmidt was inclined to make the granting of this request dependent on developments in Poland. But the hope that a renewed meeting between Brezhnev and Schmidt could, after two fruitless attempts in 1980 and 1981, favourably influence the bringing about of a summit meeting with the GDR leadership proved decisive and it was finally agreed that the third Brezhnev visit to Bonn should be fixed for 22–25 November 1981.[112] In fact, it turned out that Brezhnev expressly welcomed the Chancellor's intention of meeting General Secretary Honecker in December.[113] Also very important, given the GDR's position on West Berlin, was Soviet confirmation during the Brezhnev visit that East Germany supported the delivery of natural gas to West Berlin: the joint communiqué stated that 'In agreement with the government of the German Democratic Republic natural gas from the Soviet Union will also be delivered to Berlin (West).'[114] Both the Soviet Union and the FRG 'declared their readiness ... to do all they could to support the realisation of this project'.[115] Five years previously a similar project had failed because of the GDR's extremely restrictive interpretation of the FRG's rights arising from the Four Power Agreement to develop its ties with Berlin.

The summit meeting between General Secretary Honecker and Chancellor Schmidt took place on 11, 12, and 13 December 1981 at the lakeside resort of Werbellin to the east of Berlin and at Döllnsee in the Uckermark. It was the first meeting on German territory since Willy Brandt and Willi Stoph met in Erfurt and Kassel more than a decade before. Schmidt had met almost all of the East European leaders and knew some of them well. Honecker he had met only twice before. Despite the many uncertainties of the international situation Schmidt now felt that the time was right to talk to the man responsible for the other part of Germany openly and, he hoped, more concretely than in Helsinki and Belgrade.[116] By now he had altered his picture of Honecker. The 1981 report by the Federal Ministry for Intra-German Relations states that in view of the setbacks in intra-German relations – for example, the October 1980 increase in the minimum exchange rate – an attempt at new progress was necessary.[117] Schmidt expected no easy breakthrough but was anxious to press the East Germans to use what influence they had with Moscow to help win a negotiated settlement of the Euro-strategic missiles problem in Geneva and he also wanted to make a new bid to improve economic and other contacts between the two German states.[118]

In order to prevent the build up of hopes, the summit meeting was deliberately announced at short notice. Schmidt repeatedly warned the public not to set its expectations too high. Foreign Minister Genscher also warned against expecting 'miracles'.[119] It was emphasised that there was no fixed list of topics and that there would be no negotiations, but rather, talks would be held for the general assessment of the East–West relationship and the German–German relationship.[120] Klaus Bölling, who was the Federal Republic's Permanent Representative in the GDR at the time of the visit, writes, 'We knew that a meeting between him and Honecker could not bring the big breakthrough. We knew from the start that the other side was determined to derive political and propagandistic profit from a meeting and that brilliant results could not be reckoned on.'[121] Given the worsened climate of East–West relations, progress would be much more difficult to achieve and Schmidt felt that, 'In difficult times both sides should concentrate on preserving what has been achieved and adding and doing what is practical.'[122]

The 1981 report by the Federal ministry for Intra-German Relations stated that a comprehensive exchange of views was held about the state and potential for development of intra-German relations as well as current international questions. It also listed the individual topics discussed as being questions of family reunification, travel and visitor traffic including tourism, questions of environmental protection and co-operation in the areas of science and technology as well as education. Furthermore, opportunities for the further development of cultural co-operation as well as exchanges in other areas, questions relating to the working opportunities for journalists and the delivery of Soviet natural gas to the Federal Republic of Germany, to West Berlin and to other Western European countries were also discussed. Both sides stated their respective views on the question of nuclear weapons. On the economic side an extension of the 'swing' credit was discussed and both sides reached agreement to enter into talks over a long-term framework agreement on economic co-operation.[123]

Honecker repeated the demands that Bonn should recognise East German citizenship[124] and pressed that Permanent Representative Bölling and his East German counterpart Moldt should be made into extraordinary and plenipotentiary ambassadors.[125] Schmidt brought up the subject of the increase in the minimum exchange rate, pointing out that pensioners and those of limited means could now rarely visit friends and relatives and stating bluntly that he felt disappointed and deceived. It seems that Honecker did not give him a firm promise but indicated that things might be improved if the 'swing credit' was prolonged.[126] Apparently Schmidt did not conceal from Honecker that due to the party political situation in West Germany his own room for manoeuvre with regard to German policy was limited.[127]

One government official told the author that during Schmidt's three-day summit meeting with Honecker in the GDR, one of the talks Schmidt had with Honecker was the longest he (Schmidt), had ever had with any foreign politician, East or West, and that Schmidt was quite impressed with Honecker at Werbellinsee. His assessment of the meeting with Honecker was very positive. Klaus Bölling writes that during his visit to the GDR, 'it was ... only in Prussian heartlands that he, the pragmatist and responsibility ethicist, became fully conscious of what he personally, beset by the energy sapping tasks of crisis management, perhaps owed the topic of both states and the divided nation'. (See pp. 71–4).[128]

In his government statement on 18 December 1981 to the Bundestag, Schmidt summed up the results of the visit like this:

> The meeting between Mr. Honecker and me – the first on German territory since the meetings between Willy Brandt and Willi Stoph in Erfurt and Kassel more than a decade before ... provided a German–German contribution to the international safeguarding of peace and it signified at the same time a new effort on the difficult path to a good neighbourly relationship between both German states and their citizens. The opportunity for constructive continuation in many areas has been opened.[129]

Schmidt also said:

> It became clear in the talks that the GDR leadership is also interested in overcoming the stagnation. I quote from an interview which General Secretary Honecker gave on Wednesday to *Neues Deutschland*, an SED newspaper published in West Berlin, that he wants, in

the spirit of the meeting, to set about the practical political realisation of the results of the talks.[130]

The FRG foreign office report for 1981 stated, 'After this meeting there is hope that the phase of setbacks in intra-German relations can be overcome.'[131] It seems that both leaders were keen to continue the dialogue and Honecker was looking forward to a trip to the West, possibly before the following Easter.[132]

The fact that Schmidt and Honecker had met was significant in itself and there were also concrete results in the following period, for example in family reunification and in the travel area. The FRG renewed the 'swing' credit and this was followed by a few small improvements by the East German side in the minimum exchange rate in 1982. However, there was very little movement on the long-term framework agreement on economic co-operation. An economic framework agreement between the FRG and the GDR had been important to Schmidt for some time, more for its political aspect than for the desirable increase in intra-German trade: he viewed an agreement of this nature as a means for building confidence, similar to the 1978 agreement with the Soviet Union. He felt that if both sides could come to the understanding that a constantly growing economic co-operation would lead to a deliberate, that is positive, mutual dependency this would lead to more calculability and perhaps as a result of it an atmosphere which would gradually allow better political co-operation.[133] Klaus Bölling writes:

> Since Werbellin ... there has been little movement. We were not innocent in this. The tensions inside the social-liberal coalition increased. Our capacity for action towards East Berlin therefore also decreased for this reason. As so often in the history of German–German relations the field which had been opened up a little, was later neglected. Those forces on both sides interested in applying the brakes pushed themselves forward. In the GDR the supply situation again became complicated, the leadership appeared to be no longer sure of the future line in Moscow as Leonid Brezhnev, the friendly patron of the General Secretary, had ceased to formulate policy. On our side unemployment began to overshadow all other topics. Hardly anyone still had time for the business of intra-German relations and the necessary money was lacking anyway. It was of little use for some pro-Germany politicians to recall to mind the simple point – which I had also expressed many times to interlocutors in our and in the other Republic – that stagnation between us is not standstill but regression with the ever present risk that if misunderstandings or unforeseen events were to occur we could find ourselves

taking up position again behind new, and for neither side beneficial, fronts.[134]

On the final day of Schmidt's visit a state of emergency had been declared in Poland and martial law imposed. This overshadowed East–West relations and intra-German relations for some time. Klaus Bölling further writes that in the first months of the new year certain members of the East German Politburo who mistrusted Honecker's positive attitude to Schmidt were able to persuade their General Secretary to adopt a more restrictive course. The attempts by America to push the Soviet Union economically to the wall led to a confrontation between the superpowers which affected both German states and which provided those forces in the GDR leadership who wished to apply the brakes with the desired pretexts.[135]

> The General Secretary asserted on various occasions that he wanted to keep to the Werbellin agreements. At the time he really meant it. Only it seems that meanwhile he came more fully to the realisation that the Soviet Union, irrespective of the, for her, unsatisfactory situation in Poland, could hardly be interested in her German ally displaying even the smallest shred of détente policy.[136]

In March 1982 the GDR introduced new laws on military service and the use of firearms by border guards. The new law gave legal sanction to border guards to shoot East German citizens trying to escape to the West, something which had been going on in practice for the last nineteen years during which 186 escapers had been killed. Government spokesman Kurt Becker said that ties between the two German states were still far from being normalised.[137]

In his September 1982 report on the state of the nation in divided Germany Schmidt said, 'Since the last report on the state of the nation in April of last year the tensions in East–West relations have grown. As a result it has also become more difficult to pursue German policy in the shadow of such tension',[138] and, 'Of course the world political crisis, which we are now going through, also influences German–German relations. It raises barriers which one had already believed to have been step by step dismantled.'[139]

Conclusion

The researcher into Western–Soviet–East European relations was, until recently, faced with the notorious problem of asymmetry of information – one could, mostly, only speculate on Soviet motives and objectives. However, in the case of FRG–GDR relations, the problem was further compounded by the reluctance of West German government and party officials to discuss the Soviet dimension in this context. Presumably, one reason was that the FRG did not want to give rise to a perception of vulnerability to Soviet pressure due to her interest in good relations with the GDR (see pp. 147–50).

To an extent, it would seem that FRG–GDR relations were relatively and surprisingly unaffected by the Soviet dimension. After Afghanistan and the NATO double-track decision when East–West relations plummeted, intra-German relations actually *improved*. Even the only real break of the period during the Polish crisis in October 1980, when the minimum daily exchange rate for visitors to the GDR and East Berlin was raised and Honecker made the Gera demands, did not last long.

Where the Soviet Union did use the GDR as a channel for its own objectives *vis-à-vis* the FRG, this was generally in cases where the GDR, too, had a coinciding strong interest: for example, the protest against the establishment of the Federal Environmental Office in Berlin (a project to which both the GDR and the Soviet Union were bitterly opposed); the measures taken against journalists in spring 1979 intended to designate the limits of FRG German policy (GDR policy of *Abgrenzung*); and the raising of the minimum exchange rate and the Gera demands in response to the Polish crisis (which coincided with the GDR's priority of ensuring the internal security of her regime). Furthermore, whilst acting as a channel for the Soviet Union, the GDR often engaged in damage limitation to her relations with the FRG: despite the trouble over the Federal Environmental Office in the summer of 1974, negotiations between the two states continued as normal; none of the threats made in the last months of 1979 were carried out; as already stated, the increase in the minimum exchange rate and the Gera speech did not subsequently prove to be the break in German–German relations is appeared to signify. The GDR had, of course, a very strong economic motive for the preservation of GDR–FRG relations. Furthermore, détente in the 1970s provided the GDR, as other smaller East European countries, with the opportunity to participate in international political life as a more equal player, for example, by participation in CSCE. As a dialogue partner with the FRG, the USA's most important European ally, she probably hoped to increase her standing in the Eastern bloc. She was, therefore, concerned that the international hardening did not affect her newly won room for manoeuvre.

Why were FRG–GDR relations not affected by Afghanistan but by the Polish crisis? There are two possible explanations for this. One is that the Kremlin wished to demonstrate good relations with the Federal Republic, in order to draw attention to and exploit rising tensions in the relationship with the United States immediately following the Soviet entry into Afghanistan, and after the NATO double-track decision, and therefore gave East Germany considerable leeway in developing co-operation with Bonn.[140] The other is that it was not possible to keep German–German relations out of international turbulences if the Soviet Union did not want this or, put another way, it was only possible for as long as the Soviet Union wanted it to be. The question of geography played a part in this; it was possible with Afghanistan but not with Poland.[141] In matters which affected decisive Soviet interests and those of the bloc which it dominated, the GDR was unable to take independent action, though it would seem that most matters did not fall into the decisive category.[142]

One reason why FRG–GDR relations were able to develop relatively independently of the Soviet dimension was the posture of the Schmidt government which was to leave the reunification issue aside and deal instead more with day-to-day issues of a practical nature, thus leading to Soviet relaxation with regard to an intensification of FRG–GDR relations. Indeed, the criticism which can be made of Schmidt throughout most of his period in office – that of demotion of German–German relations to the level of negotiations between officials – most probably contributed to this and in this sense had a positive effect.

5 INF, Afghanistan and the post-Afghanistan period

The FRG's position after Afghanistan

The NATO double-track decision and the Soviet intervention in Afghanistan in 1979 caused a worsening in East–West relations. At the global level, however, East–West relations had begun to deteriorate much earlier. On the one hand, there was Soviet disappointment over trade with the United States, particularly over the tying of the most-favoured nation clause in the American–Soviet trade agreement of October 1972 to the granting of better emigration opportunities for Jews from the USSR (Jackson–Vanik Amendment). Moscow felt that a continuation of East–West détente was yielding little profit. On the other hand, the 1973 October war in the Middle East and the Soviet footholds in Angola, Ethiopia and South Yemen disappointed United States' expectations that détente would tie both sides up in a network of mutual commitments which would cause Soviet restraint in the Third World. Added to this was Soviet rearmament in the area of medium-range nuclear weapons while the American defence budget declined. The United States began to believe that détente was only giving one-sided advantages to the Soviet Union. A new tough mood took hold in the United States. It seems that one explanation of Soviet activity in the Third World could well have been a combination of two things: the USSR had always wanted to be equal with the USA in every respect, not just in a nuclear sense, and thought that détente would achieve this. The USA did not want to accept the Soviet Union as an equal power elsewhere in the world, it was only prepared to accept this in the nuclear sense. Once the Soviets realised this, one of their incentives for détente was lost. Furthermore, one West German government official put forward the view to the author that the Soviet Union always took opportunities when it saw them and the way that it did so depended on the calculability of the risk: the Soviets perceived

American political weakness after Vietnam and Watergate and took increased risks.

To Schmidt and other West European countries, the East–West relationship – apart from the need to have a proper balance of forces – was primarily political rather than military. This view was held by Nixon. One FRG government official told the author that there were no differences on East–West relations between the US and the FRG until the end of the Ford era: the situation changed with the Carter administration – Schmidt felt that Carter, Brzezinski and Cyrus Vance had no such clearcut concept as had Kissinger; furthermore, they started by pushing human rights very strongly (a policy which differed markedly from Kissinger's approach and from the West German approach and one from which the United States later had to backpedal). Under President Reagan the view was that détente had failed in that it had led to an increase in Soviet strength and to a loss in US power. The Soviet Union had achieved full parity and in some areas superiority in armaments. The Soviet Union was seen militarily and politically as an expansionist communist power. President Reagan felt that arms control should be discussed when the United States was stronger and when the Soviet Union had altered its behaviour. The FRG felt that the US had abandoned the second pillar of NATO's security policy which was détente (see p. 181 and also Schmidt's speech on p. 101). The hostage crisis in Teheran and the Afghanistan crisis had a cumulative effect on the United States, and its reaction was an all-out one.

The United States and the FRG had different approaches to détente: the United States, as a superpower, was faced with global confrontation with the Soviet Union and thus there was the tendency to regard Europe as only one of the world's regions. Moreover, the United States had only a limited dependency on the USSR arising out of mutual nuclear deterrence and therefore was not so immediately affected by deteriorating East–West relations. For the FRG, a regional power geographically and psychologically on the line between the two blocs, East–West relations were primarily a European matter. The FRG was not so directly affected by the Soviet intervention in Afghanistan and events in the GDR, for example, were of much greater importance. Although détente did not fulfil every expectation nor the early euphoria, the FRG was not burdened with the idea that it had suffered from illusion or weakness as was the United States. Brandt and Schmidt had repeatedly warned that détente was not the end of the barbed wire, and cautioned realism. While the US defence budget declined, the

FRG went on annually strengthening the Federal Armed Forces. Despite its lack of world-wide success, détente in Europe, for the FRG especially, had been a success. Bonn did not want to see the hard-won gains such as increased contacts between the two German states, travel facilitation, trade with the Soviet Union (extremely important for certain sections of West German industry and the FRG was much more dependent on foreign trade than the USA, particularly in high technology – see Appendix A, and pp. 100, 180), and the improvements in West Berlin's situation jeopardised by an abandonment of the détente process in Europe. Furthermore, the Soviet Union held the key to family reunification from the USSR, FRG–GDR relations, and to the West Berlin situation and it was firmly in Bonn's interest, therefore, that it preserved good and stable relations with Moscow. In the event of a military conflict in Europe, the FRG would have been the first and the heaviest affected and it was of vital interest to prevent such a conflict. The FRG therefore had to seek to minimise the risk of war between the East and the West by promoting stable East–West relations and by promoting dialogue and policies of moderation, especially between the superpowers at times of crisis and tension (see p. 181). And, of course, a good superpower climate was conducive to the FRG's Ostpolitik outside times of crisis. FRG policy, therefore, was to try to preserve détente, at least in Europe, and to try to achieve a better overall climate in East–West relations. Professor Hans Georg Lehmann, private archivist to Helmut Schmidt, writes in his book *Öffnung nach Osten: Die Ostreisen Helmut Schmidts und die Entstehung der Ost- und Entspannungspolitik*:

> In order to prevent a reversion into the Cold War, Schmidt saw himself more or less pressed into the role of an ambassador on both sides, trying to create, preserve and interpret understanding between East and West – not least in German self-interest. In the crisis between the world powers, the Federal Republic tried to remain a steady factor of calculability, stability and moderation. Through this she gained a world-wide importance that she had never achieved before in international politics but she also had to pay for this new weight and prestige with 'irritations' in the relationship with the USA.[1]

After Afghanistan, the FRG was the only country to exchange visits with the Soviet Union at the highest level.

With regard to 'linkage', the FRG had long been against such a concept. The FRG did not believe that anything could be achieved by using the trade lever and therefore its use would be unwise; it felt that as a state it was too weak for linkage policy against the Soviet Union and since linkage would not make the USSR pull out of Afghanistan then it would only serve to punish the USSR and the FRG felt that it was not worthwhile punishing a superpower. It also feared that punishing the USSR might jeopardize the gains achieved through détente. Moreover, as already stated, the FRG was too dependent overall on foreign trade, much more so than the Americans, particularly in high technology (see p. 180 and Appendix A). The FRG therefore, had to cultivate markets and maintain stable relationships. Sanctions would have interrupted the markets. Grain can be switched on and off but not machines – hence the differing positions on trade sanctions between the United States and the Federal Republic. Also, the FRG took the view, for example over sanctions towards Poland, that it was morally obliged for the fate of individuals, to see how it could help and alleviate their plight whilst the United States took the view that moral gestures should be made on behalf of the Polish people (see pp. 129–30).

On 17 January 1980, Schmidt said with respect to the hostages in Iran and the Soviet intervention in Afghanistan in his Government Statement on the international situation,

> There is no doubt that heavy weather has appeared in world politics. Therefore we must examine the situation with regard to German interests and the situation with regard to Western interests as a whole with a calm eye. We must steer our country through the turbulences with a sure hand. We cannot employ nervousness, or crisis outcry or excited or even agitative speeches in this. Rather we need instead ... a carefully thought out 'crisis management' ... Calm behaviour is not 'pussyfooting'. If anyone expects a policy of big words from us in this situation, then he is mistaken in the style of our state and in the interests of our state. Rather we must make it unobtrusively but unmistakably clear where we stand. And we do that. For this purpose there must be dialogue and this includes dialogue with the Soviet Union, too. Especially in difficult times our policy must be a clearly discernible one. It is especially in difficult times that we must remain in contact with one another. The so-called red telephones were first created for such situations. The Federal Government holds the view which Professor Carstens formulated in this way at the New Year's reception: 'He who wants peace must solve conflicts through negotiations and the fair balance of interests.' Therefore, I do not criticise it when, for example, the Bavarian Minister President declares his readiness to visit Moscow after the Soviet intervention in Afghanistan. Peace is not a natural state of affairs but must be brought about again and again. This has been written as early as Immanuel Kant. It

costs strength to achieve peace and it also needs at all events dialogue and negotiation. This process has suffered a severe setback through the Soviet intervention in Afghanistan. Naturally this is also felt in Europe. In my New Year's address I said, 'Co-operation between East and West in Europe will be all the more successful in relation to how strongly political action in other parts of the world is stamped with the will for détente and co-operation.' The reverse is true: the less will there is for détente in other parts of the world, the more difficult co-operation becomes in Europe, too. And precisely because this is the case, we will not let up in our efforts to secure peace in Europe but rather we will strengthen these efforts. Our détente policy is not appeasement but is one of two main elements of our security policy which is founded on the balance of military forces [see p. 181]. For us this means work continues as before in three areas: Firstly: the preservation of past achievements. This also means the strict observance and full implementation of the Four Power Agreement as well as the treaties with the Soviet Union, with Poland, with Czechoslovakia and the Basic Treaty with the GDR. It also means the preservation of the achievements of CSCE between the West and the East since 1975. Secondly: the further development of past achievements. That means: further improvements for the 'togetherness' of the people in both German states, continuation of the work in arms limitation and arms control, especially in respect of MBFR. I expressly welcome in this connection the renewed statement by President Carter that the SALT II treaty benefits the security of the United States of America and the whole world. I am assuming that this treaty will be observed even if it cannot be ratified at present. Thirdly: perseverance with new tasks. This especially means that we and all the member states of NATO do not withdraw from the table the offer of December 1979 to negotiate over medium-range nuclear missiles but continue to seriously pursue it.[2]

Chancellor Schmidt – mediator/interpreter between East and West?

It is a widely held British view that Chancellor Schmidt performed a mediator/interpreter role between East and West.[3] In West Germany, too, the term frequently occurs during the Schmidt period. The general tendency when this question was brought up by the author at interview was towards denying or avoiding affirming any mediator/interpreter role – it seems that this was to prevent giving rise to any doubts that the FRG was anything but firmly in the Western camp.[4]

According to one official source, the term mediator was launched after 1980. Schmidt first used the term mediator in a speech round about that date. According to this source, Schmidt wanted to be a mediator, to be influential, to move things forward. However, there was no issue where Schmidt used that role and there is no documentary evidence in telegrams, reports, discussions etc. In the Middle East during 1977–9, for example, Schmidt never tried to reconcile the Soviet and American positions and never tried to do so in the Third World. On arms control, he never adopted a third position between the Soviet Union and the United States. The government official said that the term mediator implied neutrality and was a term which did not fit and which he himself did not like. He said that on many occasions he had tried to explain to journalists that this mediator business was not true. With regard to the second half of the term, 'interpreter' – the same government official said that Schmidt adopted the position that the Americans were serious about arms control (i.e. at the time when many doubted Reagan's sincere will to negotiate). Schmidt never said to the Americans that the Soviets were serious but he did say to them that the Soviets had legitimate interests, please take them into account. The Soviets tried to use the FRG to influence the Americans in that they would always say to the FRG that the FRG knew the Soviets better than the Americans and would they put the Soviet case to them. The Germans never did but reported that the Soviets had asked them. The FRG always informed America and Europe after talks with the Soviet Union. Fred Oldenburg, researcher at the Bundesinstitut für ostwissenschaftliche und internationale Studien, also writes in *Sowjetunion 1982/83*. 'immediately after the Afghanistan invasion the Soviet side had made great efforts to manoeuvre the Social Democratic Federal Chancellor Schmidt into a mediator or interpreter role.'[5]

Another government official, who was in attendance during Schmidt's 1980 visit to Moscow, said that in 1980 Schmidt was in a very pivotal role due, to a smaller extent to the personality of the Chancellor, and to a larger extent – to the international situation. From the time of the NATO double-track decision and the Soviet intervention in Afghanistan up to the superpower decision to resume negotiations, Schmidt was in a position to have disproportionate influence, not as a mediator, but as a good lawyer to tell the other side what the situation was. Schmidt did not mediate, he made no proposals. What he did do was to explain the situation – for example he told the Russians Western deployment of cruise and Pershing would take place and that the Soviets would get nowhere by using the peace movement and refusing to negotiate. The Soviets believed him on this as they trusted his judgement and knew him as an honest man. The government official stressed that Schmidt did not make any proposals apart from one he once made while in Washington, that if the Soviets would stop their build-up it would be easier to negotiate. He said that Schmidt saw himself as an *interpreter* of the Western position – in a situation where tensions were high and no-one was talking, Schmidt stepped in. He denied that Schmidt had ever said to the Americans that the Soviets, too, had problems which the Americans must take into account.

One party official said that Schmidt was no mediator but the term interpreter was not completely wrong. Schmidt listened to the points of view of both sides. He tried not to mediate. He tried to find pointers for West German foreign policy as to how one could continue with a peace policy. According to the government official, Schmidt rejected the mediator role because he thought the FRG was too small a country for this. However, through their personalities, Brandt and Schmidt stood in the first row – the Americans and Russians listened.

One West German researcher and source close to Schmidt said Schmidt did not want to be a mediator as this would mean having a position of his own. However, Professor Karl Kaiser, who was one of Schmidt's advisers, describes the FRG as 'a country induced by its geostrategic position, the exposed position of West Berlin, and its links with the East Germans to act as a bridge and force of mediation with Eastern Europe' and in the same chapter writes, 'In playing from its secure Western position its systemic role as bridge builder to the East, the Federal Republic fulfils the obligation of her geostrategic position and political past.'[6]

Another West German researcher said that the FRG's experiences with the GDR, the Soviet Union and Poland made it more qualified than the rest of the Western Alliance to see problems from the Eastern point of view and its role was thus to achieve a better understanding of the East in the West and to explain to the West that a policy of restraint was the best answer; that different means to embargoes, for example working with the East, was the best answer. Another West German researcher into East–West relations said that Schmidt never used the term mediator. He tried to interpret. The Soviet Union's relationship with the West was one of antagonisms and Schmidt tried to remove misunderstandings. Neither side realised what the other side meant and Schmidt tried to interpret. Schmidt tried to contribute to the lessening of tensions between the superpowers by interpreting their behaviour, interests, and rhetoric.

When it was put to him that the author's previous interviewees had argued that Schmidt never actually played a mediator role, one party researcher was of the opinion that there was one example of Schmidt having that role: that of bringing the superpowers to the negotiating table at Geneva. After the NATO double-track decision Brezhnev said there was no reason to negotiate, the reason had gone. After the American elections, the Americans did not want to negotiate. Schmidt successfully worked at getting the superpowers to the negotiating table. It was one of his great achievements.

Another party official and source close to the Chancellor said that Schmidt was a type of teacher or interpreter to the United States regarding the Soviet Union and on the other hand he interpreted the Americans to the Soviets: the Soviets had the same foreign minister for thirty years but had the problem with the Americans that every four years they received new signals from the other side and so the Soviet reaction to this constant change was 'to wait and keep their powder dry and to put more powder in if possible'. The same party official said that the term interpreter was originally used in a speech for want of a better term and it was immediately seized on by journalists. However, he was unable to give an exact date and reference for its first use.

The earliest reference that the author was able to obtain was 10 November 1981. On this date Schmidt gave a speech to the Bundesverband Deutscher Zeitungsverleger (Federal Association of German Newspaper Publishers) on the occasion of their annual conference. In it he refers to an interpretative role for the Federal Republic:

> Today it is crucial that the two world powers do not allow the dialogue between them to be broken off and that they exercise restraint and a sense of proportion towards one another in the pursuit of their own interests. We have an important role to play in this, in the first instance towards our friends and allies in America who cannot play their role in the world without the Europeans, that also means not without the full weight of the Federal Republic on the Western side. After all we know a lot about the situation in Eastern Europe and Moscow. More than some in the other Western states who have more experience of domestic politics and are suddenly burdened with foreign policy responsibility. Therefore in the interests of the Western world there is also an interpretative role for us to play towards the Soviet Union.[7]

During a television discussion 'Bonn after the Brezhnev visit,' with journalists on 26 November 1981,[8] Schmidt gave a detailed answer on the mediator/interpreter issue. Ernst Dieter Lüg of the Westdeutsche Rundfunk put this question to Chancellor Schmidt:

> Mr. Federal Chancellor, I must come back again to the interpreter role which has been much talked about and a little too much in the three

days of Brezhnev's visit. The interpreter, as we all know, translates only what is said by others. No doubt you will have seen your role like this. Where is, so to speak, the German part, the German share within the joint Western efforts, not only to get the Soviets to the Geneva table but also to force the Soviets to make recognisable concessions? Isn't the interpreter Helmut Schmidt after all in some respect a mediator, a middleman, at the very least someone who endeavours to find the lines of compromise for Geneva or even to push them?

Schmidt's reply was as follows:

As with all images, this image of an interpreter, intended as an example, was of course not completely apt. I must say you are right there. It was the only thing we could think of when we had to give an answer publicly for the first time to journalists as to what our role would be at this meeting.

It appears, then, that the word 'mediator' *was* never used by Schmidt (this was confirmed by Schmidt's office when the author checked back with them) and that it is true that the word interpreter was only used for want of a better one.

Schmidt goes on to say:

To interpret means to translate, to translate into the language or into the conceptual world of another, to translate from the language of one person into the language of another. We have a great German interest that the Soviet side correctly understands the disarmament conceptions and all the political conceptions of the West, of which we are an important, a very important part, that this is presented to her correctly, that this is interpreted in such a way that the Soviet side fully understands it. We have a very great interest that the Soviets understand the Western position. And, vice versa: we have of course a great interest also that the West and the American leadership understands the Russians correctly. Otherwise how can a disarmament compromise come about if they do not understand one another. That is the minimum precondition for a compromise, one that is sound, to be brought about at all. If there was mutual misunderstanding and a compromise were to be brought about that rested on misunderstandings – for God's sake that would be fatally dangerous. Therefore we have an urgent German interest that they understand one another. And we are probably at present the best interpreters in both directions in the world.

According to Schmidt, then, he *did* try to interpret in *both* directions.

However, Schmidt goes on to say that he sees the FRG's role as more than this:

But our interest of course – and there you are right when you ask about German interest and about the German share – goes further than this. We do not have the ambition to become chief interpreter. It is a very important function but still a subsidiary function. The main function of the Foreign Minister, the Defence Minister, the Federal Chancellor, the political exponents of the large parties in the Bundestag at such meetings is to influence the Western negotiating position in such a way that it best corresponds with German interest. The American position which President Reagan presented in the speech to the National Press Club just over a week ago today is of course the result of the most intensive consultations within the entire Western Alliance. And I am giving away no secret, it can be guessed by everyone, that apart from the Americans themselves the Germans played the broadest role in this. It is our country at which the Soviet missiles are initially aimed. And it is our country in which the Western missiles must be stationed if the negotiations do not produce a result. Equally we have an interest in getting the Soviet Union inwardly open to negotiations ... You will remember that on 6 October 1979 the Soviet Union, anticipating the NATO decision, said through a speech by Mr. Brezhnev in East Berlin: she had no intention of negotiating. Either the West abandoned its plans now – they were not yet settled – or there would be no negotiations. Then Mr. Genscher and I – despite the entry into Afghanistan which weighed heavily upon us, despite the entire Western criticism – went to Moscow six months later. It was in the summer of 1980. And we convinced the Soviet leadership, Mr. Brezhnev, Mr. Gromyko, that they must negotiate after all. Because it lies in our interest, in the Soviet interest, that the missile armament be brought down. Then there was the election campaign in America and in Germany too, a new President, then we worked on the new administration, not only that they must negotiate – Reagan wanted to do that from the start – but how? The zero solution, which is a vital cornerstone in the Western negotiating package and also in the speech by Mr. Reagan, was propagandised by us inasmuch also pushed through by us.

Schmidt goes on, however, to put in a word of caution as to the limits of the FRG's role:

I must be allowed to add another sentence. Mr. Lüg spoke of possibilities for compromise. And that is a very complicated field. I would like to say something about this. If you read the Soviet starting position as it is presented in Mr. Wild's *Spiegel* in the form of a Brezhnev interview, then it is a maximum starting position. All the Soviet Union's interests are fully satisfied in this position. If you read the starting position of President Reagan in his Press Club speech – that is also a maximum position, a starting position which Mr. Brezhnev provoked through his *Spiegel* interview – both these positions,

as they now stand, cannot be united in a treaty. That is clear. Therefore one must acquiesce in moving down from the high level of
unrestricted demands to somewhat more realistic levels. Where compromises can be made concessions must be made to one another. A
treaty can of course only come about when both are prepared to
compromise. But it cannot be our German business to bring these
compromises into the world, Mr. Lüg. We are part of the Western
Alliance. That, by the way, is very much acknowledged by the
Soviets. Mr. Brezhnev expressed that more clearly, Gromyko clearly:
We have no intention of making any attempts to split you Germans
from the Western Alliance.

Chambers Twentieth Century Dictionary defines the verb 'to mediate'
as 'to bring about ... promote ... obtain' or 'to interpose between
parties as a friend of each.'[9] According to Mr Schmidt he did adopt a
mediator role in the sense of *bringing about* negotiations between the
superpowers. He *promoted* the cause of arms reduction through negotiation. What he did not do was mediate in the sense of the second
definition given by Chambers. He did not perform a neutral role of
aiding both sides and of going back and forth between the two parties.

On 3 December 1981 in a statement to the German Bundestag,
Schmidt refers again to his duel role of both interpreter and what
could be described as a kind of mediator role in that he promoted
dialogue between the two superpowers after Afghanistan – something
he felt to be very important: 'The term to interpret has been used; I do
not consider that to be wrong. We have indeed interpreted. But we
have in addition an important role to play that the two world powers
do not allow the dialogue with one another to break off and that they
show one another moderation and a sense of proportion in the pursuit
of their respective interests.'[10]

It seems, then, that the issue of a 'mediator/interpreter' role between
East and West appeared in the post-Afghanistan period and was,
simply, symptomatic of both Schmidt's policy objectives and how
Schmidt wanted himself and the FRG foreign policy to be perceived.
He wanted (1) to appear a loyal alliance member; he wanted (2) to
stand up for the FRG's special interests, as an ally; he wanted (3) to
salvage as much as possible of the benefits of the détente heyday after
the rejection of SALT II by the US and the invasion of Afghanistan; he
wanted (4) to influence both superpowers towards seeing where their
own 'best interests' lay. Moreover, he had to do all this from – of
necessity – a modest power base. Not all of these objectives were
mutually all that compatible. He was, therefore, involved in a balancing act: being a 'mediator' would help to accomplish objectives (3)

and (4) but it would also risk objectives (1) and (2) if to mediate one has 'not to take sides'. Being an 'interpreter' provides (4) and slightly risks (1). On more substantive issues Schmidt seems to have balanced his objectives by conceding on the unimportant and sticking to his guns on the important. Thus, the Olympics, to take an example, were unimportant so (1) was satisfied but at low cost to (2), (3) and (4).

The FRG and the NATO double-track decision

In the 1950s the USA possessed a clear nuclear superiority. This picture began to change in the 1960s when the Soviet Union began to close the gap on the United States. At this time the Soviet Union possessed more than 600 nuclear medium and intermediate range missiles which could reach targets in Western Europe but not in the United States. The United States had virtually no medium-range missiles but did possess a clear superiority in intercontinental missiles. This meant that Moscow could not attack Europe with her medium-range nuclear weapons without risking a response from the United States with intercontinental weapons fired from US territory. At the beginning of the seventies there was a decisive change. The United States lost its superiority in intercontinental missiles. Approximate parity in intercontinental missiles was established through Soviet building and stationing of these weapons. Soviet superiority in medium-range weapons remained and it began in 1975/6 to strengthen them qualitatively and quantitatively through the SS–20 missiles and the Backfire bomber, drastically increasing the number of warheads which could be directed against Europe.

The SS–4 had a range of 1,900 km and one warhead and the SS–5 had a range of 4,100 km and one warhead. The new SS–20 had a range of up to 5,000 km, three warheads and could be programmed to hit three different targets to an accuracy of about 300 m. It had a reloading capacity and was powered with solid not liquid fuel which did away with refuelling and therefore meant swift readiness for action. It was mobile and therefore difficult to combat. The Backfire was a swing-wing bomber with a range of 4,800 km. The medium-range weapons occupied a 'grey zone' between SALT and MBFR: they were not part of the negotiations in Vienna over the reduction of conventional troops and armaments, nor were they included in the US–USSR negotiations over the limitation of strategic nuclear weapons systems, i.e. intercontinental missiles, submarine-launched missiles and bombers. The SALT I agreement in 1972 codified the intercontinental nuclear balance but it did not redress the European nuclear imbalance existing in the Soviet favour. For the FRG in particular, possessing no nuclear force of its own as a deterrent, the problem now arose in connection with intercontinental parity as to whether the United States intercontinental missile response to a Soviet medium-range attack on Europe was still credible in view of the risk of a Soviet intercontinental counter-attack on the United States, i.e. would the United States really risk its own territorial security for that of Europe ('Chicago for Hamburg')?

At first the Americans had demanded that the SS–4s and SS–5s should be included in SALT but were confronted with Soviet counter-demands to include US 'Forward Based Systems'. This was decisively rejected by the Federal Government because it feared that it would affect the 'extended deterrence', i.e. the Federal Government was concerned to keep the American nuclear guarantee for Western Europe under the altered conditions of strategic parity credible. The Federal Government and other West Europeans were able to prevail on the Americans who as a result continuously rejected such Soviet requests.[11] However, from this point the apprehension that the USA could make concessions at SALT at the expense of the Europeans haunted the Federal Government.[12] Schmidt partly altered his predecessor's policy:[13] Brandt had on several occasions in 1971, 1972 and 1973 drawn the USA's attention to the 'de-coupling' problem at the conventional and tactical nuclear level arising out of the SALT parity but the Federal Government did not at that time demand that Soviet SS–4s and SS–5s be included because it was assumed that the USSR would anyway gradually deactivate them.[14] From the end of 1974, that is, after the conclusion of the SALT Interim Agreement at Vladivostock, Schmidt demanded in discussions with Ford and later with the Carter Administration that the Euro-strategic systems be included in the SALT process (apparently he was prepared to accept that this would mean the American FBS would be made an object of negotiation). His demand was not met.[15] One party official told the author during an interview that Carter and Brzezinski said that medium-range nuclear weapons had nothing to do with negotiations between the Soviet Union and the United States and that negotiations between the Soviet Union and the United States had nothing to do with Europe. This led to Schmidt's 1977 speech to the IISS in London.[16]

According to Thomas Risse-Kappen in his study on the INF policy of the Federal Republic,[17] for Schmidt, the SS–20, and to a lesser extent the Backfire bomber, was a political threat for Western Europe. He feared that if the Soviet Union were allowed under the SALT agreement to keep INF missiles which could destroy Europe it could gain psychologically the impression of having a free hand in Europe. A similar view was expressed to the author by party officials – Schmidt did not apparently fear a military intervention by the Soviet Union but he did fear that Soviet superiority could expose Europe to Soviet political pressure and blackmail.

An early 1980s publication by the Press and Information Office of the Federal Government states that the aim of the Federal Republic's peace policy was to avoid new rounds of armament and to reduce existing armament (see also p. 181).[18] Schmidt used every opportunity, therefore, to make it clear to the political leadership of the Soviet Union how seriously the West must view the modernisation and numerical expansion of the Soviet medium-range nuclear potential as added threat to its security.[19] For example, Brezhnev wanted to put in the joint declaration issued at the time of the 1978 Brezhnev visit to Bonn that there was overall balance between East and West but Schmidt said that although there was overall balance between East and West, it did not exist in Europe and he said that the striving for balance should go in.[20] A 'security-political basis consensus' was formulated:[21]

> Both sides regard it as important that no one should strive for military superiority. They proceed on the assumption that approximate balance and parity are sufficient to guarantee defence. In their opinion, appropriate measures of disarmament and arms limitation in the nuclear and conventional areas in accordance with this principle, would be of great importance.[22]

The striving for balance was therefore the crucial point in the declaration.

However, in the following period the Soviet nuclear build-up continued regardless: when Brezhnev signed the statement the Soviet Union had deployed 60 SS–20s with 180 warheads and after it Moscow continued to deploy at the rate of about one missile a week.[23] In answer to the question as to whether Brezhnev duped Schmidt or whether he was up against strong domestic rivals determined to strengthen the Soviet advantage at all costs, Jonathan Carr, who has had regular opportunities to talk to Schmidt and those close to him, writes in his biography *Helmut Schmidt: Helmsman of Germany*, that Schmidt believes there were fierce arguments in the Soviet Politburo on the missiles issue and that later Brezhnev pressed successfully for negotiations with the West when other members of the Moscow leadership were against it.[24] However, one party official and source close to the Chancellor told the author that Schmidt said that Brezhnev had cheated him over INF – Brezhnev made many statements about relative parity existing in Europe and continued to re-arm. Schmidt's own account in his book *Menschen und Mächte* published after the Carr biography and after the author's interview is that it was not clear in Bonn how far it was Brezhnev himself who had advanced the SS–20 build-up; or whether Brezhnev had perhaps underestimated its military significance for NATO and the political effect on the West or possibly had tried in vain to curb the build-up.[25] Presumably, the differing opinions given to Carr and the author are a reflection of Schmidt's uncertainty over this. (In fact, the SS–20 consisted of the upper two stages of the SS–X–16 ICBM. The SS–16 was specifically banned by the SALT II treaty but modified into an IRBM it was thus perfectly suitable for deployment in Europe.[26] It may be, then, that the SS–20 build-up gained a momentum of its own.)

During a stop-off in Moscow on his way to the annual Western Economic Summit Meeting in Tokyo in 1979 Schmidt again forcibly urged the Soviet leadership to stop their medium-range armament otherwise NATO would be forced to arm. However, despite all the FRG's attempts and urgent statements the Soviet Union continued to arm and declared at the same time that it would not hold any negotiations if NATO were to counter-arm.

On 12 December 1979, NATO foreign and defence ministers met in Brussels and approved the 'double-track decision': 108 American ballistic missiles (Pershing II) and 464 ground-launched cruise missiles (GLCM) were to be deployed in Europe but at the same time they offered Moscow negotiations on the limitation of long-range theatre nuclear forces under SALT III. The cruise and Pershing missiles would only begin to be ready for deployment from the end of 1983 and this meant that there would be four years' time for negotiation.

In the NATO debate over the stationing of the Euro-strategic weapons the Federal Government insisted on the principle of 'non-singularity' that is, that it would not become the 'nuclear aircraft carrier of the Alliance' (Herbert Wehner) and that besides the Federal Republic other West European countries must accept these weapons. In addition, the Federal Government insisted that they must be installed with United States Army units and not the Bundeswehr. The jurisdiction over their use must lie exclusively with the United States.[27] The reasons for this were the following: Bonn had become the main addressee of the Soviet Union's campaign against the NATO re-armament decision and feared a far-reaching worsening of West

German–Soviet relations if it adopted a too prominent nuclear role;[28] Bonn had to take into account opponents of the rearmament decision in the Coalition parties; West Germany already had the biggest concentration of American shorter range nuclear weapons on its soil of any other state and Schmidt, who wanted fewer weapons in the Soviet Union rather than more in Europe, did not want even more added, thus exposing the FRG even further as the number one Soviet target in the event of a military conflict.

The Germans were to deploy a few cruise missiles and 108 Pershing II missiles. Nevertheless, the West Germans did find themselves in a very 'special' position: one party official said that the FRG made a very grave mistake – and that Schmidt now accepted this – in discussions about where to deploy the missiles, the problem was overlooked that Pershing II would be installed in the Federal Republic only and in no other country. This decision was taken because of technical considerations as Pershing I was already there. It was also felt that this arms modernisation rather than installing something entirely new would be less likely to inflame domestic opposition.[29] But cruise missiles would take up to two hours to reach the Soviet Union whereas Pershing II missiles would take only about fifteen minutes. Pershing I had a range of 720 km and could not reach the Soviet Union but Pershing II had a range of about 1,800 km and it was perhaps possible that it could hit Moscow. For the first time nuclear weapons on FRG soil could reach the Soviet Union. The Soviet Union very much stressed how worried they were by Pershing II. The party official thought that this was because of the psychological impact and that the Soviet Union would probably have objected even if it had not been for Pershing II because it was German territory. The Soviet Union still remembered what happened in the Second World War when West Germany's army got as far as Leningrad, and now, for the first time, weapons were to be stationed on German territory that could hit the Soviet Union. Deep-rooted Soviet anxiety about what was going on in Germany still played a very important part in the Soviet Union. According to the party official the Soviet Union had three anxieties at this time: American intercontinental ballistic missiles, the future of Sino-Soviet relations and the FRG.

Schmidt is popularly credited with being the 'father' of the NATO double-track decision with his speech to the International Institute for Strategic Studies on 28 October 1977. However, as Simon Lunn has written in 'Cruise Missiles and the Prospects for Arms Control': 'The question of NATO's long range theatre nuclear forces had been under review well before the Chancellor spoke, and in this respect the

LRTNF modernisation must be seen as part of the continuation of Alliance nuclear planning.'[30] The early history of the double-track decision began at the beginning of the seventies.[31] In the first phase of its work from 1967 to 1974 the NATO Nuclear Planning Group (NPG) was engaged in working out guide lines for the deployment of tactical nuclear weapons in Europe in order to reify the new doctrine of 'flexible response'. In the second phase of its work the group focussed on determining the number and type of weapons systems necessary for implementation of the doctrine. In November 1973 two study groups were set up which were to examine, in particular, the impact of so called 'new technology' on the accuracy of aim, penetration capacity, guidance and command and control systems on the nuclear capability of NATO in Europe. One group dealt with the military, the other with the political implications. The 'Studies on New Technologies' submitted to the NPG in November 1976 and 1977 came to the conclusion that a modernisation of the NATO tactical nuclear weapons was unavoidable.

Already at this time, long range INF systems (800–2,500 km), which could hit military targets in Eastern Europe and the Western Soviet Union, were also at issue as the Western INF planes especially were hardly capable any more because of their lack of penetration capability due to the improved Soviet anti-aircraft defences. Also, in October 1977, around the time of Schmidt's IISS speech, NATO had decided to set up a High Level Group (HLG) as part of the Long Term Defence Programme (LTDP) to examine theatre nuclear force posture. Moreover, Schmidt did not demand any specific weapon systems in his speech. What Schmidt did say was this:

> changed strategic conditions confront us with new problems. SALT codifies the nuclear strategic balance between the Soviet Union and the United States. To put it another way: SALT neutralizes their strategic nuclear capabilities. In Europe this magnifies the significance of the disparities between East and West in nuclear tactical and conventional weapons.[32]

> strategic arms limitations confined to the United States and the Soviet Union will inevitably impair the security of the West European members of the Alliance vis-à-vis Soviet military superiority in Europe if *we do not succeed in removing the disparities of military power in Europe parallel to the SALT negotiations. So long as this is not the case* we must maintain the balance of the full range of deterrence strategy. The Alliance must, therefore, be ready to make available the means to support its present strategy, which is still the right one, and to

> prevent any developments that could undermine the basis of the strategy.[33] (Emphasis added)

Schmidt, therefore, was calling attention to the imbalance in nuclear (tactical and intermediate) and conventional weapons and the necessity of being prepared to redress the balance with appropriate weapons if it was not *achieved by negotiation*. He did not say 'the Soviets have brought in the SS–20 so let us bring in cruise and Pershing'. Schmidt himself says of his 1977 IISS speech:

> In this speech I still called for the Euro-strategic weapons to be included in SALT II, to include them in the bilateral limitations of strategic weapons. I did not demand American weapons as a counter-threat. At this stage Euro-strategic weapons on European territory were not under discussion. Nobody demanded it, nobody offered it. What was under discussion was what area SALT II should cover, if SALT II should include Euro-strategic weapons or not.[34]

However, according to Thomas Risse-Kappen's study, the Chancellor and his closest advisers were in one precise sense inventors of the double-track decision: the tying together of the decision to modernise and the offer for arms control in one decision ('Integrated Decision Document') originates from Helmut Schmidt.[35]

> Fundamentally it was a matter of concretising and making more precise the double concept of defence and détente already set out in the Harmel Report which Schmidt had supported as early as the beginning of the sixties: 'Defence and disarmament strategy have rightly been termed Siamese Twins'.[36] Arms control and deterrence had the same aim, namely stability. It was exactly this that was the foundation philosophy of the double-track decision for Schmidt. All statements from the years 1977/78 may be interpreted to the effect that he favoured an arms control political solution to the INF problem, on the other hand was not prepared to allow the Soviet Union to *one-sidedly* attack the feasibility of the Western military strategy. The decision to strive for a *double*-track decision as integration of modernisation and arms control occurred relatively early in the Federal Government, evidently already at the beginning of 1978. At this time it was not yet internally a matter of the details of the decision, but the conceptual decision as to how one wanted the INF problem to be overcome. The double-track concept was continuously advocated by the Federal Government to the USA and NATO and ultimately also carried through there.[37] (Emphasis in original)

After 1977 German–Soviet relations were increasingly overshadowed by the problem of the Soviet medium-range nuclear weapons armament. This led to the situation whereby all meetings between top Soviet and West German politicians, certainly after the Afghanistan invasion, were mostly devoted to the INF problem.

A convenient way of looking at Soviet strategy towards the FRG at this time is suggested by reading Wettig, who gives an account of the Soviet propaganda response, as aimed at the FRG, to the INF deployment decision. The Soviets used what may be termed a 'doubly divisive strategy' of attempting to divide 'people' from 'government' and the FRG from the USA. Gerhard Wettig, researcher at the Bundes-institut für ostwissenschaftliche und internationale Studien, argues,[38] citing an article in a Soviet journal,[39] that the Soviet leaders – feeling that West Germany was the decisive political factor on the European side of NATO – were determined to concentrate their efforts directed against Western armament on the Federal Republic. He reports that as early as the beginning of 1979, i.e. much prior to the NATO decision of 12 December 1979, they had set the political stage for that: they established the International Information Department in the CPSU party apparatus and staffed it with experts on German affairs; Leonid Zamiatin headed that new centre for foreign propaganda; Valentin Falin became his first deputy; and other 'germanologists' such as Nikolai Portugalov figured prominently in the work of the depart-ment. Shortly afterwards, according to Wettig, both the International Information Department people and other prominent Moscow experts on Germany – most notably Vadim Zagladin, Ponomarev's* deputy in the CPSU International Department – began systematically to give detailed and lengthy interviews to those West German media which seemed suitable for disseminating Soviet views to the West German public. Wettig adds that from then on readers and listeners in the Federal Republic always quickly received information from the Soviet standpoint through widely distributed domestic media at every poli-tical juncture. These efforts, he says, often made Soviet arguments reach the minds of people more easily and extensively than any other opinion.

Wettig goes on to say that the Soviets not only tried very hard to popularise their views in the FRG but also successfully impressed quite a few West Germans with the Soviet position through cleverly gearing their political proposals and other moves in relation to NATO towards their specifically West German audience. The picture presented by Moscow was of the Soviets as supporters of a military equilibrium in Europe and elsewhere. This military equilibrium was threatened by a

* Party functionary responsible for relations with the West.

United States drive for military superiority, the basic rationale behind which was to provide for the possibility of a limited nuclear war in Europe.

> Soviet propaganda linked that prospect, which could not but frighten any West German, to NATO's willingness to catch up in Euro-strategic armament as stated in the double-track decision of December 12, 1979. The United States, Moscow tried to persuade its West German audience, intended to prepare for the destruction of the Soviet intercontinental strategic capability from West European and West German soil. The Americans thus wanted to eliminate the USSR militarily in the course of an exclusively European war, which, besides hitting the Soviet Union, would also imply the physical extermination of the European NATO countries. In contrast to that alleged US policy, Moscow posed as the defender both of equilibrium and disarmament. Brezhnev's proposals and announcements of October 6, 1979, July 1, 1980, February 23, 1981, June 30, 1981, March 16, 1982 and May 18, 1982, reveal their strong pro-Soviet and anti-NATO biases only in expert analysis.

The general public, according to Wettig's findings, however, received an image of seeming Soviet willingness to negotiate and to compromise – even to accept unilateral sacrifice and exercise unilateral restraint. They tended not to notice the deliberate vagueness and hidden reservations which formed part of all the 'concessions' offered by the USSR and were often pretty unaware of the quantitative and qualitative imbalances which made Soviet attempts at freeze arrangements unacceptable to NATO. He points out that the extent to which the Soviet leaders based their negotiating postures on considerations of propaganda in West Germany, becomes visible when personalities are examined: Julii Kvitsinski, one of the most distinguished and perceptive German specialists in the Soviet diplomatic service, and who earlier had served in Bonn, was chosen as chief negotiator for the Geneva talks on medium-range arms limitation which began on 30 November 1981.

From the autumn of 1979, Soviet diplomatic and propagandistic efforts to prevent the NATO re-armament were concentrated on West Germany. In a paper published in 1981, Wettig stated:

> The appraisal that it is essential to persuade the West Germans more than anybody else to take sides against re-armament in Europe is also reflected in the Soviet attitude to the Federal Republic of Germany. Although the Soviet leaders fully realise that Chancellor Schmidt was the decisive initiator of the resolution to re-arm and that he continues to actively advocate the implementation of that resolution, they

nevertheless approach him with a conciliatory mien. The West German government finds itself the target of wooing appeals from Moscow while the buck of responsibility for the re-armament plans is passed to the Americans. In Soviet propaganda, too, their discretion towards Bonn is striking. While there is no form of denunciatory polemics too harsh to be used against the US, West German politics continues to get off lightly. In general, the West German government is portrayed more as a victim of sinister American machinations than as a voluntary advocate of NATO policies. In Soviet appeals to the New Peace Movement, too, the fight against the re-armament concept takes priority over the vilification of its proponents in Bonn. This does not imply that the Kremlin has committed itself to a wholesale policy of dangling carrots in front of the West German government's nose. It is also capable of using the stick where this appears to promise better results.[40]

For Soviet use, from October 1980, in its attempts to undermine the FRG's support of the NATO re-armament, of incentives and threats directed at the FRG's interest in good German–German relations, see chapter 4 above.

In October 1979, in a speech in East Berlin, Brezhnev declared that the Soviet Union would be willing to enter into negotiations over a reduction of medium-range nuclear weapons if NATO on its part dropped the introduction of such systems. At the same time, Brezhnev gave notice of a unilateral reduction in troops stationed in the GDR of 20,000 men and 1,000 tanks. In the following weeks, Moscow intensified its propaganda campaign in an effort to prevent or at least postpone the passing of the NATO resolution. The Soviet leadership warned, in particular, that a decision to introduce Euro-strategic weapons would not be without effect on German–Soviet relations. Also, there would be no arms limitation negotiations if NATO persisted in its present position.[41]

In November 1979, two and a half weeks before the NATO decision of 12 December 1979, Gromyko visited Bonn. The visit was a climax in the efforts of the Soviet government at that time to change the Bonn Social–Liberal Government's mind.[42] It proved to be a spectacular visit which left the Social–Liberal Government surprised: at the press conference at the end of his visit Gromyko replied icily to the question by the Bonn correspondent of the *Westfälischen Rundschau*, Erich Heuer, as to whether the Soviet Union wanted to negotiate after the NATO decision, 'I have said that the present NATO position and also the position of the Federal Government has destroyed the basis for negotiations. We have stated this accordingly to the Federal

Government.' Hans Gerlach from the *Kölner Stadt-Anzeiger* repeated the question and Gromyko replied, 'Should the decision be made, should our proposal to begin immediately with negotiations be turned down, then the Western position will destroy the basis for negotiations. There can be no negotiations if some countries try their luck with a new arms race.'[43] Fred Oldenburg describes Gromyko's statements as a 'publicly staged attempt at intimidation'.[44] When NATO passed the resolution, the Soviet leadership, in accordance with their stated position, refused for some time to respond to Western proposals for talks.

Moscow's first reaction to the proposal for arms control contained in NATO's double-track decision was an abrupt no, a flat refusal.[45] Carter, shocked and angered by the Soviet invasion of Afghanistan, apparently felt there was little point in pressing for negotiations.[46]

Afghanistan and the post-Afghanistan period

The Soviet intervention in Afghanistan potentially threatened to decisively burden FRG–Soviet relations. However, the FRG foreign office report for 1979 stated;

> In relations with the Soviet Union, despite the irremovable opposing positions in the well-known basic questions, the positive effects of General Secretary Brezhnev's visit to the Federal Republic of Germany in May 1978 have lasted. Recent international developments (TNF controversy, Soviet intervention in Afghanistan) with their repercussions on East–West relations throw, though, a shadow on bilateral relations with the Soviet Union.[47]

Despite the general worsening of East–West relations there was no increase in friction round Berlin. The improvements and alleviations resulting from the agreements were not affected. The FRG is the most important non-communist trading partner of the Soviet Union and even during the tense months at the beginning of 1980 the Soviet Union signalled her interest in steady trade and co-operation relations (see Appendix A).[48] Immediately after the intervention in Afghanistan the visits of the Krupp chairman of the supervisory board, Beitz, and the BP chairman of the board of directors were upgraded by receptions with Tikhonov and Baibakov (Chairman of the USSR Council of Ministers and Chairman of Gosplan respectively) as well as appearances on Soviet television. In May 1980 both sides stated at the meeting of the Soviet–West German Joint Commission for Economic, Scientific and Technical Co-operation that they did not want bilateral economic relations to be affected by the international situation.[49] It should be pointed out, however, that the FRG did not take advantage of the United States embargo policy.

United States reaction to Soviet intervention in Afghanistan was an all-out one. All important contacts and exchanges were broken off. President Carter stopped all grain export over the 8 million tons negotiated by Kissinger in a long-term agreement and he embargoed electronic and oil-producing equipment and allocated more expenditure on defence. He advised the American Olympic Committee not to go to the 1980 Moscow Olympic Games unless the Soviets withdrew from Afghanistan by 20 February. He urged his European allies to follow his example, putting special emotional pressure on the Federal Republic: Carter wanted far-reaching sanctions.[50]

Bonn's reaction was twofold: through carefully measured acts of alliance solidarity it tried to avoid causing irreparable damage to West German–United States relations through the different evaluations of the crisis (see the FRG's position on Afghanistan, pp. 97–101).[51] At the same time Bonn strove to prevent ties with Moscow from being broken off and to get dialogue between East and West going again. Bonn cancelled all exports to the Soviet Union apart from those depending on long-term agreements, the Cocom list was applied more restrictively, the Olympics were boycotted, an increase of 3 per cent on expenditure on defence was approved, four German naval units made a demonstrative passage through the Indian Ocean. The FRG adopted a rather restrictive policy on political contacts – they were cut down, for example, ministerial meetings, and exchange of delegations decreased. After Afghanistan the FRG boycotted (and continued to boycott) the May Day parade in that a counsellor instead of an ambassador was sent. The FRG was not represented by an ambassador at Marshal Ustinov's funeral. However, after Afghanistan, the FRG was the only country to exchange political contacts on the highest level. Some future projects, for example, agreements on projects for cultural exchange remained on ice. Cultural contacts, however, were not cut down.

One party official told the author during interview that Schmidt boycotted the Olympic Games even though he did not agree with America on this action: Schmidt accepted the embargo on the Olympic Games in order to get room to manoeuve – the Americans were told 'we have got interests and have to go on speaking to the Soviet Union. We follow your decisions even if we don't like them but please let us follow our interests.' The Federal Republic was the only major nation other than the United States to boycott the Olympic Games and it

appears to have been something of a sore point with the Federal
Republic – this also came across at interview with a government official
– that the West Germans were held by the United States to be slacking
or dragging their feet over the boycott. Mrs Thatcher very quickly
expressed herself to be in strong support of President Carter's stand.
She was therefore regarded by the Americans as an especially devoted
ally in spite of the fact that the British Olympic team did subsequently
go to Moscow after all.[52] Schmidt expressed support in principle for a
boycott but advised the German National Olympic Committee that
they should give the Soviets until 15 May, the last registration day for
the Olympics, instead of the date given by President Carter of 20
February. A statement of 20 March by Schmidt shows that there was
never any question of going or not going but rather the idea was first
of all to give the Russians until the last possible moment to withdraw,
and secondly, to show that Germany's decision did not depend on
orders from the USA but on her own initiative: 'The proper conditions
still do not exist, because the occupation of Afghanistan and the
constant fighting there continue unabated. But the beginnings of the
Olympic idea in classical Greece are indissolubly associated with peace
among the nations. Unless peace is restored in Afghanistan, the consequences will be inevitable.'[53] Moreover, Schmidt noted with some
irony that the British could evidently win more American goodwill
with strong words than Bonn could win with action.[54]

Already in the middle of January 1980 the Federal Government
spoke out for the continuation of East–West dialogue and the continued validity of the concluded treaties with the East.[55] At the end
of January 1980 Schmidt stated in a letter to Brezhnev a continued
readiness for dialogue.[56]

The Soviet leadership tried by propaganda, warnings and criticism
to prevent the Federal Republic from reacting too strongly against the
Soviet Union.[57] The USA was presented as an unpredictable superpower, whose policy was a 'dangerous attempt against détente' in
order to encourage the West Europeans, especially the French and
Germans, to a stronger representation of their own interests vis-à-vis
the United States and keep reactions to the Soviet intervention in
Afghanistan limited.[58] There were increased threatening noises from
the 'Soviet propaganda machine' after Schmidt's USA visit in March
1980, German help for Turkey, the more restrictive application of the
Cocom list and the passage through the Indian Ocean by the West
German navy.[59] From spring 1980 the Federal Republic was no longer
characterised as before as the victim of United States' initiatives but as

a European power which wanted to continually increase its military range.[60] The West German discussion of an economic embargo, especially, was accompanied by warning undertones in the Soviet media.[61] It was said that Washington's 'crude pressure' on the West Europeans increased their risk of 'losing what had become a traditional supply of energy'.[62]

When it appeared that the Federal Government, like other countries, would recommend its Olympic Committee to boycott Moscow, the Soviet Government, as early as 14 February, threatened that there would be consequences.[63] On 7 May 1980 Brezhnev stated to the IOC President Lord Killanin that the German Olympic boycott would not remain without consequences. In the event, Soviet diplomacy and the Soviet media behaved with restraint in order not to upset the East–West dialogue that had got going again since May 1980.[64] According to a government source, the FRG boycott of the Moscow Olympics did not long cast a shadow over FRG–Soviet relations – in the end the Soviets had to accept it. It added that there were a lot of other problems affecting FRG–Soviet relations at this time such as the SS–20s and INF modernisation so the atmosphere was not at its best anyway and so the FRG boycott action did not have such a big negative effect.[65]

On 31 March 1980 Schmidt was given an invitation to meet the Soviet Government in June of that year. The invitation seems to have been one of the initiatives with which the Soviet leadership was trying to overcome the isolation caused by its intervention in Afghanistan.[66] Fred Oldenburg writes, in connection with the visit, that immediately after the Afghanistan invasion the Soviet Union made enormous efforts to manoeuvre Schmidt into a mediator or interpreter role.[67] Schmidt had a short meeting with Brezhnev at Tito's funeral on 8 May 1980. He was the only Western leader to be granted a proper interview with Brezhnev on that occasion. This meeting was another illustration of the fact that both sides (certainly the FRG) wanted to end the West–East absence of dialogue.[68] In May 1980 Giscard d'Estaing had a hurriedly arranged meeting with Brezhnev in Warsaw but the meeting brought no clear results.[69]

In the middle of June, Schmidt received a letter from President Carter. Schmidt called the letter 'astonishing and superfluous'.[70] Carter suspected that the German Chancellor wanted to make Brezhnev, who must be punished for the Afghanistan invasion, 'respectable' again. Carter emphatically warned his German ally not to allow himself, during his Moscow visit, to be dissuaded from the NATO double-track decision through tempting offers.[71] Apparently, the

Americans were irritated by Schmidt's April moratorium offer and the general readiness of the Europeans to talk to the Soviet Union.[72] In April, Schmidt had made a remark in public that baffled many in the West and made some suspicious. He said that both sides should give up the installation of new or additional intermediate range missiles for a certain number of years and use the time for negotiations. As the West had no missiles of this type and Schmidt talked about 'both sides' and as NATO's missiles were to be ready in about three years and Schmidt talked about 'a certain number of years', many in the West, especially in Washington, felt it looked as if Schmidt was trying to slide out of his commitment to the NATO double-track decision.[73] Jonathan Carr, who, as stated earlier, has good first-hand knowledge of Schmidt and his motivations, writes:

> The fears were understandable, but groundless, Schmidt's comments were well-intentioned, but unclear. The Chancellor was trying to make a signal specifically to the Soviet Union along the lines of 'For God's sake at least stop *deploying* your missiles (even if you continue to produce them) so that talks with the West can get off the ground. Otherwise another round of arms race is absolutely certain.' Put that way, of course, the onus is on Moscow. Schmidt deliberately wrapped up the proposal in circumlocutions which might help Moscow to accept without losing face.[74] (Emphasis by Jonathan Carr)

Schmidt, who had recently tried to clear up any possible doubts of Carter by sending Washington further details about his position on the missiles was extremely angry and offended over the letter and brought the matter up in strong terms with Carter in Venice before the start of the Western economic conference being held on 23 and 24 June.[75] This resulted in Carter and Schmidt appearing before the press outside so that Carter could tell the press that he had confidence in Schmidt.

At the end of June 1980 Schmidt travelled to Moscow. The visit took place on 30 June and 1 July. One observer claims that the Chancellor had talked it over with the other Allies. They were not enthusiastic, probably because they feared that in his efforts to preserve détente he might go too far, but on the other hand they did not want to be responsible for his refusal to go.[76] Another writes that the US and some of Bonn's European allies had strong reservations about top-level German–Soviet talks when Moscow was still showing no signs of budging on Afghanistan.[77] The author's information is that there were strong reservations on the side of the British and the Americans but that Schmidt felt that Giscard d'Estaing was not against the visit.[78] Schmidt felt that he must go to Moscow because of the lack of superpower dialogue since the Soviet intervention in Afghanistan. He felt that such a time of crisis and tension was just when dialogue between the superpowers was most important. Most importantly, he hoped to gain Soviet agreement to negotiate on INF.

On Monday evening, 30 June, the German delegation and almost the entire Politburo attended a banquet in the Kremlin. During his speech, Schmidt spoke very, very frankly about Afghanistan. One government official said during an interview that he spoke so openly that he held his breath. The government official did not think that the Soviets had ever been spoken to like that before. Schmidt himself called it 'the toughest speech any Western leader has given in the Kremlin, although I delivered it in a courteous tone'.[79] A senior *Die Zeit* journalist writes, 'When he spoke his mind on the subject of Afghanistan, Suslov, the ideological eminence in the Politbureau, who was sitting beside him, suddenly slapped his typescript down on the table. A few others followed his example and laid down their copies though not quite as noisily and demonstratively.' At the end there was a frightening silence and then Brezhnev clapped and they all joined in.[80] She goes on to say, 'I myself was in Washington at the time, and when I went to the State Department next morning they said with great admiration, "Your Chancellor made a very courageous speech."'[81]

On the subject of INF one government official gave this account at an interview: Schmidt spoke very softly to the Politburo but made it absolutely clear that there would definitely be deployment if the Soviet Union did not negotiate. He spoke very softly but in substance absolutely firmly, saying that it was now up to the Soviet Union. Suslov stood up and called the whole Politburo out of the room. There was no contact between both delegations for the whole night and the German delegation thought that it was an absolute failure and that they would have to leave. At 9.30 am there was a signal from the Soviet side that there would be a meeting at 10 am and then shortly before 10 am there was a signal that they would meet at 11 am. The messages meant that the Politburo had spent all night and morning in discussion. The German delegation felt that Ostpolitik and the whole political idea of negotiating before deployment was about to collapse and then Brezhnev came in and said they would negotiate.

On Tuesday morning, Brezhnev began to answer the questions which President Carter had given Helmut Schmidt. On the question as to whether both sides could keep to SALT II without ratification, Brezhnev replied that the Soviet Union takes a commitment in international law seriously when the treaty is in force. On the second question as to whether the Soviet Union would be prepared before the ratification to explore the ground for SALT III, Brezhnev said that they were prepared to enter into pre-negotiations but the conclusion of these negotiations could only take place after the ratification of SALT II. Schmidt's April moratorium proposal was rejected as 'Unfair'. However, the Soviets also put up new hurdles. The Soviets said that the so-called Forward Based Systems, i.e. those American long-range bombers and aircraft stationed in Europe, should be included in the medium-range nuclear talks.[82]

On 1 July an implementation agreement to the 1978 long-term economic agreement was signed. The signature was a good sign for German trade and industry with the Soviet Union, which had been unsure as to how it stood after Afghanistan. The White House would have liked a Western and Japanese economic boycott after the Soviet invasion of Afghanistan. Although the West German side insisted that the agreement should be signed by ambassadors Wieck and Semenov, and not, as the Soviet side wanted, at high level, the United States was unhappy about the agreement. As Jonathan Carr writes, 'It would surely have been better if the signature had been postponed altogether. In the long history of US–German friction, it was not only Washington which displayed insensitivity to its partner's concerns.'[83] On 3 July 1980, Schmidt said in a statement to the Bundestag:[84]

> The aim of this visit is achieved. It has proved that direct talks in a world situation unchangingly marked by a series of severe crises are not only necessary but also useful. The most important aim of our visit was to bring first hand to the Soviet leaderships' attention our view of the present world situation, to convey to the Soviet leadership a first-hand impression of our deep concern and vice versa to really get to know in detail the Soviet views.

On the matter of medium-range nuclear weapons negotiations he said,

> the General Secretary ... introduced a new constructive proposal. The Soviet leadership declared readiness to enter into bilateral talks about the limitation of medium-range nuclear weapons with the United States of America before the ratification of SALT II. The subject matter of these talks must cover the medium-range weapons of both sides with due regard to all factors which influence the strategic situation in this area. And he made it clear also that the so-called Forward Based Systems should be included ... He added that agreements arising out of such talks could, though, according to

his, the General Secretary's view, only come into force after ratification and implementation of SALT II ... It seems important to me that a new situation has been created with this. The demand that the NATO decision be dropped no longer stands in the way of the start of talks over mutual limitation of medium-range weapons. The normal process in the forefield of negotiations has now been set in motion. A proposal from the United States and her allies to the Soviet Union has been answered by it with a qualification. I do not regard this as a breakthrough yet; for a successful result of such talks, which will last a long time, is not yet foreseeable. But it appears to me that the chance has been opened up to avoid an unchecked arms race in this field.

The 1980 talks showed the progress in bilateral questions and increased world political weight of the Federal Republic.[85] In 1970, at Brandt's visit, bilateral questions were in the foreground and so was the state and development of German–German relations. During Brezhnev's first visit to Bonn, in May 1973, bilateral questions were dealt with almost exclusively and much time was devoted to trying to find a formula for the Four Power Agreement on Berlin which resulted in the 'strict observance and full implementation' formula. This passage in the joint communiqué figured prominently in the subsequent discussion in the Federal Republic on the results of the visit. During Schmidt's 1974 visit to Moscow the talks were almost exclusively about German–Soviet questions, whereby Berlin was in the foreground and both sides, as at earlier visits also discussed the Hitler period. At the 1980 visit world political topics were in the foreground: 'Afghanistan which lies thousands of kilometres away in another continent and ... nuclear weapons which don't even belong to us, but to the Americans.'[86] The joint communiqué states, 'The talks which they held in accordance with their hitherto existing practice of consultations covered a wide range of political and economic questions with European and world-wide bearings, which characterise the present international state of affairs. Current questions of the state and prospects for the development of bilateral relations were also discussed.'[87] Only three paragraphs in the joint communiqué were devoted to bilateral questions with a mere repetition of the 1973 Berlin Formula.

How much did Schmidt influence the Soviets to come to the negotiating table at his 1980 visit? Fred Oldenburg writes that Brezhnev convinced Schmidt that he (Schmidt) had managed to get the, at first reluctant, USSR to resume disarmament talks with the USA.[88] However, Jonathan Carr writes, 'Could it all have been a put-up job? Had the Russians perhaps already decided before Schmidt turned up that they would have to negotiate anyway? "I don't know," Schmidt says simply, "I can't tell you."'[89] In fact what emerged from the author's interviews with government and party officials was that the Soviets were ready to negotiate but wanted to find out from Schmidt whether there was any other way to stop the stationing of cruise and Pershing other than by negotiating. Schmidt told them no, stationing would take place and, believing him, they came to the conclusion that it was a mistake to block negotiations, i.e. the Soviets were ready to negotiate and what Schmidt did was to tip the balance. They also used the visit to tell Schmidt, and, therefore, the Americans that they were ready to negotiate. A government official put it to the author this way: the question for the Soviets was, is it right to negotiate or not to negotiate, and there Schmidt influenced them. They thought Schmidt had a certain insight and so they invited him to Moscow to ask his opinion. Soviet diplomats worked by intimidation. They would get themselves into an impasse and each time they would have to back-pedal. They said they were ready to negotiate partially because Schmidt said deployment would take place.

As one party official put it during interview, Schmidt returned to Germany with the Soviet agreement to negotiate but then the Americans were not willing – President Carter would have liked to negotiate but he lost to President Reagan in the elections; Reagan said no and then Schmidt's 'Ostpolitik' had to start in Washington and this took up the whole of 1981.

In the margins of the 1980 United Nations General Assembly the foreign ministers of the USA and USSR agreed that talks about the limitation in Europe of medium-range weapons would begin in Geneva in the middle of October. A first round of talks took place in Geneva from 17 October to 17 November. They did not get past preliminaries as the impending change of government in the United States did not allow meaningful negotiations.

President Reagan apparently believed that there was little point in discussing arms control until America was stronger and until the Soviet Union had changed its behaviour.[90] Thomas Risse-Kappen writes in his study on the FRG's INF policy, 'Just as at the beginning of the year 1980 the Federal Government had to secure Soviet readiness to negotiate, it now had, a year later, to strive equally hard for a resumption of the INF talks by the USA.'[91] He goes on to say that European pressure, above all by the Federal Government, for a binding undertaking by the US Government for the resumption of the INF negotiations finally achieved initial success. On 26 February 1981 Reagan declared his support of the double-track decision to Mrs

Thatcher, and the joint declaration by US Secretary of State, Al. Haig, and Foreign Minister Genscher on 9 March 1981 read similarly. Finally, at the NATO Council in Ministerial Session on 4/5 May 1981, the United States committed itself to the start of INF talks before the end of the year. During Schmidt's visit to Washington, Reagan, at Schmidt's request, concretised this undertaking on 22 May 1981 to the effect that the negotiations could begin between the middle of November to the middle of December.[92]

It had taken almost six months before the United States government accepted the integrated decision document as the basis for business, it now took another six months before the Reagan administration agreed on a negotiating position. On 18 November 1981 President Reagan said in a speech to the National Press Club in Washington that he had written a letter to General Secretary Brezhnev and proposed that negotiations be entered into on 30 November in Geneva on the limitation of medium-range nuclear weapons. The United States was ready, he said, as a first step, not to go ahead with the stationing of Pershing II and cruise missiles if the Soviet Union on its part would dismantle its SS–20, SS–4 and SS–5 missiles. The zero-option, favoured by its NATO partners and above all by the Federal Government, was thus raised to be the official negotiating aim.[93] Thomas Risse-Kappen in his study on the FRG's INF policy maintains that the idea of a zero-option did not first arise in 1981 but goes back to the SPD party's internal debate ahead of the NATO 1979 double-track decision. The Federal Government, as a response to the increasing domestic demands for an abandonment of stationing, took over the idea mainly for internal political reasons. He points out that from the first there were different variations of the zero-option under discussion.[94] Schmidt has himself taken credit in public for the American adoption of the zero-option.[95]

With regard to Schmidt getting the Americans to the negotiating table, Patricia Clough wrote in *The Times* that Schmidt had apparently persuaded President Reagan 'that any other course would accelerate the Europeans' loss of confidence in the United States and seriously threaten the cohesion of the Alliance. Thus the peace movement, which at first so irritated the Chancellor, turned out to be a useful ally in bringing psychological pressure on the Americans.'[96]

The talks between the USSR and the USA resumed again on 30 November 1981 after a year's break.

The FRG foreign office report for 1981 stated that 'the Federal Government tried to make her contribution to the reduction of tension [in East–West relations] and to get the dialogue going again between

West and East. Expression of this policy was the visit of General Secretary Brezhnev in Bonn and the meeting between Federal Chancellor Schmidt/General Secretary Honecker in the GDR.'[97] With regard to FRG–USSR relations the report stated that 'The relations between the Federal Republic of Germany and the USSR developed on the whole satisfactorily ... The strains of East–West relations, in particular the continued Soviet occupation and the development in Poland restricted the development of German–Soviet relations ... in 1981, too, the Federal Government continued the top-level political dialogue with the Soviet Union.'[98]

On 1–2 April 1981, Foreign Minister Genscher returned Gromyko's 1979 visit to the Federal Republic with a trip to Moscow. International controversies rather than bilateral controversies were the focus of his discussion with Gromyko.[99] Gromyko stated to Genscher that the USSR would no longer make pre-conditions for the speedy resumption of talks and negotiations with the USSR. Genscher was also received by Brezhnev and handed him a letter from Schmidt which contained the invitation, already expressed in June 1980, to a third visit by Brezhnev to the Federal Republic.[100]

From 22 to 25 November 1981 General Secretary Brezhnev and Foreign Minister Gromyko paid a return visit to Bonn for the working visit of the Federal Chancellor and Federal Foreign Minister in the summer of 1980. It was the only foreign visit Brezhnev undertook that year. The FRG foreign office report for 1981 stated:

> In the talks the Federal Chancellor and the Federal Foreign Minister stated the firm stance of the Federal Government on the basis of the common Western positions, among them the NATO double-track decision of 12 December 1979. At the same time the German interest was emphasised in the continuous further development of bilateral relations with the Soviet Union in all those areas where this is necessary and possible. With the continuation of their personal talks with the Soviet leadership the Federal Chancellor and the Federal Foreign Minister are pursuing the aim of reducing mistrust and avoiding misjudgements and thus to contribute to a successful outcome of the – for the international stability and safeguarding of the peace important and necessary – negotiations between West and East.[101]

The emphasis of the discussions during the visit was on the medium-range missiles issue.[102] Apparently the aim of the political talks from the Soviet point of view was to foster doubts about the USA's will to negotiate and to represent American policy altogether as lightweight and insincere. The Soviet side emphasised its readiness to come to an agreed reduction at Geneva of several hundred Soviet medium-range weapons. In addition to this the USSR confirmed the proposal which it had already made before of a moratorium* lasting for the duration of the Geneva negotiations. The Soviet Union declared itself ready to unilaterally decrease the medium-range missiles stationed in the European part of the USSR.[103]

Sixteen months after the creation of the trade union Solidarity, a state of emergency was declared in Poland and martial law imposed on 13 December 1981. According to Fred Oldenburg's report in *Sowjetunion 1982/83* the measures of repression adopted by the Polish military regime, with the approval of the Soviet Union, resulted in a renewed period of stagnation between Bonn and Moscow and this phase was only ended by Brezhnev's death on 10 November 1982.[104] Oldenburg may, however, be overstating the case because when the author put this view to a government official, he was reluctant to endorse it, stating that the real chill in FRG–USSR relations occurred in 1984 with the revanchism campaign. The United States pressed for sanctions against the Soviet Union and Poland, but Bonn and the other European countries were reluctant. As Helga Haftendorn writes:

> The worsening of the situation in Poland confronted the Federal Republic with a double dilemma: a way out of the Polish crisis appeared only possible through an economic and political stabilisation of a repressive regime and thus ran contrary to Western values, whilst the policy pursued by the USA of isolating Poland and 'punishing' the Soviet Union would certainly not bring about liberalisation in Poland and in addition would expose East–West relations to an intolerable strain.[105]

The Federal Republic adopted a middle course of political condemnation of the military regime but continuation of a limited economic co-operation.[106] One party official told the author with regard to the FRG's position on the upheavals in Poland that the FRG did not want to endanger the whole process of East–West relations. The FRG kept the most silent about the Soviet instigated declaration of martial law but helped the Poles the most. According to the party official, the French were great on speeches for freedom but the FRG sent 1 million parcels a month (privately, not through government).

On 25 December 1981, Schmidt stated that Federal Government's position on Poland in a letter sent to General Secretary Brezhnev: no

---

* General Secretary Brezhnev proposed several times a moratorium lasting for the duration of the negotiations but it was rejected by the West on the grounds that it would only insignificantly affect Soviet planning but would prevent the fulfilment of the NATO decisions according to schedule.

state, not even the Soviet Union, had the right to determine the political and social development of another state. Poland must solve its problems without external interference.

On 23 December, Reagan announced in his Christmas speech a shortlist of steps against Poland which included the suspension of Polish fishing rights, suspension of Polish flights to the United States, restrictions on high-technology exports, and the further extension of Ex-imbank credits was stopped. It was felt that some tangible gesture of protest was needed and the administration took the position that these measures were against the Polish authorities on behalf of the Polish people.[107] Perceiving the Soviets as instigators of the declaration of a state of emergency and the imposition of martial law in Poland, the United States imposed, in actual fact quite modest, sanctions on the Soviet Union by the end of December 1981. The sanctions included postponement of a new docking rights agreement for Russian ships, an indefinite delay in talks for a new grain agreement, suspension of Aeroflot flights to the United States and cancellation of new export licences for high-technology and equipment for the trans-Siberian gas pipeline.

Bonn's position was that sanctions would not help the Polish people and it appealed to Warsaw to end martial law, release all detainees and resume dialogue with Solidarity, indicating that if this was carried out more official economic aid could be expected. The European Community agreed to cut back imports of some Soviet goods as a political signal. The United States increased pressure on its allies when no sign of any real improvement emerged from Poland.[108] Bonn agreed to one key demand that there should be no state-subsidised credit for trade with the East but did not have a policy of giving subsidies anyway. At the Western economic summit conference in Versailles in June 1982 a compromise was found between the United States and its main partners on the trade issue.[109]

In 1980 negotiations over a vast new European gas pipe deal had begun. (Bonn had signed gas pipe deals with the Soviet Union in 1970, July 1972 and 1974.) A consortium of West European firms concluded the deal with the Soviet Union for the delivery of items of equipment for the trans-Siberian natural gas pipeline against future delivery of gas to Western Europe. German firms and banks had a special share in the deal. Forty billion cubic metres of Siberian natural gas from the Yamal Peninsula, where 15 per cent of the world's known reserves were situated, would be supplied to Europe scheduled for 15 January 1985. France and West Germany expected the Siberian natural gas to supply 5 per cent of their total energy requirements for the next quarter of a century.[110] In 1980 the Federal Republic was importing 16 per cent of its gas from the USSR and 6 per cent of its oil.[111] The agreement meant that by 1990 the FRG would be importing 28 per cent of its natural gas from the USSR.[112] The West German firm of Mannesmann was to sell pipe valued at 15 billion DM to the Soviet Union and financing was to be provided by a bank consortium at an interest rate of 8 per cent.[113] For the Soviet Union this deal meant that Moscow could boost its hard-currency earnings by around £100 billion.[114] For the big international banks there was large commission and interest payments on the deals. For the West German firm Mannesmann, in the depressed Ruhr, such orders were vital.

The American view over the gas pipe deal was this: 'If we help the Soviets develop their energy resources, they earn hard currency and can continue to put a number of their resources domestically into the military sector' and 'Administration concern stems from both because of the energy dependency that will be created on the part of Western Europe for Soviet gas, and because it would accelerate the creation of dependency on the Soviet Union as a market for the exports of certain West European countries.'[115] Both Carter and Reagan had tried unsuccessfully to block or slow down the deal. West Germany's position on the issue of dependency on the Soviet Union for energy was that this was exaggerated and that it would be taking less than one third of its gas imports from the Soviet Union, which would represent about 6 per cent of its total primary energy needs.[116] The biggest purchaser Ruhrgas claimed that it could easily absorb a total shut-off and that it would feel far safer with energy from Siberia than from the unreliable North African and Middle Eastern alternatives.[117]

In response to the imposition of martial law in Poland the United States had banned the sale of 200 giant trench-diggers, and, more seriously, the export of various General Electric components and technical licences vital to the completion of the forty-one compressor stations the Soviet Union had ordered to a General Electric design. Bonn's position was that it needed all the energy it could get from any source to sustain its oil-starved economy and that this was far more important in preserving the stability of the Western alliance than dubiously effective sanctions.[118] A fortnight after the Versailles economic summit President Reagan suddenly banned the supply of certain crucial parts: those of the key pumping components made by the US companies or by Europeans under US licence. The European Community condemned Reagan's action as 'contrary to the principles of international law'. They made it clear that the pipeline project would be completed even if it were delayed.[119] What made the dispute between the West Europeans and the United States worse was that soon after the latest steps against the pipeline deal, the United States agreed to deliver more grain to the Soviet Union. The issue was only resolved after difficult negotiations conducted partly between the USA and the Europeans in the EPC and partly in the Bonn Group (the FRG and the three Western Allies): this resulted in the USA giving in during November 1982 – Schmidt was then no longer in office – and lifting the sanctions against the Europeans whilst the Europeans undertook to exercise greater restraint in trade with the East.

One government official said during interview with regard to Schmidt's political and intellectual influence *vis-à-vis* the Soviet Union that the Soviets went ahead with the stationing of SS–20s in the seventies without any consideration to Schmidt, despite the fact that Schmidt was worried all the time about them and repeatedly brought the matter up with the Soviets. The same applied to Afghanistan – the Soviets went ahead. However, it was a bit different with Poland and the fact that the Soviets never militarily intervened – there the warnings of the Chancellor did play a role. Schmidt told the Soviets that co-operation with the FRG would stop if the Soviets invaded.

In 1982 there were no meetings between the FRG and the USSR at summit or foreign minister level. Brezhnev was in poor health and died in November and Schmidt was absorbed by the tension inside the Social–Liberal Coalition and the threat to the SPD's survival in government. With regard to the superpower talks on medium-range nuclear missiles, the United States, despite an undertaking to the European allies to conduct close consultations with them at all stages of the Geneva talks, did not keep Schmidt informed as to what was going on.[120] An example of this was the 'walk in the woods' proposal of July 1982.[121] Paul Nitze and his Soviet counterpart Kvitsinski put forward a plan whereby there would be no deployment whatsoever of Pershing II, a smaller deployment of cruise missiles and a drastic cut in the number of SS–20s. Schmidt would have welcomed the plan because this would have solved the problem of only West Germany having the Pershing II and it would also have stabilised a balance at a relatively low level, but he was not informed of it by the American camp.[122] The author's information is that the plan came to nothing because the American military rejected it and because the Soviets thought that Brezhnev would die and so the Soviets tried to keep down any movement.[123]

On 17 September in a bid to clear the uncertain domestic political situation Schmidt proposed new elections in the FRG, announcing that Social Democrat ministers would replace the four FDP ministers who had resigned to forestall dismissal. He himself took over Genscher's post as Foreign Minister. On Friday, 1 October 1982, Schmidt lost a constructive vote of no confidence brought by Kohl and Genscher. Under the West German system this means that Kohl immediately and automatically became Chancellor, thus bringing thirteen years of SPD/FDP coalition to an end.

6 Assessment of the Federal Republic of Germany's relations with the Soviet Union, 1974–1982

There is a view held both in the FRG and abroad that during the Schmidt period Ostpolitik was demoted, that Ostpolitik and FRG–Soviet relations began to stagnate, that the great 'visionary' period of Brandt was over. For example, Henri Ménudier writes in his article 'La Politique à l'Est de Bonn': 'The policy towards the East has lost the priority character which it had under the Brandt governments: Mr Helmut Schmidt often gives the impression that foreign policy amounts essentially to action by the Government in the field of energy and of economics.'[1] But Schmidt has his defenders. A close party colleague and long-term observer of Helmut Schmidt, does not see Schmidt as having in any way undervalued the importance of Ostpolitik. A politician wants, however, to go down in history for something – Adenauer was famous for his Westpolitik, Brandt for his Ostpolitik, so Schmidt chose economics. Schmidt, it seems, never saw foreign policy as being one-sided. Furthermore, external circumstances and world interdependency and the fact that the FRG as a trading country is especially dependent on global trading conditions forced Schmidt to concentrate on economics when he came to office. The same source says, interestingly, that Schmidt saw the prominence of economics in international relations as transitional and that he did not think it would last as long as it did. And there was, of course, also the consideration that a politician would like to be re-elected and must therefore take into account that the electorate tend to 'look at their purses rather than at foreign policy'.[2]

That Schmidt was a man for the times is a view taken by more objective observers too. As Marion Dönhoff says, the second half of the 1970s saw a change in what 'high' foreign policy was, with the rise to the top of the agenda of matters of international finance.[3] Schmidt's background meant the man and the moment were well suited. His reputation abroad and at home benefited accordingly.

134

Certainly, there seem to be several different factors contributing to a change in 'character' in Ostpolitik and FRG–Soviet relations. One was the actual characters of the two chancellors, Brandt and Schmidt, and their personal attitudes to politics, to East–West relations and to the Soviet Union. Although it must be pointed out that Brandt cautioned realism and many times warned that détente did not mean the end of the barbed wire, the characters of Schmidt and Brandt *were* different and Schmidt's character was not only naturally pragmatic but he also consciously believed in the wisdom of adopting a pragmatic approach to politics. According to a close party colleague, Schmidt mistrusted emotional politics and wanted to get away from the emotional politics of Brandt, in fact the two had argued about an emotional approach to politics. In his 1986 farewell speech to the Bundestag, Schmidt said:

> I would ... like to call on us to reflect on the ethos of a political pragmatism on a moral basis. That means: that which we achieve and that which we want to do must be morally well-founded. The way in which we seek to achieve the objective must be realistic, it must not be illusionary. And – whatever we do – we must not forget: he who wants to achieve a distant goal must take many small steps.[4]

The tone of the Schmidt–Genscher period was less grandiose, less large conceptionally. The large concept of the Brandt period had gone. Schmidt concentrated on the 'substance' of East–West relations: both he and Genscher concentrated on the details. They saw the difficulties and tried to solve the difficult little details of East–West relations.

And, after all, Schmidt and Brandt were the products of different pasts. Brandt had had more contact with the communists in the past whereas Schmidt started in politics when the SPD had a strong anti-communist stance having seen the SPD persecuted in the GDR after the Second World War. Schmidt had a very dispassionate attitude towards the Soviets and saw them as a power among powers whereas Brandt had a different, an ideological approach, to the communist countries arising from the fact that he grew up when people still made pilgrimages to the USSR. Brandt and Brezhnev were friends whereas Schmidt and Brezhnev met together as people who had both fought in the Second World War and who both believed that, as a result of past experiences, it was genuinely the case that neither wanted another war. Schmidt and Brezhnev trusted one another but did not especially like one another. They had a good relationship but the emotional warmth was not there. Schmidt is not an emotional man but there was also the fact that the emotion was not there in their relationship as it was between Brandt and Brezhnev.

Personalities are not, of course, everything. The change in external and internal challenges when Schmidt came to power was as important as the change in personalities. There was a refocussing of West German policy of a necessary kind. Schmidt's convictions with regard to Ostpolitik were the same as Brandt's – with regard to Poland, Schmidt, according to a close party colleague, was even more committed than Brandt having fought there during the war and because he took the suffering of the Polish people to heart. But when Brandt came to power there was the need for Ostpolitik, and when Schmidt came to power, as Marion Dönhoff says, there was a need to see to the economy. In fact, there is very likely justice in the view held within the SPD that internal politics, economy and the 'oil-price shock' were Brandt's undoing, not the Guillaume spy affair.[5]

Another factor was time itself; the major Ostpolitik treaties had been signed, the big moves had been made by the time Schmidt and Genscher came to office and this was bound to lead to comments that the ensuing period was less 'spectacular' than the preceding one. What might be termed as the 'second phase' of Ostpolitik – that of putting the treaties into practice – was bound to be slower and more difficult and to bear fruit on a long-term basis. Indeed Ostpolitik was intended to be a long-term process. The achievements of détente such as increased travel and family contacts, and a quieter Berlin situation became accepted by the public, and people tend to have very short memories – in fact, it was a measure of the success of détente and the 'normalisation' of East–West relations that they should have been so regarded. Furthermore, after the bi-lateral Ostpolitik treaties had been signed, détente moved into a multilateral phase with many issues being dealt with through CSCE and MBFR negotiations and through contacts between East and West in the Economic Commission for Europe (ECE).

Also, as was the case with FRG–GDR relations, the FRG's Ostpolitik in general and FRG–USSR relations in particular were affected by and dependent on the superpower climate. During the seventies the superpower climate began to deteriorate, greatly accelerating after Afghanistan. Although bad superpower relations gave the FRG certain opportunities which it could exploit, there is no doubt that a positive climate of détente was much more conducive to Ostpolitik and FRG–USSR relations.

There may have been another factor. William E. Griffith writes in *Die Ostpolitik der Bundesrepublik Deutschland* that from 1975 a certain trend towards the right became noticeable in the FRG and that Schmidt was therefore inclined not to supply the CDU/CSU with election campaign ammunition through a too active Ostpolitik.[6] A party official's comment on this view to the author (perhaps not unexpectedly) was that this was absolute nonsense and that Schmidt certainly did not alter his FRG–USSR relationship out of fear of losing votes. However, the West German author Klaus Mehnert writes about Schmidt's 1974 visit to the Soviet Union (Klaus Mehnert was in Moscow covering the visit) that the successful performance of the CSU in Bavaria and the CDU in Hessen on the eve of the negotiations meant that Schmidt's room for negotiation was narrowed down by the result of the election and he was forced to prove that he was harder than Willy Brandt.[7] At any rate Schmidt seems to have been less accommodating in negotiations with the East. Schmidt saw himself as 'mild in der Art, aber ganz hart in der Sache' (mild in manner but very hard in substance), whereas there is a view within the party that Brandt was mild in substance. It is perhaps fair to say that although Schmidt might have been harder in *person* than Brandt, he was harder in *negotiations* because of the demands of the situation. The USSR through détente gained political equality and Schmidt saw that the USSR gained influence in the West and that it could be the case that the Soviets thought they could push too much. Schmidt was of the opinion when he came to power that the political possibilities for the Soviets should not be unlimited, that they should not all be on the Soviet side.[8]

When asked for his assessment of FRG–USSR relations, one government official was of the opinion that very little had been achieved because the potential was very limited.[9] In fact, the approach to assessments of FRG–USSR relations often met with during interviews conducted in the 1984–5 period tended to be polarised – either maintaining that FRG–Soviet relations were 'wonderful' and making out a case for this, or pointing at how little had been achieved and bitterly condemning it all. One could assume that these two views were mutually exclusive and at opposite ends, but there was, however, a middle view and one which the author finds more reasonable:[10] although given Soviet behaviour, not much could have been expected to begin with, this did not mean that Ostpolitik should not have been tried – things became clearer with regard to Soviet behaviour in the seventies. Ostpolitik was trial and error. Of course, the FRG would have preferred more outcome but given its problems caused by the Second World War and given the general deterioration of détente, the FRG managed quite well. Ostpolitik had to be given a try to find out how much could be achieved, and one had to try for as much as possible. It was, in fact, *an opportunity* to be tried out. In the early seventies things looked different and it was hoped that there would be a much quicker real pace of détente. The basic reason why this did not occur lay with the Soviets. Détente had to be explored as far as possible – it was not a question that there were too many illusions. Once it was seen that the limits were narrower than had been first thought, then the FRG had to work on them. Schmidt was more realistic than Brandt or Bahr. In 1972 in order to carry the day the SPD had to exaggerate the case for Ostpolitik in a way that it might not have done had it had a solid majority. Thus, Ostpolitik became very emotionalised in a way that was arguably not necessary as it rested on a good case anyway. This was the reason why the term 'realistic' (*realistische Entspannungspolitik* – realistic détente policy) became so popular during the 1974–82 period.

The middle attitude said rightly that the FRG had to live with the Soviet Union because of the GDR and that neither the USSR nor the FRG could solve problems by forcing a solution on the other side. FRG–Soviet relations were basically a matter of strength of will – the Soviets wanted the FRG to accept Soviet *de facto* domination on the continent, especially in Eastern Europe, by keeping quiet and co-operating with the Soviets economically. The Soviets wanted to prevent the Europeans from helping the Americans in their conflict with the Soviet Union. The FRG could not accept that because its security was guaranteed by the United States. Denying the Soviets fulfilment of their goals was a victory for the West. If the FRG was able to achieve things not by confrontation but by keeping lines of communication open then FRG–Soviet relations may be said to have been a success.

What then were the concrete achievements and disappointments in FRG–USSR relations during the 1974–82 period? The author feels that FRG–Soviet relations were well summed up by Brezhnev during his 1978 visit to Bonn when he was asked in an interview with the West German Social Democratic Party newspaper *Vorwärts* how he assessed the state of relations between the FRG and the Soviet Union,

> The relations between the USSR and the FRG have assumed a qualitatively new character. Co-operation has become the norm. A certain trust has been established in each other's word, in the signatures put to joint documents. Members of government, parliamentarians and political and public leaders meet; numerous delegations are sent. Cultural and tourist exchanges are being put on a regular basis. In short, a great experience of diversified links has been accumulated. It

Table 4. *Western–Soviet high-level meetings, 1974–1982*

	France		FRG		Britain		US	
	Summit	FM	Summit	FM	Summit	FM	Summit	FM
1974	2		1	1			2	1
1975	1				1			
1976								
1977	1					1		2
1978		1	1					4
1979	1				1		1	
1980	1	1	1					
1981			1	1	1			
1982								1

Source: R. Smith, 'Soviet policy towards West Germany', *Adelphi Papers*, no. 203, p. 14.

is clear that summit meetings have been playing the dominant role in establishing and strengthening fruitful ties between the USSR and the FRG. On each occasion these summit meetings introduce something new and positive and make it possible to untie difficult knots, to take decisions which signify further progress.[11]

With regard to an assessment of FRG–Soviet relations, Chancellor Schmidt has also stressed the dominant role of meetings between the two sides, 'It is gratifying to note that particularly in our relations with the Soviet Union we have achieved an exchange of views and consultations of remarkable intensity. We are thus able to gauge the interests and problems of the other side better.'[12]

Roland Smith gives figures for Western–Soviet high-level meetings (including meetings at summit and foreign minister (FM) level only and excluding conversations in the margins of occasions such as the UN General Assembly, CSCE and state funerals) for the period 1974–82 as shown in Table 4.[13]

As Roland Smith points out, Brezhnev met Helmut Schmidt more often than any other Western leader and after the Soviet intervention in Afghanistan in December 1979, there were more high-level contacts between the Soviet Union and the FRG than between the Soviet Union and any other major country, and Brezhnev's visit to Bonn was the only one he made to the West after Afghanistan.[14] One government official said this of FRG–Soviet relations to the author: all views were contradictory and remained so. There was no political *rapprochement*. The strange thing was that the more they discussed, the more they quarrelled and the more they quarrelled the better they got on psychologically. The more relations in public got tense, the better the personal ones were. Personal relations between Genscher and Gromyko were excellent. In his speech in Moscow on 30 June 1980, Chancellor Schmidt said, 'Our bilateral relationship is, I feel, a good illustration that problems can be settled, conflicts resolved and tension alleviated by a readiness for negotiation and by a will for the reconciliation of interests. In this way the Governments of our two countries have made a contribution towards equilibrium and stability.'[15]

One example of this, and one of the great achievements of the 1974–82 period of FRG–Soviet relations, was the breakthrough over Berlin which occurred during the 1978 Brezhnev visit to Bonn. The talks that were held resulted in the quietening down of the Berlin question – until 1978 the city was the subject of considerable bilateral friction. Another great achievement, given the extreme importance to the FRG of German–German relations, was that during the 1974–82 period the FRG convinced the Soviets that it was safe for the Soviet Union to sit back and allow intra-German relations to develop.

Another positive development of the period was that ethnic German emigration figures, though they did not reach the West German Government's aim of 10,000 re-settlers a year, constantly increased to peak in 1976 and 1977. Much of this was due to the Helsinki Final Act but the state of FRG–USSR relations also played a major role.

With regard to the economic side of FRG–Soviet relations, the FRG remained the Soviet Union's leading Western trading partner (see Appendix A). During the 1974–82 period two economic agreements were signed: the 1978 'Agreement on Developing and Deepening the Long-Term Co-operation between the Federal Republic and the Union of Soviet Socialist Republics in the Economic and Industrial Fields' and the implementation agreement signed in 1981. The long-term economic agreement was one of the most important results of the period. It provided a firm base for economic relations for decades ahead. Its political value lay in the unusual length of twenty-five years providing a stabilising basis and expressing the mutual trust that had been built up in FRG–Soviet relations (see Appendix C).

The progress in bilateral questions in FRG–Soviet relations is also shown in the change of subject matter of the summit talks (see chapter 5). In 1974 during Schmidt's visit to Moscow the talks were almost exclusively about German–Soviet questions, with Berlin in the foreground. During Schmidt's 1980 visit to Moscow world political topics were in the foreground. However, this was not just the result of bilateral progress but also of the increased world political weight and stature of the Federal Republic.

The FRG's relations with the Soviet Union greatly increased its political weight and stature during the Afghanistan crisis period and up to the point where the FRG persuaded the superpowers to the negotiating table. Furthermore, as Karl D. Bredthauer points out:

> a substantial part of the Federal Republic's present room for manoeuvre in foreign policy, which as Schmidt's Moscow trip showed, makes a certain independence towards the USA possible too, was in fact only created in the course of détente through the establishment and development of relations with the Soviet Union and the other East European countries and can only be preserved through a continuation of this policy.[16]

The obtaining of Soviet agreement, during the May 1980 Schmidt visit to Moscow, to go to the negotiating table – in fact bringing *both* superpowers to the table and getting the superpower dialogue going again – was one of the FRG's chief foreign policy successes of the 1974–82 period.

One very great achievement was the survival – indeed the fact that they were relatively unaffected – of FRG–Soviet relations through the seventies when the overall climate of détente began to decline, and also through Afghanistan and the difficult post-Afghanistan period. The dialogue between the two states was never affected nor was there a significant effect on their relations overall (with the exception of ethnic German emigration). Naturally the survival of FRG–Soviet relations was very much in the interests of both sides but it is also a measure of the personality, views and achievements of Helmut Schmidt and of the state of FRG–Soviet relations. As Chancellor Schmidt said in a speech made during his visit to Moscow after the Soviet intervention in Afghanistan:

> The relations between our two countries, which we set on a sound foundation about ten years ago with the German–Soviet Treaty of 12 August 1970, must prove to be stable, durable and capable of development in difficult times, too. Otherwise we would not be able to live up to the obligations we have assumed in the Treaty itself and in our joint declarations of 1973 and 1978.[17]

On the negative side there were occasions when the FRG felt let down and deceived by the Soviet Union. One example of this was the continued stationing of the SS-20s (see chapter 5). In May 1978, when Brezhnev visited Bonn, a Joint Declaration was issued in which both sides stated that they regarded it as important that no one should strive for military superiority and in which both sides gave their support for balance and parity and for disarmament and arms limitation. Brezhnev made many statements about relative parity existing in Europe, yet the Soviet Union continued to deploy the SS-20s. Schmidt felt that Brezhnev cheated him over INF.

Another instance was the treatment of dissidents in the Soviet Union, in particular, the sentencing of the dissident Professor Orlov, head of the Moscow Helsinki Group (in 1976–7 the dissident 'Groups to Assist the Implementation of the Helsinki Agreements' were set up in Moscow, Ukraine, Lithuania, Georgia and Armenia, their aim being to monitor violations of human rights and fundamental freedoms by the Soviet government and to make them known to the governments and public of the CSCE signatory states). R. Russell, pseudonym for a West German government official, writes:

> In the Federal Republic of Germany, the Government virtually felt it had been deceived by the Soviet Union because Orlov was sentenced 12 days after the signing of the Joint German-Soviet Declaration on 6 May 1978 during Brezhnev's visit to the Federal Republic in which both sides have expressed a) their willingness to expand the process of détente, and b) their joint efforts to make all principles and provisions of the CSCE Final Act become fully effective 'for the good of human beings'.[18]

Another disappointment, given the great importance and high priority attached by the Federal Republic to family reunification and emigration rights for ethnic Germans living in the Soviet Union, was the constant decline in ethnic German emigration from the Soviet Union since 1976 and 1977. This was to drop in 1982 to below the quota of 3,500–4,000 exit permits a year which Brezhnev informed Chancellor Schmidt during his October 1974 visit to Moscow that the Soviet Union would keep to. Economic relations did not reach the level of intensification called for by both sides. One government official when giving his opinion on FRG–Soviet relations to the author said that the FRG was disappointed with regard to the 'substantial relationship' – the government official said that although the fairly regular dialogue proved that the Moscow Treaty had worked and FRG-Soviet relations survived the Afghanistan and Polish crises, the two sides did not make agreements with too much substance. They were formal but empty. He said it was important to distinguish between a materialised relationship where lots of problems were solved and one in which, on the whole, not much was achieved.

In 1975, 1976 and 1977 there were no meetings between the two sides at summit or foreign minister level. Perhaps, the word 'stagnating' should not be used for 1975 because although there were always problems as usual there was also a lot of talking going on, and also 1975 was CSCE year; and 1976 can be specifically seen as a year of stagnation of East–West relations as a whole. It was the year in which there was the American election and reaction in the USA against détente policy. But in 1977 there certainly was the feeling that the political dialogue between the FRG and the USSR was stagnating a little.[19] Roger Morgan writes that the FRG's foreign policy in 1977 was 'surprisingly inactive' and gives as a major reason, apart from economic pressures, internal problems due to the coalition being returned with a reduced majority causing limited room for manoeuvre. Also, in two of the more important provincial parliaments, the FDP had entered into alliances with the CDU. Furthermore, in 1977 the FRG had the increasing problem of terrorism.[20] It seems that from the second half of 1976 to the end of spring 1977, relations between the Soviet Union and the Federal Republic stagnated – above all, the differences over West Berlin were an important stumbling block, hindering development and agreement between the two sides and generating an atmosphere of distrust and tension. But although from 1975 onwards there was a 'sobering up' (to borrow a phrase used to the author in Bonn) on both sides, there was no conscious chilling in FRG–Soviet relations until 1984, after the Schmidt–Genscher period.[21]

How far was the FRG able to influence the Soviet Union during the 1974–82 period? One way to begin to answer this question is to take a survey of informal Bonn opinion. One government official said during interview that Schmidt had a very high reputation in the Kremlin – he played a kind of role but in fact the FRG did not influence the Soviets very much, the FRG influenced them only a little. The government official gave two examples where the FRG had influenced the Soviet Union during that period: Berlin – the Brezhnev visit and the talks they had during it contributed to the calming down of Berlin after the visit; Soviet relaxation with regard to an intensification of FRG–GDR relations – during this period the FRG convinced the Soviets that the FRG was not a threat in this respect and that it was safe for the Soviets to let FRG–GDR relations develop.

Another government official said that the Soviets had a very precise assessment of power ratios and they never forgot power relations. He said that he felt one should be careful making statements with regard to influence: that it was not right to speak of individual politicians and leaders as having had great personal connections with the Soviets. He did not think that a West German Chancellor was able to influence the Soviets a lot *but* that the Soviets, that is Brezhnev and Gromyko, knew that Schmidt was an extremely clever politician and that it was always worthwhile listening to him. They knew that his opinion on American policy and Western Europe was very sound and that they should listen to it. They knew that he spoke the truth. The government official said that Schmidt said the same in the Kremlin as he did in the White House (i.e. he did not alter his statements to suit his audience) and that this probably impressed Brezhnev and Gromyko. Schmidt was never in a position to apply diplomatic pressure (however, the government official did give one example where the warnings of the Chancellor with regard to the consequences did play a role: the Soviet decision not to invade Poland. Schmidt had warned the Soviets that co-operation with the FRG would stop if the Soviets invaded), but he was in a position to tell the Soviets about the real situation and they believed him. The government official gave as a concrete example the Soviet agreement given during the 1980 Schmidt visit to Moscow to go to the negotiating table at Geneva. He did not think that the Soviets did this to please Schmidt but because they believed him when he said that stationing of the new cruise and Pershing missiles would take place and that the only way to stop it would be to negotiate. They came to the conclusion that it was a mistake to block negotiations. The government official said that the political and intellectual influence of Schmidt was bigger through his personality than the weight of the FRG, but not to the degree that the Kremlin in *crucial* questions as a result departed from its policy – for example, Schmidt had no influence over the stationing of the SS-20s (see pp. 110–11). In the question of 'to negotiate or not to negotiate', there Schmidt influenced the Soviets. The government official said that in 1980 (at other times FRG influence was very reduced) Schmidt was in a very pivotal role – he could have disproportionate influence within limits, to a smaller extent because of the personality of the Chancellor, to a larger extent because of the international situation. A weaker chancellor would not have been able to exploit the situation in 1980. In the time from the NATO decision, through Afghanistan and up to the decision to resume negotiations, Schmidt was in a position to have disproportionate influence.

A party official said he assessed FRG influence on the Soviets this way: firstly, at the very least Schmidt made them reflect on their policy or proposed policy. Secondly, in some things he was able to convice them that it was not anti-Sovietism when he pointed out wrong foreign policy behaviour by the Soviet Union and this was appreciated by the Soviets to the extent that they recognised that his statements were not malicious. According to the party official, the Soviets put proposals on the table at the Geneva negotiations which the FRG had made: in November 1983 Andropov made proposals that SS-20 forces should be reduced to the strength that England and France had in strategic nuclear weapons (about 200 missile launchers): according to the party official the FRG had suggested this to the Soviets in 1980 as they felt this would be enough for the Soviets. The party official said that a lot of proposals made by the Soviets at several different international conferences were influenced by the FRG with regard to what was realistic and what was not.

Another source close to Chancellor Schmidt said that Helmut Schmidt's political weight as head of the FRG was small but his personal weight was strong. He was accepted as an interlocutor by the Soviets and trusted by them. He said that because the Soviets knew that Schmidt was not a 'yes-man' in his dealings with the Americans, and spoke his mind, they respected and sought his opinions on American and on Soviet policy, even when Schmidt agreed with American positions and criticised Soviet positions.

Another party official told the author (corroborated by Schmidt in his autobiography)[22] that in one of the discussions between Schmidt and Brezhnev during the 1980/1 period, Schmidt said to Brezhnev that he had never lied to him and that Brezhnev replied that it was indeed the case that Schmidt never had. The party official said that Schmidt said the same in Washington as he did in Moscow and the Soviets knew this and trusted him. The party official said that Schmidt was a factor of stability between both sides.

The overall picture that emerges from this 'opinion poll' is one of fair (and unsurprising) unanimity that the Soviets responded to power, and that whilst Schmidt's personal qualities acted for the FRG as a kind of 'power multiplier', the net FRG influence on the USSR would always be greatest on those issues the latter saw as secondary. This is not to say that the FRG's influence was negligible. The economic levers in the FRG's hands may have caused Schmidt's warning over Poland to be especially heeded. And Schmidt's known expertise in the Euro-missile issue could have given the FRG suggestion, that SS-20s should be balanced with the British and French strategic nuclear forces, a credibility in Moscow. Neither of these issues can be described as secondary. On the other hand on neither of these issues was Bonn the only persuasive voice.

The same technique of informal opinion survey yields interesting reactions on another matter concerning the nature of FRG influence in Moscow. There is a conventional view of postwar FRG–USSR relations that when relations between the superpowers were good, then the Soviets were not interested in West Germany. They would have liked to have had a settlement between themselves and the USA whereby Europe was divided into spheres of influence ('you can look after your Germany and we'll look after ours'). When relations between the superpowers were bad, then the value of West Germany went up for the Soviets and they viewed West Germany as an intermediary. For example, *The Times*, 23 November 1981, states:

> Generally speaking, when relations with Washington are good they are attracted by the idea of joint super-power control of Europe – 'You look after your Germans and we'll look after ours'. Cementing the status quo becomes the main task. When relations with Washington are bad, as they were under President Carter and remain under President Reagan, they become more tempted by the idea of splitting and weakening the alliance by offering special terms to the Europeans.[23]

When this view was put to a party official by the author during an interview, his reply was that he agreed with the first part of this view but not the second. He said that after 1946–7 the USSR only had one thing in mind, to become equal to the American superpower, and that the USSR had three fears: US ICBMs, China and the West German conventional army. Western Europe and the FRG just played a role in this big game of chess. The USSR's main interest was Washington – the FRG just played a marginal role. He felt that the above view was too simplistic, too balanced. According to the party official it was not true that when relations between Washington and Moscow were bad, then the USSR became very smooth towards the FRG. He said that, on the contrary, the value of the FRG to the USSR was nearly objectively stable.

When the conventional view and that of the party official were put by the author to a government official his reaction was this: to say that the superpowers were primarily only interested in one another was correct. It was also correct that when the American–Soviet relationship was tense, the Soviets tried to activate the European relationship. However, the government official stated that he used to think that this was automatic but over the years he had come to the belief that the

Soviet policy was more sophisticated than a rising and falling of the value it placed on the FRG. The government official said that such a view was too neat. He also felt that another conventional view was wrong: he did not believe that the Soviets really needed the threat of the FRG and the West towards their satellites – he thought that it was not true that the Soviets always needed a choice enemy in the shape of either the USA or the FRG. The government official said that on balance the FRG was always better off when American–Soviet relations were good even if it sometimes meant that the FRG's own role was reduced. Even if the FRG's role was enhanced by American–Soviet tensions or even if these tensions gave the FRG a more important role to play – even if this was the case, the FRG felt very uneasy when the superpowers did not talk.

While it is impossible to state, without rare specialist insight, just where, and how constant, the FRG was in the scale of Soviet policy values, the above view of the government official providing a more sophisticated version of the conventional view would appear to be the most plausible. The FRG saw itself as benefiting from good super-power relations, but when these did not materialise it could work to improve them. Its situation made a 'good officer' approach feasible. Good superpower relations meant a more secure environment for the FRG. Less good relations perhaps made the FRG more 'important'. It is certainly the case, that after Afghanistan, when relations between the USSR and the USA were at their lowest of the 1974–82 period, the FRG was the only Western country, and remained so till the end of the Schmidt–Genscher period, to exchange visits with the Soviet Union at the highest level (i.e. the summit meetings in Moscow in 1980 and Bonn in 1981).

How far did the FRG modify her foreign policy out of consideration for or as a result of (e.g. Soviet direct or indirect pressure) her bilateral relations with the Soviet Union? Obviously, in view of its interest in ethnic German emigration from the Soviet Union, intra-German relations and West Berlin, where, *at the very least*, Soviet goodwill could do much to promote Bonn's cause, the FRG had to seek to achieve and maintain good relations with the Soviet Union, and in view of its vulnerable geographic position, too, it was in its interests to seek good relations with its Soviet neighbour. This was borne out in its position after Afghanistan and its very early signalling to the Soviet Union that it wished to continue the dialogue. The FRG position after Afghanistan may also have been a response to a tacit Soviet threat of reprisals against West Berlin.

The West German authority on Soviet Berlin policy, Gerhard Wettig, wrote of 'Soviet reservations with regard to the non-use of a potential for pressure *vis-à-vis* Berlin.'[24]

> The leadership round Brezhnev regards the restraint embodied in the Four Power Agreement as a correlate to the Western détente obligation to show appropriate consideration for the USSR in Berlin and to pursue in general a non-confrontative policy towards the Warsaw Pact States. The main addressee of the Soviet demands is the USA. For Moscow the leading Western power is the decisive force in the Western camp on whose conduct a great deal more rests than on the action of other Western states. The Soviet pursuit of securing American readiness for co-operation has become a more pronounced concern the more tendencies towards withdrawal from the policy of détente have arisen in the United States since the middle of the seventies. What the Soviet leadership cannot achieve directly in Washington it tries to enforce indirectly. The Federal Republic of Germany presents itself here as the Western state which, because of her immediate human interest in the welfare of West Berlin, is the most easily responsive to counter requests. In May 1978 Federal Chancellor Schmidt and General Secretary Brezhnev came to an understanding on mutual restraint with regard to West Berlin. In addition it is clear that the Soviet restraint with regard to measures against the city is subject to the tacit proviso that the Western Alliance will not take up a confrontative position towards the USSR.[25]

Gerhard Wettig went on to say,

> In view of the fact that the West European states and above all the Federal Republic of Germany continued with détente in Europe, participated only in a limited way in the American policy of confrontation and worked within the Alliance towards an improvement in East–West relations it appeared advisable to the Soviet leadership to continue the state of peace in Berlin.[26]

The FRG avoided taking up a sharply censorious and punitive stance over Afghanistan but it must also be pointed out that there were reasons for this other than bilateral considerations – as a medium power the FRG felt itself too small to punish a superpower and furthermore doubted the wisdom and efficacy of sanctions.

On the issue of human rights in the Soviet Union, the FRG adopted a non-confrontational policy. 'She does not apply sanctions and polemical or provocative measures against Warsaw Pact countries in reply to human rights violations. Thus the West German government did not apply any sanctions when the sentence on Shcharansky was passed except to reduce the size of its military team attending the

World Helicopter Championships in Vitebsk.'[27] This was certainly partly out of consideration for bilateral relations and FRG gains through détente. R. Russell writes, for example, that, although the FRG government virtually felt deceived over the sentencing of the dissident Orlov twelve days after the Joint German–Soviet Declaration of 6 May 1978, in which the two sides had expressed their willingness to expand the process of détente, and after their joint efforts to make all principles and provisions of the CSCE Final Act become fully effective for the good of human beings, 'Nevertheless, in its statement on the sentencing of Orlov the Federal Government did not mention this Joint Declaration out of consideration for its relationship with the Soviet Union.'[28] R. Russell further writes, 'West Germany regards the progress so far achieved in both the area of human rights (in particular in comparison to the Stalinist period) and in other fields of détente not related to human rights as a relative success and as an "acquis de détente" which is worth being safeguarded.'[29] and 'West Germany worries that, if the West reduces or terminates its détente policy or applies sanctions because of Eastern human rights violations, opposition to détente within Eastern communist parties might be fuelled and the East might scale down or stop its détente as well and jeopardise this "acquis de détente."'[30]

However, there were also other reasons for the FRG position on human rights in the Soviet Union, for example Jonathan Carr (who, as stated earlier, has had regular opportunities to talk to the Chancellor), writes of Helmut Schmidt:

> He shared Henry Kissinger's view that a 'policy of state-to-state confrontation on human rights with the Soviet Union can bring nothing but a demonstration of Western impotence, a worse condition for the dissidents and no significant progress on human rights'. Kissinger had managed by quiet diplomacy to win permission for the emigration of thousands of Soviet citizens. Successive governments in Bonn had quietly and methodically secured the release of hundreds of thousands of ethnic Germans from communist states. Schmidt feared that by overt action, which would cause the Soviet Union loss of face, Carter would achieve the opposite of what he wanted.[31]

Despite considerations for the benefits of good relations with the Soviet Union, the FRG did not allow itself to be deflected from support for the NATO double-track decision, even though it found itself from the autumn of 1979 the main target of the Soviet campaign against that decision, nor did it allow itself to be influenced by the Soviet use of the

FRG's interest in good German–German relations in its attempts to undermine the FRG's support of the NATO rearmament, or by Soviet 'sanctions' over ethnic German emigration from the USSR (see pp. 30–1). The FRG stood firm in participating in the US Olympic boycott despite Soviet propaganda, warnings and criticism (see pp. 119–21). During Schmidt's 1980 visit to Moscow he spoke out in no uncertain terms over the Soviet intervention in Afghanistan (see p. 123). On the issue of human rights the FRG government made public statements criticising the Eastern human rights policy, for example the conviction of Orlov and Shcharansky and, in fact, initiated the statement made by the Nine on Shcharansky.[32]

The 1970 Treaty of Moscow between the USSR and the FRG was meant to 'normalise' relations between the two countries. FRG–USSR relations may be said to have been 'normal' during the 1974–82 period in that contacts at all levels, including summit meetings, and trade and cultural relations, came to be accepted, even regarded as commonplace. They were as 'normal' as relations between the Soviet Union and any Western state, with the important exception that in FRG–Soviet relations there was always the question of the GDR and Berlin. However, it may be argued that towards the end of the 1974–82 period, and certainly immediately after the Soviet intervention in Afghanistan, relations between the FRG and the USSR were 'abnormal' in the sense that had they followed the pattern of Britain, France and the United States' relations with the Soviet Union, then they would have deteriorated.

Conclusion

In a situation where, contrary to earlier hopes and expectations, the potential for the development of FRG–USSR relations proved to be limited and in a difficult period in the overall climate of détente, Schmidt consolidated on the Brandt period. He developed FRG–USSR relations, putting them on the solid basis that they are on today. As one Western journalist put it to the author in an interview, 'Brandt had a vision and Schmidt translated it into cash and hard politics.' It was a period when East–West relations became increasingly dominated by security issues and this was reflected in FRG–USSR relations. However, the growing dominance in FRG–USSR relations of security issues was not only due to the overall superpower climate but also to the emphasis placed on security by Helmut Schmidt, to the INF problem, the increased weight of the Federal Republic and to the progress made in bilateral FRG–USSR issues. A measure of mutual trust was established. Schmidt had a very high reputation in the Kremlin and this was translated into a certain limited influence on the Soviets – influence which, from the end of 1979 to the end of 1981, was increased due to the international situation. Through relations with the Soviet Union, the FRG's international political weight and stature increased. Again, this was particularly the case from the time of the NATO double-track decision, through Afghanistan and up to the superpowers going to the negotiating table in Geneva. It is a measure of the success of the period that when Schmidt fell from office in 1982, the CDU/CSU[33] more or less continued Schmidt's foreign policy with no change, no change sometimes even in style.

7 The Federal Republic of Germany's political relations with the Soviet Union after 1982

Initially, continuity was the hallmark of FRG–USSR relations after 1982. In 1984, however, the first real conscious chilling since the signing of the 1970 Moscow treaty occurred in bilateral relations, and this was to last until 1986. In January 1988 FRG–USSR relations entered a dynamic phase. It was a fast moving period which saw the opening of the Berlin Wall in November 1989, followed eleven months later by the historic reunification of Germany.

This chapter is aimed at providing an overview of the post-Schmidt period of FRG–USSR political relations until the reunification of Germany in October 1990.

Ethnic Germans

After the end of the Schmidt period the numbers of ethnic Germans allowed out of the Soviet Union continued to drop: 1983 (1,447), 1984 (913), 1985 (460), 1986 (753). But from the middle of 1987 a sharp change of direction occurred. From January 1987 ethnic German applications were subject to a new regulation, however the proximate cause seems to have been President Richard von Weizsäcker's visit to Moscow in July 1987. For 1987 as a whole the numbers of ethnic Germans allowed out totalled 14,488. In 1988 the figures took another quantum leap upwards to 47,572.[1] The explanation in terms of the analysis given in chapter 2 would seem to be a confluence of two linked factors favourable to increased emigration. One is fairly obvious: the improvements in East–West relations sought by the Gorbachev administration.[2] The other is more internal to the Soviet Union. As pointed out above, Soviet policy on their nationalities question has not always been consistent in the period since the Revolution: the problem – of maintaining essential unity between the centre and the periphery – may have been consistent but the method of tackling it has sometimes been repressive of ethnic diversity, and sometimes much more tolerant. In 1987 a new phase of toleration was set in motion under Gorbachev.

Despite nationalist unrest emerging in 1988 as the then greatest threat to democratic reform in the Soviet Union this policy of toleration was continued.[3] In 1989 tentative Soviet soundings were made to the FRG with regard to the establishment of a special German–Soviet trade zone combined with a new republic for ethnic Germans in Kaliningrad (before 1945, the old German port of Königsberg, East Prussia). Apparently the proposal was intended to combine Soviet interest in attracting Western capital and technology with the FRG's interest in former territories and in the treatment of Soviet ethnic Germans. The proposal was initially welcomed by Chancellor Kohl but later the German view became more sceptical because of Polish worries.[4] One reason for FRG approval was that the large numbers of ethnic Germans arriving in the FRG from Eastern Europe were presenting Bonn with considerable problems. The number of ethnic Germans emigrating to the FRG in 1989 was approximately 98,000.[5]

In March 1989 the ethnic Germans in the Soviet Union formed a pressure group 'Gesellschaft Wiedergeburt' (Society for Regeneration). Numbering 50,000, the aim of the majority of its members was territorial autonomy in the area of the former Volga republic. On 28 November 1989 the Supreme Soviet passed a resolution resulting in the setting up of a commission to work towards ethnic German autonomy. This commission, however, was unable to make progress due to opposition among the Russian population in the Volga area.

On 13 September 1990, the FRG and the USSR signed the Treaty on Good Neighbourliness, Partnership and Co-operation, in which the signatories *inter alia* supported the recognition of the cultural rights of ethnic Germans in the Soviet Union and of Soviet citizens in the Federal Republic. From January to November 1990 approximately 132,000 ethnic Germans were allowed to emigrate.[6]

It is obviously too soon to say how, at what point, or even whether the historical pattern of inconsistency over how to deal with the nationalities question will reassert itself. It would seem, however, that the changes in the Soviet Union and in Eastern Europe have been too fundamental to allow any such reverse.

Berlin

The calming down of the Berlin question, achieved in 1978, continued after 1982 despite the international and bilateral problems. On the negative side, however, there was no progress either until 1986 when, during the visit of Foreign Minister Genscher to Moscow, the agreement on scientific and technological co-operation was signed on 22 July. This agreement had hitherto remained unsigned because Moscow was unwilling to compromise on the practical inclusion of West Berlin.

In the autumn of 1987 expert talks were held with the aim of enabling West Berlin to be included in further agreements. However, a breakthrough was only achieved during the Shevardnadze–Genscher meeting in September 1988 at the UN General Assembly. The matter had become pressing because of the imminent visit of Chancellor Kohl to Moscow. During that visit in October, as a result of the breakthrough, an agreement on environmental protection was signed which fully included West Berlin, and a two-year implementation program for 1988/9 to the cultural skeleton agreement of 1973 was finally signed, too.

FRG–GDR relations

After the death of Brezhnev in November 1982, and the election of Chancellor Kohl in March 1983, both sides tried to keep relations going. It seems that Andropov had agreed, with the GDR, apparently in May 1983, to a policy of dialogue between the two German states and had even sacked the unpopular Soviet Ambassador Abrasimov, which made increased contacts between Bonn and East Berlin easier.[7]

During the Kohl–Chernenko period, the GDR, despite pressure from Moscow, steered a less punitive and isolatory course *vis-à-vis* the FRG and continued the policy of dialogue apparently agreed with Andropov in May 1983, thereby becoming a side target in the revanchism campaign.

Immediately after the death of Chernenko, on 10 March 1985, Honecker signalled unchanged interest in security and economic co-operation with Bonn. It seems Honecker believed that Gorbachev, who was considered to be part of the Andropov wing of the party, would allow greater German–German room for manoeuvre. However, this calculation proved to be incorrect and Honecker felt obliged on 4

September 1985 to cancel his visit to the FRG scheduled for the end of September.[8]

From February 1987 there was a more relaxed atmosphere between the Soviet Union and the GDR over agreed German policy. The overall marked improvement in East–West relations and in superpower relations was reflected in an improvement in German–German relations. From 7 to 11 September 1987 Honecker visited the FRG. It was the first visit by an SED General Secretary to the Federal Republic.

Throughout 1988 the GDR gave strong support to the Soviet led campaign, targeted at the West German public, to prevent the modernization of short-range nuclear forces (SNF), indeed eventually playing the more active role.[9]

Gorbachev's reforms in the Soviet Union were met with opposition by the GDR. Honecker rejected following a policy of perestroika, denying any need for reform and reconstruction in East Germany and attributing Soviet attempts at perestroika to the Soviet Union's less advanced state of development. East Germany, with its legitimacy problem and its border with democratic West Germany, had much to fear from a questioning of the past and from demands for openness and publicity. It therefore resisted implementing glasnost also.[10]

The Kohl/Andropov period

Even before the actual breakup of the SPD/FDP coalition, the Soviet Union expressed the wish for continuity in FRG–USSR relations in the event of a CDU/CSU (i.e. conservative) government. The Soviet Union expressed the same sentiment at Brezhnev's funeral and again before the elections of March 1983. Immediately after the Bundestag elections, Andropov conveyed an invitation to Chancellor Kohl to come to Moscow.

On coming to office, the CDU/CSU/FDP coalition declared continuity in foreign policy. Indeed, as stated above, after Schmidt's fall from office the CDU/CSU more or less continued his foreign policy with no change, no change sometimes even in style.

FRG–USSR relations, which had been stagnating, were given a new impetus by Andropov at Brezhnev's funeral. Soviet interest in a reanimation of the dialogue at top level was shown on that occasion by the unusually long discussion between General Secretary Andropov, Federal President Carstens and Foreign Minister Genscher.[11] The summit meeting between Kohl and Andropov held in Moscow in July 1983 was the first meeting Andropov had had with a Western leader and was an indication of the importance, at that time, of the FRG in Soviet Western policy.[12]

FRG–USSR relations continued to be dominated by security issues, i.e. Western rearmament and Soviet countermeasures. Up until, and also after, the Federal Government's ratification through the Bundestag, on 22 December 1983, of the decision to install 108 American Pershing II missiles and 96 cruise missiles, the Soviet Union attempted to interrupt or prevent this actually being carried out.

The Kohl/Chernenko period

Owing to its failure to prevent the stationing of cruise and Pershing missiles, the Soviet Union tried from 1984 to isolate the FRG and up to the beginning of 1985 attempted to establish alternative focal points around the Federal Republic. The break in relations was also due to the Soviet desire to keep face by carrying out previously stated countermeasures and reprisals.[13]

The FRG also suffered a loss in status. Although the loss of status did not mean that the substance of the USSR's political or economic relations with Bonn was affected, indeed Foreign Minister Genscher met his Soviet counterpart Gromyko four times in 1984 and economic and cultural relations continued to thrive with closer co-operation in environmental protection being initiated, it did mean that the FRG lost the role of special partner which had been accorded to it since the concluding of the Moscow Treaty. FRG–USSR relations now played an even more subordinated role than previously to superpower relations and to the safeguarding of Soviet hegemony over Eastern Europe. The reason for the loss of status was that the Soviet Union expected the FRG to show more consideration for the Soviet Union's security interests and to distance itself more from the United States. Also, the Soviet Union was annoyed that the new coalition government's declarations that the German Question was still open were being delivered in a more positive fashion than had been the case under Schmidt.[14]

In May 1984 the Soviet Union began its 'revanchism campaign'. This was, in fact, a delayed reaction to the differing emphasis placed by the Kohl government in the FRG's Ostpolitik, emphasis on statements on the German Question and on the Eastern borders, whereas the Schmidt government had tended towards playing down these, i.e. no strong public verbal statements (see, e.g., pp. 65–6 above). The revanchism campaign took the form of harsh criticism in the Soviet media of 'militaristic and jingoistic tendencies' of the new Kohl/Genscher government. It is possible that one of the reasons was that the Soviet Union wanted to revive old enemy images of a neo-nazi and revanchist West Germany to legitimise Soviet hegemony over Eastern Europe – after the Soviet Union walked out of the INF talks (November 1983) it became clear that several Warsaw Pact states were revolting against Moscow's confrontation course.[15]

FRG–USSR relations under Gorbachev

Initially the new Kremlin leadership continued the policy of keeping a distance from Bonn. This was for the following reasons:

continued Bonn–Washington axis;
fear of co-operation between the FRG and the USA on SDI research;
to underpin the Eastern Bloc co-ordination of Western policy and Eastern Bloc discipline;
as FRG–USSR economic relations were unaffected there was no incentive to improve political relations;
Soviet analysts probably thought that the CDU/CSU/FDP coalition would lose the January 1987 election.[16]

Future bilateral relations with the FRG were explicitly linked by Gorbachev to the 'good conduct' of the FRG towards the USSR and her allies in matters of security policy.[17]

The continued demotion of the FRG was shown in the protocol accorded to Chancellor Kohl during his visit to the Soviet Union to attend Chernenko's funeral and the reserved acceptance of an official invitation. In May 1985, the fortieth anniversary of the surrender of the German army, the Soviet media defamation campaign reached its height.

However, the Soviet leadership was still interested in continuing a minimum of official relations – a delegation of the Supreme Soviet visited the FRG, from 15 to 21 April 1985, and foreign ministers Gromyko and Genscher met in Vienna on 16 May, in Helsinki on 1 August and in New York on 24 September and 25 October 1985. For its part the FRG remained determined to adhere to a policy of dialogue and co-operation.

In 1986 a change in Soviet FRG policy occurred. The Soviet Union apparently came to the conclusion that the political and economic weight of the Federal Republic meant that it could not afford to ignore the FRG if it wished to refashion its relations with Western Europe and to influence United States' security policy through the West Europeans. Also, there was increased Soviet interest in imports of advanced

Western technology after the reactor accident at Chernobyl. From the spring of 1986, therefore, the Soviet Union gradually began to revise its perception of the FRG.[18]

Early in the summer of 1986, when it became apparent through Landtag elections and opinion polls that the present coalition would be re-elected and not the SPD, as the Soviet Union would have preferred, the Soviet Union decided to include Chancellor Kohl in a more active European policy.[19] An invitation was issued to Genscher to visit Moscow from 20 to 22 July. During the visit both sides agreed to 'open a new page in relations.'[20] Consultation agreements were made to pave the way for an intensification of the political dialogue at political and expert level.

However, in October 1986, Chancellor Kohl gave an interview in which he linked the public relations abilities of Gorbachev with those of Nazi propaganda minister Goebbels.[21] This led to the Soviet Union cancelling or postponing all agreed ministerial meetings up to the Federal elections. Relations remained overshadowed until immediately before the elections.

During the course of 1987 there was a marked improvement in West German–Soviet relations. The state visit of Federal President Weizsäcker from 6 to 11 July 1987, to the USSR, the first for a Federal head of state for thirteen years, was a particularly clear expression of this. At the talks with General Secretary Gorbachev and President Gromyko, both sides agreed to a comprehensive development of relations. As we have seen, in 1987 there was a significant rise in the number of Soviet ethnic Germans allowed to emigrate to the FRG; at 14,488 (1986: 753) it was the highest figure since emigration began in 1950.[22]

In 1988 FRG–USSR relations entered a dynamic phase. Already in January 1988 during Foreign Minister Shevardnadze's visit to the FRG, both foreign ministers had signed a protocol on bilateral consultations and on 30 July 1988 Genscher met Shevardnadze in Moscow in accordance with the protocol. Among other agreements signed by the foreign ministers during Shevardnadze's visit was an agreement on the establishment of general consulates in Kiev and Munich and an agreement which extended the 'Agreement on Developing and Deepening the Long-Term Co-operation between the Federal Republic of Germany and the Union of Soviet Socialist Republics in the Economic and Industrial Fields' of 6 May 1978 (see p. 174, 176–9 above) by five years. On 24–7 October 1988, Helmut Kohl made an official visit to Moscow with the aim of beginning 'a new future-orientated chapter' in FRG–USSR relations.[23] He held talks with Gorbachev totalling ten hours. Several agreements and declarations of intention were made covering almost all areas of bilateral co-operation. The number of ethnic Germans allowed to emigrate in 1988 shot up to 47,472.[24]

During this period security issues once again began to dominate bilateral relations. With the signing of the US–Soviet INF treaty on 8 December 1987, NATO turned its attention to the question of modernisation of its short-range nuclear forces (SNF) in Europe, which for West Germany would mean modernisation of the ageing Lance missile launchers – a move which was very unpopular not only with the West German public and the left-wing opposition but even with some members of Chancellor Kohl's conservative party. The Soviet Union initiated a campaign for the removal of short-range nuclear forces. It was aimed at fuelling West German fears of weapons which, in the campaign's words, were 'only designed to kill Germans.'[25] During his January 1988 visit to Bonn, Shevardnadze warned that nuclear modernisation would 'scuttle all that has been achieved in arms control so far.'[26] This was also strongly expressed to Chancellor Kohl during his visit to Moscow in October 1988.[27]

In the middle of February 1989 Gorbachev and Kohl agreed to install a direct telephone link between the Kremlin and the Chancellor's office. In June, Gorbachev made a four-day visit to the FRG, the first Soviet leader to do so since Brezhnev's visit in 1981. Soviet officials called the visit a milestone in German–Soviet relations.[28] The two sides issued a six-page joint declaration which had taken the two Foreign Ministries nearly a year to draw up. It was a wide-ranging policy statement covering such areas as human rights, disarmament, Europe, economic and environmental co-operation. Eleven agreements on bilateral co-operation were also signed.[29]

Gorbachev at this time enjoyed immense popularity with the West German public. The results of a survey, published in *Der Spiegel* shortly before his visit to the FRG, placed him way above Mitterand, Bush and Margaret Thatcher.[30]

The year 1989 saw the rapid fall of communist governments across Eastern Europe and the opening of the Berlin Wall.[31] In May 1989 a liberalising Hungary began to dismantle its barbed wire border with Austria. Increasing numbers of East Germans began to cross illegally into the West via Hungary. Hungary initially reacted by tightening border security, meanwhile housing growing numbers of East Germans in government camps. On 10 September Hungary opened its border with Austria and more than 30,000 East Germans left for the

West. This was followed by refugees sheltering in Bonn's Prague and Warsaw Embassies taking trains to the West and as the trains passed through the GDR, people jumped on board. Meanwhile, in the GDR, New Forum was created to press for reform. In October riots and protests broke out in the GDR. On 18 October Honecker resigned to be replaced by Egon Krenz. The mass demonstrations and meetings continued into November.

On 4 November, Czechoslovakia opened its border after 5,000 refugees occupied the West German Embassy. A mass exodus began. Between 4 and 6 November 23,000 East Germans arrived in the FRG from Prague and 50,000 had come through Hungary since mid-September. Details of a new travel law announced on 5 November failed to stem the exodus. On 7 November the East German government resigned, followed twenty-four hours later by the East German Politburo. Hans Modrow became Prime Minister and a new Politburo was formed. The Party announced that it was ready for multi-party elections. On 9 November the GDR declared that all citizens could leave East Germany for visiting purposes through all crossing points in the Wall and the border with West Germany. This measure meant in practice the general opening of the Wall.

It does seem that the opening of the Berlin Wall was a response to instability within the country – a gamble which was taken to stem the mass exodus and save the economy rather than as a consequence of any changes at this stage in Soviet German policy as such. Around 225,000 people out of a population of only 16.7 million, mostly between the ages of twenty and forty, had left East Germany between the beginning of the year and the opening of the Berlin Wall.[32] It seems that the overriding Soviet concern was still the stability of the GDR. The opening of the Wall was followed by Soviet statements to the effect that the GDR must remain in the Warsaw Pact, the elimination of the borders would not be tolerated and that it did not mean that the question of reunification was up for discussion.[33] In line with all Soviet leaders since the Second World War, Gorbachev was still insisting that the 1945 borders, giving the Soviet Union a considerable amount of territory, were not open to negotiation.

Rather, the changes in East Germany at this point should be seen in the context of the Soviet policy, under Gorbachev, of allowing the Warsaw Pact states to follow their chosen political course without interference from outside and of adopting a position of detachment, thus enabling the Soviet Union to turn inward to concentrate on domestic events, but at the same time of ensuring the durability of its military alliance. However, this policy was accompanied by reference to Mr Gorbachev's vaguely defined concept of a common European (anti-American?) home and the ultimate dissolution of NATO and the Warsaw Pact. It is possible, or more likely probable, that Gorbachev at this stage had the long-term aim of playing the German card to bargain with the West and that his later volte-face on the reunification question was caused by his urgent need for West German and Western help for economic reforms at home, and by the fact that the GDR proved so near collapse that reunification was almost forced on him. He, in effect, saw the need to play the German card much sooner than he had anticipated. The opening of the Berlin Wall should also be seen in the context of Soviet aims *vis-à-vis* disarmament. Whilst announcing the opening of the Berlin Wall, Günter Schabowski, the East German Politburo member responsible for the media, hinted that the Berlin Wall might become a bargaining chip in disarmament negotiations. Western disarmament moves would have a 'positive influence' on its future.[34]

At the end of November 1989, Chancellor Kohl presented a ten-point programme for overcoming the division of Germany and Europe to the Federal Parliament in Bonn.[35] Unification was to be achieved by developing confederative structures between the two states in Germany with the goal of ultimately creating a federation. The plan was immediately condemned by the Soviet Union with the accusation that it was an attempt to fan GDR nationalism. The USSR reiterated her position that she had no wish to see changes in the borders, stating that reunification could only occur as part of a comprehensive process of overcoming the division of Europe.[36]

A turning point in Soviet thinking on German reunification appeared to have been reached in January 1990. In talks with the East German Prime Minister, Hans Modrow, President Gorbachev declined to rule out the possibility of a united Germany. It seems that Modrow warned that the GDR risked economic and social chaos if its separate existence were prolonged and that the two leaders discussed a stage by stage union.[37] On his return Modrow unveiled a unification plan of his own, along similar lines to that of Chancellor Kohl, but with the proviso that a united Germany must be neutral, and this was immediately rejected by the NATO General Secretary, Manfred Wörner.

With the economic and political situation in the GDR reaching crisis point, the East German government decided that the date of the country's first free elections would be brought forward from May to 18 March. Chancellor Kohl's response to the situation in the GDR was to offer immediate talks with East Berlin on a West German Mark based currency union linked to economic reforms. By this time (February 1990), East Germans were pouring into the FRG at a rate of more than 3,000 a day.[38]

At the weekend of 10 February, Chancellor Kohl and Foreign Minister Genscher paid a lightning visit to Moscow and after significant breakthroughs in the talks the Soviet Union gave the go ahead for German reunification later in the year, with Moscow stating that it would not impede reunification and that the timing and method was a matter for the two Germanies to decide alone.[39] It seems that Moscow was not only concerned about the security aspect of a united Germany but also about the prospect of economic losses if the present Soviet–East German economic relationship were affected. This problem was discussed by the two Foreign Ministers, Shevardnadze and Genscher, at the Moscow talks, and Genscher gave an assurance that Moscow's economic interests would be fully taken into account.[40]

Apparently the breakthrough was due to reports of the imminent collapse of the GDR's economy, enabling Chancellor Kohl to argue that bankruptcy and anarchy were much more likely to be a danger to Soviet security than any fears of a newly united Germany committed to peace.[41] On his return from Moscow, Chancellor Kohl took care to emphasise that the process of unification would only take place in collaboration with the Western allies and that they would be closely involved in resolving questions of NATO membership and the security concerns of the Soviet Union.

During the February 'Open Skies' conference of NATO and Warsaw Pact foreign ministers held in Ottawa, the 'two plus four' formula was devised, under which the two Germanies would agree on unification terms between themselves and then meet the four Allies to discuss the security implications for Europe.

One problem which emerged at this period, causing consternation particularly to Poland, East Germany and to the FRG coalition, was Chancellor Kohl's equivocal position on the issue of Poland's borders, i.e. the former German Oder–Neisse territories placed under Polish administration by the Potsdam Agreement pending a final peace treaty. The 1970 Warsaw Treaty between the FRG and Poland had been seen by most observers as virtually a settlement of the border question.[42] Mainly for domestic political reasons, Kohl refused to accept unconditionally the Oder–Neisse line as the western border of Poland stating that this was legally something only the parliament of a united Germany could do. He established a link between recognition of the Oder–Neisse line and Warsaw's renunciation of claims for war reparation. However, in early March he backed down on the issue.

The chief stumbling block to unification remained Soviet opposition to a united Germany's membership of NATO. Following three days of talks in early April between President Bush and the Soviet Foreign Minister, Eduard Shevardnadze, in Washington, the two sides had reached deadlock, with the West equally adamant that a unified Germany must remain in NATO. It did appear, however, that the Soviet Union no longer took the view that West Germany should be neutral. A compromise was then suggested by the Soviets that united Germany should be part of both NATO and the Warsaw Pact during a transitional period leading to the disbanding of the two blocs. As the first 'two plus four' meeting on 5 May approached, there were signs of a toughening Soviet stance with the Soviet side signalling they would insist that the reunification of Germany be synchronised with the creation of a European security system. It seems that the West, however, at this stage, was taking the view that with the right package of economic and security incentives, e.g. reductions to the German army, renunciation of its own nuclear and biological and chemical weapons, Soviet agreement could probably be obtained.[43] Certainly in a long session of talks held shortly before the 'two plus four' meeting, Chancellor Kohl offered Mr Shevardnadze a significant expansion of bilateral ties, particularly economic co-operation.[44]

According to a report in *The Times* such a deal was, in fact, reached, with the Soviets apparently reluctantly accepting that a united Germany could be a member of NATO if it wished to be, but that in return the three Western Allies and the FRG must provide satisfactory economic and security guarantees. If they failed to do so, then Moscow would still retain a veto over reunification.[45]

In June the West German magazine *Der Spiegel* claimed that during a meeting between Mr Shevardnadze and Mr Genscher at the margins of the Conference on Security and Co-operation in Europe, Mr Shevardnadze had indicated that Moscow was prepared to accept membership of a united Germany in NATO in return for Western economic help. According to reports circulating in Bonn, West Germany was putting a package together totalling 20 billion DM (£7 billion). Genscher subsequently refused to confirm the figure but stated in a television interview that the FRG government was indeed discussing closer economic and financial co-operation with the Soviet Union. The FRG position was that although NATO allegiance could not be bought or sold, economic stability for the Soviet Union was important both for that country and for Europe.[46]

Two important steps towards unity were taken in June: in simultaneous parliamentary sessions in East Berlin and Bonn, the GDR and the FRG gave formal recognition to the postwar border between Germany and Poland by voting in identical resolutions to acknowledge the Oder–Neisse line by treaty and they also ratified a treaty introducing monetary union on 2 July.

On 14 July Chancellor Kohl flew to the Soviet Union for a two-day meeting with Mr Gorbachev in Moscow and in Mr Gorbachev's home town of Stavropol. Although the ground had been prepared in the previous two months in six meetings between Foreign Ministers Shevardnadze and Genscher, it seems that the speed of agreement may have come as something of a surprise to Chancellor Kohl and certainly to his Western allies. At Zheleznovodsk, a resort spa in the Caucasus, Kohl and Gorbachev announced that the last significant obstacles to reunifying Germany by the end of the year had been removed: Germany could join NATO in exchange for FRG concessions to Soviet economic and security concerns. The likely explanation of the breakthrough was that Gorbachev, faced with the urgency of solving domestic problems, wanted to settle the issue of German reunification and not least by securing thereby urgently needed West German finance and technical assistance to ease the Soviet Union's desperate economic situation.[47] Parallel talks were held between finance ministers Valentin Pavlov and Theo Waigel as well as between foreign ministers Shevardnadze and Genscher. It seems that the West Germans pledged aid to the Soviet economy totalling 5 billion DM.[48]

An eight-point plan was agreed: German reunification would involve East and West Germany and Berlin; the USSR, USA, Britain and France would lose their occupation rights; a united Germany would be free to decide to which alliance it wished to belong; the country would sign a treaty for the withdrawal of Soviet troops within three or four years; NATO structures would not apply to eastern Germany as long as Soviet troops remained there; Germany would limit its army to 370,000 men; Germany would renounce chemical and nuclear weapons.

On 31 August the two Germanies signed a political unification treaty. Unification was to take place on 3 October. On 12 September the two plus four agreement on German reunification, the Treaty on the Final Settlement with Respect to Germany was signed by the foreign ministers of the two Germanies and the four wartime allies

Britain, the United States, France and the Soviet Union. This historic treaty which officially ended the Second World War was hailed as signifying the end of the division of Europe and the end of the Cold War. Its provisions were basically the same as those agreed in the Kohl–Gorbachev Eight Point Plan, though it did terminate the Four Power rights ahead of reunification and the exact details of the agreement and contentious points had meanwhile had to be solved by negotiation and compromise. The date of Soviet troop withdrawal, for example, was reportedly agreed by President Gorbachev in a telephone call with Helmut Kohl when West Germany agreed to provide 12 billion DM towards the cost of the provisional keeping of Soviet forces in Germany, of removing, rehousing and retraining them in the Soviet Union.[49]

On 13 September, West Germany and the Soviet Union signed a treaty in Moscow on 'Good Neighbourliness, Partnership and Co-operation'. It was intended as a further development to the 1970 treaty between the Federal Republic and the Soviet Union which had opened the way to expanding co-operation. The new treaty, as its successor, strengthened its provisions and provided the Soviet Union with additional security guarantees.[50] The treaty included a non-aggression clause with each side pledging not to attack the other, nor to support an attack by anyone else, and to settle disputes by peaceful means. It reinforced clauses on United Germany's borders contained in the unification treaty. Both states undertook to reduce weapons in their territory, to promote the Helsinki process on co-operation in Europe and to hold regular consultations, including twice-yearly at foreign minister level. They gave their support to a significant increase in economic, scientific, technical and ecological co-operation and an easing of visa procedures, especially for businessmen. The treaty was a declaration of general principles with specifics left for separate agreements.

On 24 September, East Germany left the Warsaw Pact in readiness for formal reunification. On 3 October, after more than half a century, the division of Germany was finally ended and the country united, with Chancellor Kohl becoming the first all-German Chancellor since the end of the Second World War in May 1945.

Soviet strategy towards the FRG, 1974–1990

During the Schmidt–Brezhnev period, one of the aims of Soviet policy towards the FRG was to influence the FRG towards a favourable view of Soviet policy to the West, to influence FRG policy and to use Bonn as a mediator to Washington of Soviet positions. This was particularly the case during the late seventies when security issues began to dominate bilateral FRG–Soviet relations and the international scene and as East–West relations began to deteriorate. This was done by using a policy of incentives and sometimes threats (see pp. 114–18). This policy was carried on during the Kohl–Andropov period, wherein the incentives and the threats were alternated. During the Kohl–Chernenko period, threats outweighed incentives. During all these years use had been made of the FRG's geographical position, its vulnerability in the event of a war, its economic interests, and of Bonn's interest in good German–German relations. However, it seems that at no time during this period had German reunification been used by the Soviet side.[51]

From 1984 onwards, when it appeared that threats had failed to have any effect on the process of installation of cruise and Pershing missiles, Soviet policy switched to one of isolating the Federal Republic and of building alternative focal points around her. As stated above the reasons for this were varied but one contributing cause could have been the person of the Chancellor, Kohl did not appear at this time to command the personal stature of Schmidt *vis à vis* the Soviets. Also, on the diplomatic side, he did not adopt the Schmidt view that public statements of principle could sometimes be counterproductive.

Initially this policy of demotion of the FRG as special partner was continued by Gorbachev. One of the reasons for this was the particularly close relations of the Thatcher government to the Reagan administration; the Soviet leadership therefore felt that it was now important to try to influence London. Instead of just ignoring it as Brezhnev had done, striking efforts were made to cultivate better relations with Great Britain. Even before coming to office in December 1984, Gorbachev visited Britain, and in July 1986, Shevardnadze emphasised that Great Britain was a great power with nuclear weapons and considerable armed forces in Europe. A further advantage in view of the Soviet Union's economic problems was that far-reaching financial agreements were made with Great Britain to give new impetus to bilateral economic and scientific-technological co-operation.[52]

Soviet Western policy under Gorbachev consisted of creating a political relationship of trust and a climate of economic co-operation with the West with the twin aims of lowering the costs of the foreign policy 'load' through the reduction of tension and through disarmament, and of economically supporting perestroika through its Western partner states. After a while, a decisive role was accorded once again to FRG–Soviet relations. This coincided with the switch in emphasis of Soviet activities from the USA to Europe, partly because important security agreements had already been secured with the USA and there was an approaching change in the administration in Washington.[53] Moscow resumed its earlier policy of incentives and threats, whereby, as before, security issues dominated bilateral relations, i.e. according to the Soviet view, Bonn should advocate the prevention of modernisation of nuclear weapons and further steps in disarmament.

However, unlike the Brezhnev period when the German question was striking by its absence from efforts to woo the FRG out of fear that even non-binding words could lead to destabilisation in Eastern Europe and especially the GDR, general verbal suggestions were made to the West German public that positive changes would occur but without any of these suggestions actually taking on concrete, binding form. It seems that the idea was to stimulate FRG interest in good relations with the USSR but that there was no actual interest in altering things – Soviet policy remained restrictive over the Berlin question and over its German policy. It seems that the over-riding concern of the Kremlin was still not to risk instability in the GDR.[54]

By December 1989, after the fast-moving events in Eastern Europe and the opening of the Berlin Wall, the FRG was playing a central role both in the eyes of the United States and those of the Soviet Union, with US officials privately admitting that Britain's importance was being 'eclipsed by Bonn's special role in managing the East–West relationship' and Soviet diplomats taking the position that while 'Mr Gorbachev recognises the great debt of gratitude he owes Mrs Thatcher for championing his cause, even before he became the Soviet leader ... he no longer needs her as an intermediary with the United States, and questions her relevance to the great East–West issues now on the international agenda.'[55] By this time, also, President Bush was regularly having telephone talks with Chancellor Kohl. He opted to have dinner with Chancellor Kohl before reporting to other NATO leaders on the Malta summit.[56]

After January 1990 when a turning point in Soviet thinking on reunification had occurred, the German Question was used by Moscow to try to buy either the neutralisation of Germany (a harking back to the Stalin note of 1952 in which he proposed a sovereign, reunited, armed, but neutralised Germany and which was rejected by Adenauer and the Western Powers) or the creation of a European security system which would involve the dissolution of NATO and the Warsaw Pact.

Appendix A   The Federal Republic of Germany's economic relations with the Soviet Union

Since 1971 the FRG has been the Soviet Union's leading Western trading partner. As Chancellor Schmidt said in his statement on the 1978 Brezhnev visit to Bonn, there are good possibilities for the two economies of the FRG and the Soviet Union to complement one another. 'The Soviet Union possesses ... energy and raw materials we do not have. We, on the other hand, can offer exceptionally perfected technologies, capital goods, techniques'.[1] The FRG has been the largest Western supplier of advanced technology to the Soviet Union: in 1977, for example, 34 per cent of Soviet imports of high technology came from the FRG, followed by Japan with 17 per cent of high technology exports to the Soviet Union.[2] In the 1970s the USSR earned 75 per cent of its hard currency from the FRG through the sale of energy, raw materials, chemical materials, wood and cotton.[3]

However, actual trade levels have never, in spite of exhortations, reached the sort of shares that were attained in 1931.[4] Although trade expanded – between 1971 and 1978 the volume of exchange quadrupled[5] – it did not match up to the grandiose possibilities which Brezhnev outlined during his visit to Bonn in 1973.[6] The main underlying reasons for this were the, for the FRG side, unacceptable Soviet desires for large amounts of credit and for as much business as possible to be done on the basis of barter transaction, i.e. the costs of plants installed in the Soviet Union by West German firms to be paid for by deliveries from future production.[7]

There was a tendency at the author's interviews during the 1984–5 period for both government and party officials – presumably in order to discourage a perception of vulnerability – to play down the significance of the FRG's trade with the Soviet Union, stating that it was only a small percentage of West German trade.[8] Obviously it is certainly true that the figure for trade with the Soviet Union *was* a small percentage of the overall trade[9] but as a reliable source in Bonn, close to both government and party officials, stated to the author during an interview it should not be looked at overall but in terms of the industries involved: the Ruhr was an area of very high unemployment and its trade with the Soviet Union, especially in steel, counted very much (see also pp. 130–1). The same source stated that every government had to listen to sectional trade interests citing Presidents Carter and Reagan as being no exception – Carter was not strong enough to keep up the grain embargo and Reagan was eventually forced to stop the embargo when he came to office as he could not keep it up either. This view was confirmed to the author by an employee of the Ruhr steel producing firm of Mannesmann. Roland Smith, too, in his *Adelphi Paper* on Soviet policy towards West Germany, found that exports to the Soviet Union were 'critical for certain companies, notably Mannesmann'.[10] He further writes, 'In 1982, it was estimated that 90,000 people in the FRG were employed directly or indirectly in connection with exports to the Soviet Union – or 0.4% of the total number of employed persons'.[11] In fact, the FRG had the largest involvement of any West European country in trade with the Comecon countries[12] and the lobby for Eastern trade was a powerful one. It is probable that if all Eastern trade were to have come to an immediate stop in the early 1980s, the unemployment figures in the FRG would have exceeded 2 million.[13]

And it is interesting to note that it seems that the Soviet side, well aware of the Ruhr's difficulties, was on one occasion anyway prepared to take advantage of this in a business deal. An article in *Der Spiegel* in 1978 states,

> The Soviets know how to fully use tactical negotiating advantages towards capitalist partners. In 1977 when Mannesmann's export managers wanted to agree a new slice of their swop transaction of pipes for natural gas, the Russians took their guests by surprise with extremely low price limits for steel products: they had discovered that the Düsseldorfers were dependent on follow-up orders from the East to employ to capacity their underemployed works.[14]

Furthermore, the FRG is a very export orientated country and it also does not possess an abundance of natural resources; it is very dependent on foreign trade, particularly exports in high technology and therefore had to cultivate the market, maintain all lines of service and maintain stable relationships, including those with Eastern Europe. The FRG foreign office report for 1978 listed 'the dependency of her economy on the export of industrial goods and foreign deliveries of raw materials' as one of the factors constituting the FRG's political starting position.[15] Karl Hardach writes: 'Almost one-quarter of all German jobs [in 1980] stemmed from export activities, a fact that made Germany dependent on the smooth functioning of world trade like no other major industrial country in the West. As the world's second largest exporter, Germany sold goods valued at $193 billion in 1980.'[16]

The FRG must diversify its export markets. The recession in the Western industrial countries and its negative effect on export possibilities, meant increased West German interest in trade with Eastern Europe. The Soviet planned economy meant that it was relatively shielded from the cyclical fluctuations of the world market. The oil crisis meant increased West German interest in the opening up of Soviet raw material and energy sources. In his 1977 Alastair Buchan Memorial Lecture to the IISS, Schmidt said:

> The East, due to its large potential of raw materials and energy, affords the West the possibility of diversifying, to a certain extent, its raw material and energy imports. At the same time it offers markets which are especially attractive for the West because they are not, or not fully, involved in the synchronization of Western business cycles. In 1975, for instance, due to the world recession, German exports dropped by almost 4 per cent in nominal terms whereas the exports to the Soviet Union rose by 46 per cent, thus making a valuable contribution towards improved use of capacities and a better employment situation in my country.[17]

Exports to the Soviet Union were relatively more important to the FRG than exports to the FRG were to the Soviet Union due to the FRG economy being more export dependent than the Soviet one.[18]

Has the Soviet Union or the FRG used economic relations for linkage or for leverage? Roland Smith in 'Soviet Policy Towards West Germany' published in 1985, gives examples of possible implied, implied and actual Soviet threats (April 1972, for example, at the time of the Bundestag debate on the ratification of the Moscow Treaty when Suslov said that non-ratification of the treaty would mean the FRG losing the political confidence of other states and so its significance for the Soviet Union as a serious economic partner).[19] He also states that there have been a number of examples of generalised Soviet threats suggesting that any adverse developments in West German–Soviet political relations would have adverse consequences for trade. He goes on to say, however, 'But in practice it is not possible to point to any case where the Soviet Union has applied negative linkage in her trade with the FRG and has deliberately cut back on trade as a sign of political disapproval.'[20]

Angela Stent writes that the Soviet Union has generally been unable to initiate negative economic leverage towards the FRG because of its weaker bargaining power and that it has only been able to implement those linkage strategies involving political levers.[21]

> The Soviets have occasionally used negative political levers ... to try to induce the Germans to make economic concessions. The Soviets have not pursued negative linkage strategies too often, because in general they were concerned to increase their trade with the FRG. They resorted to utilizing negative political levers only when they realized that the Germans would not yield and when the economic stakes were not so important. The most usual form of linkage for the Soviets has been the use of positive political levers involving secondary issues ... In 1972, they were willing to include Berlin in the trade treaty with Germany in return for the promise of more trade.[22]

She goes on to say 'The Soviets have never attempted to wrest major concessions from the Germans through the use of linkage.'[23]

The FRG position was that trade should not be dependent on politics except in the most serious circumstances. The feeling was that as long as the FRG did not become dependent on the Soviet Union and as long as trade did not jeopardise the FRG's security position – and she believed that none of this had happened – then why should the FRG not benefit. The FRG was against using trade *directly* as a lever as it believed that it did not work and would only hurt its own interests (see pp. 99–100) but it did believe in the 'spill-over' and long-term effects (see pp. 173–4 and Appendix B). Foreign Minister Genscher said:

> the Soviet economy – unlike those of other Eastern European countries – is largely self-sufficient and not reliant on the West. While the Soviet Union's economic relations with the West have reached a magnitude making the country seriously interested in co-operation, they have not reached a volume that affords the West leverage for inducing the Soviet Union to make major political concessions. The 'carrot' and 'stick' are simply too small for this purpose. The prospect of trade may perhaps prompt the Soviet Union to make concessions in the humanitarian sphere. But trade incentives cannot make the Soviet Union abandon its arms buildup if it sees in this an opportunity for acquiring superiority. Nor can they prompt the Soviet Union to exercise restraint in the Third World if it sees chances of expanding its predominance there without incurring any risks. The Soviet challenge is political and military in nature – it can be countered effectively only by political and military means. There is even less hope of making the Soviet Union incapable of continuing its arms buildup by denying it trade. The Soviet economy is made up of two components: the military economy and the civilian one. The

military economy is given virtually absolute priority, and there can be no doubt that the Soviet leadership will and can at all times allocate to it the resources it considers necessary. While Soviet policy can thus not be influenced in the short-term by either economic incentives or economic 'punishment', it must be clearly recognised that economic ties are of major importance for the long-term development of East–West relations. Maintaining the Western readiness for trade means maintaining the offer of co-operation and constantly reminding the Soviet Union of the possibility of comprehensive East–West economic co-operation – that is, if the Soviet Union abandons its policy of predominance and seeks 'genuine coexistence'.[24]

On the question of any future threat of Soviet use of the gas pipe deal against the FRG, Genscher has said that dependency would not

result from the planned increase in natural gas imports beginning in the middle of the 1980s. These imports will only compensate, at best, for the expected decrease in Soviet oil deliveries. Thus the five or six per cent of overall German primary energy consumption provided by energy imports from the Soviet Union will not rise, but may decrease. It is true that the share of Soviet gas in our overall gas consumption will increase to 30 per cent; but we have taken precautionary measures to ensure that the major industrial customers can shift from natural gas to coal or oil on short notice. It should also be kept in mind that the Yamal Pipeline is an export pipeline. An interruption in gas deliveries – which would inevitably affect all of Western Europe – would thus be expensive for the Soviet Union too: it would interrupt the flow of hard currency and probably also curtail production.[25] (See also p. 131 this volume.)

As Roland Smith writes, it is therefore not likely that the Soviet Union would 'cut off gas supplies in isolation, but only as part of an international crisis so grave that the gesture would not create a significant additional problem for West German decision-makers'.[26]

Trade is, of course, part of 'normal' relations with any state, but Chancellor Schmidt looked on trade with the Soviet Union as something more than this. One party official when asked about Schmidt's view of trade with the Soviet Union, said that he could best illustrate this with reference to the German philosopher Immanuel Kant and his 'Schrift vom Ewigen Frieden' (essay on 'Perpetual Peace') and the passage dealing with trade and the peace-making capacity of trade relations. The party official said that mutual dependency is a 'political peace institution' (friedenspolitische Institution), each side looks for the welfare of the other side because they want trade with them.[27] In his after-dinner speech on 5 May 1978 during the Brezhnev visit to Bonn,

Schmidt said, 'East–West trade is a significant instrument in the safe-guarding of peace.'[28] Jonathan Carr writes in his book on Schmidt, 'he had long found in Kant's works a valuable guide to the principles of political action. That applied especially to Kant's treatise 'On Perpetual Peace' which Schmidt admired for its logic and sense of realism.'[29] And in a paper which he gave to a congress of philosophy and politics on 'Kant in Our Time', organised by the Friedrich Ebert Stiftung in Bonn, Schmidt said 'important for peace in Kant's view is a continuous process of economic integration. Economic integration for the sake of peace was also the motive of the social-liberal coalition in developing closer trade relations with the Soviet Union and with Eastern Europe.'[30]

Schmidt put forward this view of trade with the Soviet Union during an interview with *The Times*: 'You know, the Soviet Union is a very close neighbour to central Europe. We are interested in having good economic relations because there is a psychological and political spill-over from there into other fields'.[31] A government official told the author that Schmidt was a great believer in strong economic relations as a part of German–Soviet relations because of the spill-over and he pointed out that there were two economic agreements signed with the Soviet Union during the Schmidt period – the 'Agreement on Developing and Deepening the Long-Term Co-operation between the Federal Republic and the Union of Soviet Socialist Republics in the Economic and Industrial Fields' of May 6, 1978, and the implementation agreement to this signed in 1981. (See Appendix B for these agreements and their evaluation by Schmidt.)

The doubters of Kant's realism and logic who have not always seen greater trade with the USSR as an uncovenanted benefit and who have worried about negative linkage and vulnerability do, on the other hand, have some history on their side. The state of USSR/Russian–German trade in 1914 and in the 1930s was at an unusually high level.[32]

On coming to office, the new CDU/CSU/FDP coalition government announced its intention of further developing trade and co-operation with the USSR under the maxim of 'continuity and commercial good sense'.[33] In 1984 the Soviet Union endeavoured to detach economic relations from the deteriorating bilateral relations and the FRG remained the USSR's number one Western trading partner, exports to the FRG being the most important Soviet source of foreign currency. Although the general deterioration of the state of Soviet foreign trade and payments since 1985 led to a decline in bilateral trade which corresponded with a fundamental decrease in Soviet trade with the

West, trade was, in fact, on a high level in the years 1985 to 1986. Despite fluctuations in bilateral political relations the FRG again remained the number one trading partner of the USSR.[34]

It seems that the USSR under Gorbachev regards the FRG as its most important partner in the realisation of its economic strategy and this was evident, for example, at the sixteenth conference of the bilateral trade commission, on 11–12 May 1988.[35] In the months before reunification, Gorbachev negotiated 20 billion DM (£670 million) in aid packages from the FRG.[36] In connection with the Soviet consent to the unification of Germany and the disastrous state of the Soviet economy in 1990, President Gorbachev and Chancellor Kohl developed the grand design for intensive and privileged bilateral economic co-operation and German economic help for the Soviet Union in the decades to come.

Appendix B   The 'Agreement on Developing and Deepening the Long-Term Co-operation between the Federal Republic of Germany and the Union of Soviet Socialist Republics in the Economic and Industrial Fields', 6 May, 1978

On 6 May 1978 an agreement on developing and deepening the long-term co-operation between the FRG and the USSR in the economic and industrial fields was signed which came into force on 27 December. As Chancellor Schmidt pointed out, the agreement had of course been prepared by the two sides before the Brezhnev visit: at the press conference on 7 May 1978 Schmidt personally warned that the agreement should not be regarded as 'having been born off the cuff, as it were'.[1] Fred Oldenburg and Christian Meier write that Schmidt claimed to be the initiator of the agreement but that in fact Brezhnev had expressed great interest in such an agreement already during his first visit to Bonn in 1973.[2]

The agreement was called a co-operation agreement, not a trade agreement. This meant that it was not subject to the EEC ruling that trade agreements might only be concluded with the Soviet Union by the Community and no longer bilaterally. Co-operation agreements were only subject to the requirement that the EEC be consulted. The agreement was a very broad framework agreement to be concretely filled out through further negotiations. It did not establish any new projects but was meant to give new impulse to trade and industry between the two states. It applied for twenty-five years but had an initial period of validity of ten years with the possibility of its being renewed three times for a period of five years each time. The Soviet Union had wanted an initial period of validity lasting till 1990 which would have been in its interest because of the Soviet centralised foreign trade planning and five-year plans but the FRG did not agree to this.

The agreement consisted of a preamble stating that the Soviet Union and the FRG were 'seeking constantly to develop and deepen the entire complex of relations between the two states', and ten Articles.[3]

In Article 1 both sides committed themselves to economic, industrial and technical co-operation which should expand as free from disturbance and as continuously as possible. Raw material and energy especially were named as areas for the intensification of co-operation. Jürgen Nötzold writes in an article published after the visit in October 1978 that the building up of long-term raw material and fuel dependencies such as gas and mineral oil brings up the question of trust in the partner keeping to the agreement and thus Article 1 may in as much be regarded as a confidence-building measure.[4]

Article 2 lists the areas and branches of industry which are to be specifically singled out for co-operation: vehicle building and mechanical engineering, metallurgical engineering, chemistry, electrical engineering including the electronics industry as well as the consumer goods industry. Article 2 lists a new area, ocean mining, as an area for co-operation – something which could mean the extraction of mineral oil and natural gas in areas close to the coast or deep-sea mining. West German industry had won a leading role in the technology of both types of ocean mining and Article 2 could therefore mean the employment of West German industrial ocean technology for the development of mineral oil and natural gas in the Soviet coastal areas, apart from the Far Eastern areas where Japan was offering itself as a co-operation partner.[5]

Article 3 laid down the specifications for economic exchange, business contacts and conditions of work for both sides. Jürgen Nötzold writes that the 'as comprehensive as possible exchange of economic information' mentioned in Article 3 is not only an important requirement for economic relations with the Soviet Union but may also be regarded as a confidence-building measure in the sense of CSCE. This point was taken into Basket II of the CSCE Final Acts and the reference to it in a bilateral agreement under international law represents a further development as the Helsinki Final Acts are only a political declaration of intention.[6]

Article 4 deals with barter transaction – unpopular with West German industry but wanted by the Soviets. Article 4 states that such transactions may be done in large or long-term projects if it is in the interests of both sides. Article 5 deals with the granting of credit. Article 6 directs the West German and Soviet commission for economic and scientific-technical co-operation to draw up a long-term programme on the main establishments involved in the co-operation.

Article 7 was very important at the time of signing in that it states that Berlin is included in the agreement (see chapter 3). As Meier and

Oldenburg have pointed out in a paper published on the 1978 Brezhnev visit, Berlin was generally included in agreements with the Soviet
Union if the Soviet Union had enough interest in the bilateral project.[7]
Article 8 stipulates that the treaty shall not affect earlier concluded two
or more sided treaties and agreements, and deals with necessary
consultations resulting from these. Article 9 deals with the validity
period of the agreement and Article 10 deals with the enactment of the
Agreement.

The long-term economic agreement was one of the most important
results of the 1978 Brezhnev visit to Bonn, indeed of the Schmidt
period. West German participation in the large development projects
in the Soviet Union needs a long-term period for their development
and utilisation. However, its importance was the political value which
lay in the long-term length of the agreement: twenty-five years. This
was much longer than the usual duration of ten years for agreements
between the Soviet Union and Western industrial states on economic-
technical co-operation and longer than the new economic agreements
which the Soviet Union had signed with France and Finland extending to 1990.

In his government statement of 11 May 1978 to the Bundestag on
Brezhnev's visit, Schmidt said,

> I am ... for political reasons glad that we were able to sign this
> agreement. It displays – over and above the individual business deals
> – the long-term aspects for the economic co-operation between these
> two important European industrial nations. The aspects, the pros-
> pects in this agreement extend beyond the end of this century. Both
> governments have made it clear that they are determined not to
> make the development of economic relations dependent on indi-
> vidual projects, however important and spectacular, but rather to
> give them a firm basis for decades to come. The agreement thus
> extends far beyond the field of economics. It provides an orientation
> for the development of political relations altogether, for a long-term
> peaceful development between our two countries, a peaceful devel-
> opment that presupposes that the people in both states will acquire a
> lasting interest in the good economic health of the people in the other
> state.[8]

According to a government spokesman, Schmidt saw the long-term
economic agreement as a 'political act without parallel in the recent
history of the world'.[9] As Nötzold writes in his article published after
the Brezhnev visit: 'The extraordinarily long term of validity of this
agreement expresses the changes which have occurred in bilateral
relations since the 1970s. For a long-term planning of bilateral

economic relations of this nature presupposes mutual trust in the long term advantages of co-operation'.[10] Herr Hoppe, FDP, said during the Bundestag debate on the 1978 Brezhnev visit, that the agreement was indeed 'a stabilising element for the development of bilateral relations'.[11] Carl-Christian Kaiser summed up the agreement in *Die Zeit* this way, 'its political function lies in materially providing security for détente through an ever increasingly closer mesh of economic relations – to the point where the mutual mixing-up of interests makes serious political collisions increasingly unlikely ... the aim is unmistakably not just to simply pursue a foreign trade policy but to embed economic relations in the political détente and to make it its underlying lining'.[12]

On 1 July 1981, during Schmidt's visit to Moscow, an implementation agreement to the 1978 long-term economic agreement was signed by Ambassadors Wieck and Semenov.

Appendix C The Federal Republic of Germany's foreign policy in the early 1980s

The FRG Government position in the early 1980s was that FRG foreign policy was based on a number of clearly defined basic tenets. Government foreign policy was set out on pp. 5–12 of *Aspekte der Friedenspolitik: Argumente zum Doppelbeschluss des Nordatlantischen Bündnisses* published in June 1981 by the Press and Information Office of the Federal Government. Those main features implicitly or explicitly relevant to this study are set out below.

In the author's view the original is a somewhat unclear and repetitive document and, therefore, selected and extracted quotations are presented here not in the order they occur in the original, but without doing violence to the sense of the document. Translations of the quotations are the author's own.

Published by the Federal Press and Information Office, *Aspekte*, is of course, a declaratory document, i.e. it is designed to affect foreign perceptions and domestic perceptions more than it is meant to be an objective analysis. But it is, however, a useful statement of the broad upper and lower limits within which practical policy was conducted and as such the author needs to refer to it and the reader needs to know about it.

> The foreign policy starting position of the Federal Republic of Germany is determined in particular by three main factors:
> the existence of two German states and the special situation of Berlin, the exposed situation of the Federal Republic of Germany on the boundary position between East and West and with it her special need for security,
> the dependence of her economy on industrial export goods and foreign raw material deliveries.
> Because of this German foreign policy is compelled to have as its fundamental aim the preservation and securing, together with our partners, of the peace in Europe and the world. Only in a condition of peace is it possible to guarantee the security of our state and its

people and at the same time uphold the option of a future realisation of the right to self-determination for all Germans.

The policy of the Federal Government is directed at the preservation of the peace and security in Europe. Its means are defence through the Western Alliance and arms limitation between East and West on the basis of an approximate balance of the military forces. This balance is to be achieved and preserved with the help of arms limitation between NATO and the Warsaw Pact at the lowest possible level of armament. This is to be achieved through negotiation. The relaxation of relations with Eastern Europe is possible as long as the security in Europe is preserved. Superiority of the one side over the other involves the danger of political vulnerability to blackmail or even to a military attack. Therefore superiority of military forces must be reduced or balanced out.

... the Federal Republic together with her partners in the Atlantic Defensive Alliance has developed a decisive concept for its security policy which still stands today. In December 1967 the NATO Council in Ministerial Session approved the guideline "Report on Future Tasks of the Alliance" known as the Harmel Report. The basic lines of our security policy are described in this report:

'The Atlantic Alliance has two main functions. Its first function is to maintain adequate military strength and political solidarity to deter aggression and other forms of pressure and to defend the territory of member-countries if aggression should occur ...'

The Western Alliance defines the second function as being:

to pursue the search for progress towards a more stable relationship in which the underlying political issues can be solved. Military security and a policy of détente are not contradictory but complimentary.

The Federal Government is guided ... by the four guiding points which the Federal Chancellor set out in the following way at the special General Assembly of the United Nations on Disarmament:

Political, strategic and military balance;

Relaxation of tension, the stemming of conflict and the balance of interests;

The capability for effective crisis management;

Foreseeability and calculability of political and military conduct.

In accordance with these principles the Federal Government advocates that in times of international crisis – such as the one triggered by the Soviet intervention in Afghanistan – the dialogue with the other side should not be broken off. Especially in a time of international hardening the Federal Government, with her peace policy, holds fast to the will to co-operate, to readiness for dialogue and to an understanding of the interests of the other person but also to the demand for moderation in political action.

Notes

Introduction

1 See, especially, the following publications listed in the bibliography, those listed under the headings Bundesinstitut für ostwissenschaftliche und internationale Studien and Radio Liberty Research; the articles listed in the journals *Osteuropa, Osteuropa Wirtschaft, Problems of Communism*; and the following authors listed in the section 'Books': Renata Fritsch-Bournazel, Boris Meissner, Maria Elisabeth Ruban, Angela Stent, Gerhard Wettig; also the articles by Gerhard Wettig in the journal section.

2 With regard to FRG government statements in general on FRG–USSR relations, one FRG foreign office official put forward the view to the author during an interview in 1984 that the statements were not slanted for Soviet consumption but were straightforward statements, perhaps a little embellished – he was, he said, amazed at how straightforward West German politicians were in foreign policy and felt that it would be better in the context of relations with the Soviet Union if they operated more like diplomats.

3 Günter Gaus, *Wo Deutschland liegt: Eine Ortsbestimmung*, Munich, Deutscher Taschenbuch Verlag, April 1986, p. 183.

4 Angela Stent, *From Embargo to Ostpolitik: The Political Economy of West German–Soviet Relations, 1955–1980*, Cambridge University Press, 1981.

1 The Second World War and its aftermath, 1945–1974

1 For the widely held high expectations of the US elite see, for example, Harry Gelman, 'Rise and fall of détente', *Problems of Communism*, vol. 34, March–April 1985, p. 51 and note 1. With regard to Soviet expectations see, for example, Brezhnev's statements during his visit to Bonn in May 1973 when he 'expounded upon the practically unlimited potential for economic co-operation between the two countries', cited in F. Stephen Larrabee, 'Soviet–West German relations: normalization and beyond', RL 203/75, 16 May 1975, p. 2.

2 See Hans-Adolf Jacobsen, 'Deutsch-sowjetische Beziehungen: Kontinuität und Wandel 1945 bis 1987', *Aus Politik und Zeitgeschichte*, B3, 15 January 1988, p. 43.

3 See, for example, *Der Spiegel*, 17 March 1975; Alexander Korab, *Der Tagesspiegel*, 19 March 1975; Karl Christian Kaiser, *Die Zeit*, 14 March 1975, cited in Larrabee, 'Soviet–West German relations', p. 2.

4 For Soviet and American disappointment in détente, see Gelman, 'Rise and fall of détente', p. 53. Also, this volume pp. 97–101.

5 Helmut Schmidt, *Menschen und Mächte*, Berlin, Siedler Verlag, 1987, p. 50.

6 Paul Frank, 'Bonn und Moskau – was ist möglich? was ist nötig?' in *Wir und die Russen: Fakten, Chancen, Illusionen*, ed. Guido Knopp, Aschaffenburg, Paul Pattloch Verlag, 1983, pp. 84–5. Paul Frank was State Secretary in the Foreign Office of the Federal Republic of Germany from 1970 to 1974.

2 Ethnic Germans

1 'Nationality Composition of the USSR (1979 Census)', in *The Cambridge Encyclopedia of Russia and the Soviet Union*, eds. Archie Brown, John Fennell, Michael Kaser and H. T. Willetts, Cambridge University Press, 1982, p. 61.

2 Ibid., p. 61.

3 Kemal Karpat, 'Moscow and the "Muslim Question"', *Problems of Communism*, vol. 32, November–December 1983, p. 71.

4 Compare, for example, Hélène Carrère d'Encausse, *Decline of an Empire*, New York, Newsweek Books, 1979; Mary MacAuley, 'In search of nationalism in the USSR', unpublished paper delivered at the Annual Conference of the National Association for Soviet and East European Studies, Cambridge University, March 1982; Joseph Rothschild, *Ethnopolitics: A Conceptual Framework*, New York, Columbia University Press, 1981, pp. 226–7, cited in Zvi Gitelman, 'Are nations merging in the USSR?', *Problems of Communism*, vol. 32, September–October 1983.

5 'The social sciences – a combat arm of the party in the building of communism', *Kommunist*, January 1972, pp. 18–30, cited in Teresa Rakowska-Harmstone, 'The dialectics of nationalism in the USSR', *Problems of Communism*, vol. 23, May–June 1974, p. 17.

6 'Preparations for the 50th anniversary of the formation of the Union of Soviet Socialist Republics', *Partiinaia zhizn* (Moscow), no. 5, March 1972, p. 12, cited in Rakowska-Harmstone, 'Dialectics of nationalism', p. 17.

7 L. I. Brezhnev's report to the 26th Congress of the CPSU, *Pravda* (Moscow), 24 February 1981, cited in Gitelman, 'Are nations merging in the USSR?', p. 37.

8 Figures from: Wolf Oschlies, 'Deutsche in der Sowjetunion – Versuch einer Bestandsaufnahme', in *Sowjetunion 1982/83*, Bundesinstitut für ostwissenschaftliche und internationale Studien, Munich, Carl Hanser, Verlag, 1983, p. 103. (Further references, including to articles in other years will give author, journal and year.)

9 See Andreas Lorenz's report on the ethnic Germans, 'Wir sind stolz, dass wir Deutsche sind. Andreas Lorenz bei den Deutschen in der Sowjet-Republik Kasachstan', *Der Spiegel*, no. 43, 1982, pp. 183–92; and Oschlies *Sowjetunion 1982/83*, pp. 102–12. Andreas Lorenz visited the ethnic Germans in Kazakhstan. Wolf Oschlies' report is based on the findings of a confer-

ence of experts held in 1982 by the Koordinationssekretariat of the Bundesinstitute für ostwissenschaftliche und internationale Studien, under the chairmanship of Dr A. Buchholz. This account (pp. 17–21) of the situation of the ethnic Germans living in the Soviet Union is based on these two sources and the author is indebted to them for the material. Other publications by the Landsmannschaft der Deutschen aus Russland (organisation of ethnic Germans from Russia) are *Die Kirchen und das religiöse Leben der Russlanddeutschen*, Stuttgart, Verlag der Landsmannschaft der Deutschen aus Russland, 1978. Karl Stumpp, *Die Russlanddeutschen*, Stuttgart, Verlag der Landsmannschaft der Deutschen aus Russland (no year). However, for reasons of objectivity it was felt that the above two independent sources should be used. A recent publication on the ethnic Germans is Ingeborg Fleischhauer and Benjamin Pinkus, *The Soviet Germans Past and Present*, London: Hurst, for Marjorie Mayrock Centre for Soviet and East European Research, Hebrew University, Jerusalem, 1986. Like the Oschlies' report it has been revised from conference papers; it uses both existing material and material not previously analysed. However, with regard to the situation of the ethnic Germans living in the Soviet Union, in general it adds little but detail to the reports by Oschlies and Lorenz.

10 Figures from Oschlies, *Sowjetunion 1982/83*, p. 105.

11 Lorenz, 'Wir sind stolz', p. 190.

12 Oschlies, *Sowjetunion 1982/83*, p. 106.

13 Ibid., p. 104.

14 *Neues Leben*, 7 April 1982, cited in Oschlies, *Sowjetunion 1982/83*, p. 106.

15 Th. Kussmann and B. Schäfer, *Berichte des BIOst*, vol. 46, 1982, cited in Oschlies, *Sowjetunion 1982/83*, p. 109.

16 Der Bundesminister des Innern, *Betrifft: Eingliederung der Vertriebenen, Flüchtlinge und Kriegsgeschädigten in der Bundesrepublik Deutschland*, p. 104.

17 Renata Fritsch-Bournazel, *Die Sowjetunion und die deutsche Teilung: Die sowjetische Deutschlandpolitik 1945–1979*, Opladen, Westdeutscher Verlag, 1979, p. 159.

18 Lorenz, 'Wir sind stolz', p. 188.

19 Written personal communication. The Red Cross figures seem to show that the number of requests to leave did not diminish with the granting of requests, which would be the case if there was a fixed 'pool' of potential emigrants.

20 Renata Fritsch-Bournazel, 'La RFA et l'Europe de l'Est: voie royale ou impasse?', *Politique Internationale*, 15, Spring 1982, p. 85.

21 See F. Oldenburg on USSR–FRG relations during that period: 'Das Verhältnis UdSSR – Bundesrepublik Deutschland', in *Sowjetunion 1976/77*, Bundesinstitut für ostwissenschaftliche und internationale Studien, pp. 232–40.

22 Ibid., p. 239.

23 Presse- und Informationsamt der Bundesregierung, *Bulletin*, no. 44, 9 May 1978, p. 435.

24 Ibid., pp. 429–30, Figure 2 regarding CSCE on p. 429, makes no specific mention of family reunification.

25 Ibid., p. 402.
26 Foreign Office report in *Jahresbericht der Bundesregierung 1979*, Presse- und Informationsamt der Bundesregierung, p. 43.
27 Foreign Office report in *Jahresbericht der Bundesregierung 1981*, Presse- und Informationsamt der Bundesregierung, p. 58.
28 Ibid., p. 40.
29 Oldenburg, p. 226.
30 Oschlies, *Sowjetunion 1982/83*, p. 103.
31 If one is looking for an explanation of this in broad sociological terms, one need not look beyond the frustration–aggression hypothesis: the greatest frustration of would-be emigrants coincided with the period when the gap between applications and permits was greatest (see Table 2 and Table 3).
32 See Oschlies, *Sowjetunion 1982/83*, pp. 110–11.
33 Internationale Gesellschaft für Menschenrechte, *Deutsche in der Sowjetunion. Dokumentation*, Frankfurt-on-Main 1982, cited in Oschlies, *Sowjetunion 1982/83*, pp. 110–11.
34 Ibid.; and *Frankfurter Allgemeine Zeitung*, 26 May 1979, cited in Oschlies, *Sowjetunion 1982/83*, pp. 110–11.
35 E. Dutengefner, in *Komsomolskaya pravda*, 14 July 1982; W. Kreutzahler, in *Kulturpolitische Korrespondenz*, 469, 1982, pp. 3–5, cited in Oschlies, *Sowjetunion 1982/83*, p. 111.
36 Oschlies, *Sowjetunion 1982/83*, p. 111.
37 Figures from ibid.
38 Ibid., p. 111.
39 Ibid., p. 105.
40 Ibid.
41 Ibid., p. 110.
42 Lorenz, 'Wir sind stolz', p. 188.
43 Author's interview with a government official.

3 Berlin

1 For the text of the Quadripartite Agreement on Berlin and the agreements between the competent German authorities, see *Documentation Relating to the Federal Government's Policy of Détente*, Presse- und Informationsamt der Bundesregierung, Bonn 1978, pp. 87–152.
2 The opposition criticised from the start the lack of unequivocalness in some of the formulations. 'Die Bundesrepublik Deutschland 1966–1974', *Informationen zur Politischen Bildung*, 191, 1981, p. 24.
3 Helmut Schmidt and Willy Brandt, *Deutschland 1976 – Zwei Sozialdemokraten im Gespräch*, Hamburg, rororo aktuell, 1976, p. 136.
4 For the 'back-channel' negotiations see H. Kissinger, *White House Years*, Boston and Toronto, 1979, pp. 534, 807ff., 825ff.; and the interview of Kenneth Rush on German television on 26 March 1980 (SFB), cited in Helga Haftendorn, *Sicherheit und Entspannung: Zur Aussenpolitik der Bundesrepublik Deutschland 1955–1982*, Baden-Baden, Nomos Verlagsgesellschaft, 1983, p. 353, note 174.

5 Egon Bahr, 'Von Moskau über Helsinki nach Wien', *Deutschland Archiv*, 12, 1975, p. 1336.
6 Ibid., p. 1337.
7 *Informationen zur Politischen Bildung*, p. 23.
8 Bahr, 'Von Moskau über Helsinki', pp. 1336–7.
9 Martin J. Hillenbrand, 'The future of Berlin', in *The Future of Berlin*, ed. Martin J. Hillenbrand, Montclair, NJ. Allenheld, Osmun, 1980, p. 291.
10 Bahr, 'Von Moskau über Helsinki', p. 1337.
11 The East Germans also retreated from an agreement to clarify the meaning of the English 'not to be a constituent part of the FRG' as applied to the Western sectors. The East German version 'kein Bestandteil' does not convey the full implication of the English 'constituent part' which indicates that it is only in the sense of its being an actual state of the Federal Republic that West Berlin may not be regarded as part of West Germany. The Russian 'sostavnaya chast' is like the East German 'Bestandteil' and is not so very different from the Soviets' originally preferred world 'chast' (part). The clause which limits the maintenance and development of the ties ('taking into account that these sectors continue not to be a constituent part of the FRG and not to be governed by it') is more strongly accentuated in the Soviet than in the Western formula. Furthermore, the English text of the Quadripartite Agreement states that the Western Sectors 'continue' not to be a constituent part of the FRG, i.e. that no new state of affairs has been created, that the hitherto existing state of affairs is merely being recorded. The Russian text (and both German texts, in fact) do not show this continuity quite so clearly. See Gerhard Wettig. 'Die Bindungen West-Berlins als Verhandlungs- und Vertragsgegenstand der vier Mächte 1970/71', *Deutschland Archiv*, 3, 1979, pp. 278–90; Gerhard Wettig. *Das Vier-Mächte-Abkommen in der Bewährungsprobe: Berlin im Spannungsfeld von Ost und West*, Berlin, Berlin Verlag, 1981.
12 Foreign Office report in *Jahresbericht der Bundesregierung 1979*, Presse- und Informationsamt der Bundesregierung, p. 28.
13 Schmidt and Brandt, *Deutschland 1976*, pp. 136–7.
14 *Europa-Archiv*, 12, 1973, D.334–8.
15 See Klaus Mehnert, 'Mit Bundeskanzler Schmidt in der UdSSR', *Osteuropa*, January 1975, p. 7.
16 In 1972–3 the Soviet Union and the GDR objected to the extension of an agreement over the rescue and repatriation of astronauts and the Vienna convention on diplomatic relations to West Berlin. On 21 December 1972 the Soviet Union questioned the legality of the inclusion of West Berlin in the Basic Treaty and in West Germany's entry into the United Nations because reference was made in the Bundestag's act of consent to the 'Land Berlin' instead of the Western Sectors of Berlin. On 16 October 1972 the GDR expressed its displeasure through its Foreign Minister that the Bundestag's act of consent to the German–German traffic agreement contained the term 'Land Berlin', and on 28 February 1973 the GDR objected to the use of this term in the extension of the International Telecommunication Agreement to West Berlin. On 11 April 1973 the Soviet Union maintained

that the term must be generally eliminated from the Federal Republic's political vocabulary. See *Das Vierseitige Abkommen über West Berlin und seine Realisierung: Dokumente 1971–1977*, (The Quadripartite Agreement on West Berlin and its realisation) Ministerium für Auswärtige Angelegenheiten der DDR und Ministerium für Auswärtige Angelegenheiten der UdSSR, Berlin, Staatsverlag der Deutschen Demokratischen Republik 1977, pp. 117, 121, 134, 131ff., 128, 122ff., 158ff., 132ff. Cited in Gerhard Wettig, 'Das Problem der Bindungen West-Berlins bei der Anwendung des Viermächteabkommens', *Deutschland Archiv*, 9, 1979, p. 921, note 4. The publication *Das Vierseitige Abkommen* is a collection of documents edited jointly by the foreign ministries of the USSR and the GDR. It contains protests, responses to protests, and communications and statements made during the 1971–7 period. A very few Allied communications are included. It is herein subsequently referred to as *Das Vierseitige*. The author is indebted to Gerhard Wettig for his above-mentioned article 'Das Problem der Bindungen', pp. 920–37 for some of the material for pp. 44–54, this volume

17 Wettig, 'Das Problem der Bindungen', p. 925.

18 Martin J. Hillenbrand, 'The legal background of the Berlin situation', in *The Future of Berlin*, ed. Martin J. Hillenbrand, p. 79, note 62.

19 Wettig, 'Das Problem der Bindungen', p. 925.

20 Ibid., p. 925, and *Das Vierseitige*, pp. 164ff., 177ff., 196–8, cited in ibid. p. 925, note 18.

21 *Das Vierseitige*, pp. 168–71, 180, 184, 186, cited in Wettig, 'Das Problem der Bindungen', p. 926, note 19.

22 Ibid., pp. 129ff. Cited in Wettig, 'Das Problem der Bindungen', p. 922, note 6.

23 Wettig, 'Das Problem der Bindungen', p. 922.

24 Ibid., p. 924; Ernst Levy, 'Der politische Kleinkrieg gegen West-Berlin hat nie aufgehört', *Frankfurter Allgemeine Zeitung*, 3 June 1976, p. 6.

25 Wettig, 'Das Problem der Bindungen', p. 924; Ernst Levy, 'Der politische Kleinkrieg', p. 6.

26 Wettig, 'Das Problem der Bindungen', p. 923.

27 For the text to the declaration by the Federal Constitutional Court, see *Texte zur Deutschlandpolitik*, Bundesministerium für innerdeutsche Beziehungen, Reihe II, Bd. 1, Bonn: October 1975, pp. 79–110, cited in Wettig, 'Das Problem der Bindungen', p. 923, note 7.

28 See Otmar Hennig, *Die Bundespräsenz in West Berlin*, Cologne 1976, pp. 39ff. and reprint of a statement by the GDR government from 4 October 1973 in *Das Vierseitige*, pp. 15ff., cited in Wettig, 'Das Problem der Bindungen', p. 923, note 8.

29 *Das Vierseitige*, pp. 153, 157ff., 160ff., cited in Wettig, 'Das Problem der Bindungen', p. 923, note 9.

30 *Das Vierseitige*, pp. 154ff., cited in Wettig, 'Das Problem der Bindungen', p. 923, note 10.

31 *Das Vierseitige*, pp. 153, 157ff., and 160ff., cited in Wettig, 'Das Problem der Bindungen', p. 927, note 22.

32 Part IIB and Annex II1 of the Quadripartite Agreement on Berlin.

33 *Der Spiegel*, 15, 7 April 1975, p. 22. See also Helmut Schmidt, *Menschen und Mächte*, Berlin, Siedler Verlag, 1987, pp. 55–6.
34 'Berlin back again', *The Times*, 6 August 1974, p. 13.
35 Wettig, 'Das Problem der Bindungen', p. 928.
36 'Point made', *The Economist*, 10 August 1974, p. 60.
37 Schmidt, *Menschen*, pp. 55–72.
38 Cited in ibid., p. 69.
39 Schmidt, *Menschen*, p. 72.
40 Ibid., pp. 81–2.
41 F. Oldenburg, 'Das Verhältnis UdSSR – Bundesrepublik Deutschland', *Sowjetunion 1976/77*, Bundesinstitut für ostwissenschaftliche und internationale Studien, Munich, 1979, Carl Hanser Verlag, p. 237. See also Ernst Levy, 'Der politische Kleinkrieg gegen West-Berlin hat nie aufgehört', *Frankfurter Allgemeine Zeitung*, 3 June 1976, p. 6.
42 Wettig, 'Das Problem der Bindungen', p. 929.
43 *Das Vierseitige*, pp. 166–8, cited in Wettig, 'Das Problem der Bindungen', p. 929, note 29.
44 Dan van der Vat, 'The cold War revisited', *The Times*, 27 May 1975, p. 6.
45 *Pravda*, 30 January 1977, cited in Oldenburg, *Sowjetunion 1976/77*, p. 237.
46 *Frankfurter Allgemeine Zeitung*, 15 February 1977, cited in Oldenburg, *Sowjetunion 1976/77*, p. 237.
47 Charles Hargrove, 'West tells Russians four power status of Berlin must stand', *The Times*, 29 May 1975, p. 5.
48 *Das Vierseitige*, p. 251, cited in Wettig, 'Das Problem der Bindungen', p. 931, note 36.
49 Gretel Spitzer, 'Tug-of-war over West Berlin's possibilities', *The Times*, 16 June 1976, p. III.
50 'Russians reject West's Berlin protest', *The Times*, 28 August 1976, p. 3.
51 Wettig, *Das Vier-Mächte-Abkommen*, p. 208.
52 Oldenburg, *Sowjetunion 1976/77*, p. 237.
53 Ibid.
54 Ibid.
55 Ibid.
56 Deutsches Fernsehen (1. Progr.), Sendereihe 'Kontraste', 26 June 1978, cited in Wettig, *Das Vier-Mächte-Abkommen*, p. 210 and note 55.
57 Paul Noack and Reiner Eger, 'Der Fortgang der deutschen Ostpolitik: innerdeutsche Beziehungen und die Berlin-Frage', *Die Internationale Politik 1977/78*, eds. Wolfgang Wagner, Marion Gräfin Dönhoff, Gerhard Fels, Karl Kaiser, Paul Noack, Vienna, R. Oldenburg Verlag, 1982, p. 158, note 36.
58 See Roger Berthoud, 'West to resist change in status of East Berlin', *The Times*, 10 May 1977, p. 6; Dan van der Vat, 'Treaties stalled over status of West Berlin', *The Times*, 22 June 1977, p. ix; Noack and Eger, 'Der Fortgang der deutschen Ostpolitik', pp. 157–8.
59 'Der politische Kleinkrieg gegen West-Berlin geht ohne Pause weiter', *Frankfurter Allgemeine Zeitung*, 8 October 1977, p. 9.
60 Bahr, 'Von Moskau über Helsinki', p. 1337.
61 Ibid.

62 Presse- und Informationsamt der Bundesregierung, *Bulletin*, no. 24, 10 March 1978, p. 221.

63 Interviews with, and personal communications from, government officials.

64 The so-called 'Petersberger Formula' of the 'strict observance and full implementation of the Quadripartite Agreement of 3 September 1971' originated from the Brezhnev visit to Bonn in May 1973 (see also p. 43 of this study).

65 Presse- und Informationsamt der Bundesregierung, *Bulletin*, no. 44, 9 May 1978, p. 430.

66 *Plenarprotokoll 8/90*, Deutscher Bundestag, Bonn, Thursday, 11 May 1978, 7064C–7065A.

67 Foreign Office report for 1978, Auswärtiges Amt, Referat Öffentlichkeitsarbeit, p. 6.

68 Presse- und Informationsamt der Bundesregierung, *Bulletin*, no. 64, 18 May 1979, p. 594.

69 *Plenarprotokoll 8/90*, Deutscher Bundestag, Bonn, Thursday, 11 May 1978, 7065A.

70 See Wettig, 'Das Problem der Bindungen', p. 933.

71 See Hillenbrand, 'The legal background of the Berlin situation', p. 75; '"Serious breach" of Berlin accord', *The Financial Times*, 29 June 1979.

72 In the run up to the European elections this warning was given by the German language service of Radio Moscow and was reprinted in all East Berlin newspapers: 'The Soviet Union again draws the attention of the Western Powers to the illegal actions connected with the inclusion of the city in Western European integration. Neither in Washington, London, Paris or Bonn does one seem to be listening to these warnings. As a participant in the Four Power Agreement, the Soviet Union will not be indifferent to these violations. She will find it necessary to take measures to protect her interests and to insure normal functioning of the Agreement', cited in Hillenbrand, 'The legal background of the Berlin situation', p. 75. See also 'Moskau droht mit Konsequenzen: "Keine Berliner Abgeordneten in das Europa-Parlament"', *Frankfurter Allgemeine Zeitung*, 7 June 1979.

73 'Wenn es regnet', *Der Spiegel*, 20, 15 May 1978, p. 28.

74 Personal communication from a government official.

75 The Berlin press files at the IISS include amongst their coverage cuttings from all the main British, German, French, and American sources and Soviet English-language publications.

76 Noack and Eger, 'Der Fortgang der deutschen Ostpolitik', pp. 159, 160.

77 It may be, however, that in actual practice, long before 1978 even, practices were found to circumvent the treaty (see Christian Meier and Fred Oldenburg, 'Das Deutsch-sowjetische Verhältnis nach dem zweiten Breschnew-Besuch', *Berichte des Bundesinstituts für ostwissenschaftliche und internationale Studien*, 40, 1978, p. 30). In the field of culture an interesting way round this problem certainly developed in more recent years: according to an article in *Der Spiegel* ('Neuer Flügel' 13, 25 Mar. 1985, pp. 206–8) the 'Deutsche Bank' was using its good business relations with the Soviet Union to set up cultural exchanges. In 1983, for example, an exhibition of contemporary

German painting and graphic arts was shown in Moscow and Leningrad. It had been negotiated by the Deutsche Bank at the edge of the natural gas pipeline transaction. It is interesting to note that it was often possible for exceptions to be made when private institutions of the Federal Republic negotiated with Soviet officials: a third of the exhibits in the exhibition sponsored by the Deutsche Bank were from West Berlin.

4 The Federal Republic of Germany's relations with the German Democratic Republic

1 Josef Joffe, 'All quiet on the Eastern Front', *Foreign Policy*, no. 37, Winter 1979–80, p. 168.
2 Gerhard Wettig, 'Die Bundesrepublik Deutschland als Faktor der sowjetischen Westpolitik', *Beiträge zur Konfliktforschung*, 12, 1982, p. 50.
3 Ibid.
4 Klaus Bölling, *Die Fernen Nachbarn: Erfahrungen in der DDR*, Hamburg, Stern-Buch im Verlag Grüner und Jahr, 1983, pp. 134–5.
5 Ibid., pp. 149–50.
6 'Das Verhältnis UdSSR–DDR', *Sowjetunion 1975/76*, Bundesinstitut für ostwissenschaftliche und internationale Studien, Munich, Carl Hanser Verlag, 1976, p. 212.
7 Joachim Nawrocki, *Relations between the Two States in Germany: Trends, Prospects and Limitations*, Bonn, Verlag Bonn Aktuell, 1985, p. 57.
8 Ibid.
9 Ibid.
10 Patricia Clough, 'Two Germanies hoping for closer links at summit', *The Times*, 11 December 1981, p. 6.
11 Klaus Mehnert, 'Mit Bundeskanzler Schmidt in der UdSSR', *Osteuropa*, no. 1, January 1975, p. 10.
12 Ibid.
13 Ibid., p. 11.
14 Klaus Mehnert, 'Mit dem Bundespräsidenten in der UdSSR', *Osteuropa*, no. 1, January 1976, p. 4.
15 'Bundesrepublik Deutschland', *Sowjetunion 1975/76*, p. 245.
16 Mehnert, 'Mit dem Bundespräsidenten in der UdSSR', p. 4.
17 Ibid.
18 Angela Stent, *From Embargo to Ostpolitik: The Political Economy of West German–Soviet Relations, 1955–1980*, Cambridge University Press, 1981, p. 229.
19 Mehnert, 'Mit dem Bundespräsidenten in der UdSSR', p. 4–5. See also Stent, *From Embargo to Ostpolitik*, pp. 229–30.
20 Presse- und Informationsamt der Bundesregierung, *Bulletin*, no. 79, 13 July 1978, p. 750.
21 Presse- und Informationsamt der Bundesregierung, *Bulletin*, no. 36, 10 April 1981, p. 313.
22 Presse- und Informationsamt der Bundesregierung, *Jahresbericht der Bundesregierung 1977*, p. 27.

23 Presse- und Informationsamt der Bundesregierung, *Documentation Relating to the Federal Government's Policy of Détente*, Bonn, 1978, p. 20.

24 Ibid., p. 182.

25 See, for example, Foreign Office report in *Jahresbericht der Bundesregierung 1979*, Presse- und Informationsamt der Bundesregierung, Bonn, p. 29, and *Jahresbericht der Bundesregierung 1980*, p. 29 and Regierungserklärung by Chancellor Schmidt on 17 June 1977 in Presse- und Informationsamt der Bundesregierung, *Bulletin*, no. 64, 21 June 1977.

26 Presse- und Informationsamt der Bundesregierung, *Ein Land lebt nicht für sich allein*, Bonn, 1980, p. 104.

27 Nawrocki, *Relations between the Two States*, p. 122.

28 Ibid., p. 125.

29 Ibid., p. 6.

30 Dr Wilhelm Bruns, Departmental Head at the Friedrich-Ebert-Stiftung Research Institute, lecturer at the University of Bonn.

31 Wilhelm Bruns, *Deutsch-Deutsche Beziehungen: Prämissen, Probleme, Perspektiven*, 4th edn, Opladen, Leske und Budrich, 1984, p. 136.

32 'Die Bundesrepublik Deutschland 1974–1983', *Informationen zur Politischen Bildung*, no. 202, 1984, p. 35.

33 Bölling, *Die Fernen Nachbarn*, p. 178.

34 Ibid., p. 179.

35 Frank R. Pfetsch, *Die Aussenpolitik der BRD 1949–1980*, Munich, Wilhelm Fink Verlag, 1981, p. 180.

36 William G. Hyland, 'The Soviet Union and Germany', in *West German Foreign Policy 1949–1979*, ed. Wolfram Hanrieder, Boulder, CO, Westview Press, 1980, p. 123.

37 Bölling, *Die Fernen Nachbarn*, p. 179.

38 Ibid.

39 Ibid.

40 Ibid., p. 110.

41 Hans Georg Lehmann, *Öffnung nach Osten: Die Ostreisen Helmut Schmidts und die Entstehung der Ost- und Entspannungspolitik*, Bonn, Verlag Neue Gesellschaft, 1984, p. 197.

42 Bölling, *Die Fernen Nachbarn*, p. 179.

43 Ibid., p. 180.

44 Ibid.

45 Ibid., p. 178.

46 Ibid., p. 121.

47 Helmut Schmidt and Willy Brandt, *Deutschland 1976–Zwei Sozialdemokraten im Gespräch*, Hamburg, rororo aktuell, 1976, pp. 147–8.

48 Dieter Mahncke, 'Abschluss der Neuordnung der Beziehungen zwischen der Bundesrepublik Deutschland und Osteuropa', in *Die Internationale Politik 1973/74*, eds. Wolfgang Wagner, Marion Gräfin Dönhoff, Wolfgang Hager, Karl Kaiser, Norbert Kloten, Paul Noack, p. 211.

49 Wolfgang Jäger and Werner Link, *Republik im Wandel 1974–1982: Die Ära Schmidt*, Stuttgart, Deutsche Verlags-Anstalt, 1987, pp. 357–8.

50 Bölling, *Die Fernen Nachbarn*, p. 78.

51 Marion Dönhoff, *Foe into Friend: The Makers of the New Germany from Konrad Adenauer to Helmut Schmidt*, Weidenfeld and Nicholson, 1982, p. 167.

52 Ibid.

53 *Der Spiegel*, no. 18, 1978, p. 25.

54 Christian Meier and Fred Oldenburg, 'Das Deutsch-sowjetische Verhältnis nach dem zweiten Breschnew-Besuch', *Berichte des Bundesinstituts für ostwissenschaftliche und internationale Studien*, 40, 1978, p. 26. Also Renata Fritsch-Bournazel, *Die Sowjetunion und die deutsche Teilung: Die sowjetische Deutschlandpolitik 1945–1979*, Opladen, Westdeutscher Verlag, 1979, p. 159.

55 Bulletin des Presse- und Informationsamt der Bundesregierung, no. 44, 9 May 1978, cited in Meier and Oldenburg, 'Das Deutsch-sowjetische Verhältnis', p. 26.

56 Anton Böhm, 'Aus dem Osten nichts Neues. Die deutsch-sowjetischen Beziehungen nach Breschnews Besuch', *Die Politische Meinung*, 178, May/June 1978, p. 50.

57 Meier and Oldenburg, 'Das deutsch–sowjetische Verhältnis', p. 27.

58 Helmut Schmidt, *Menschen und Mächte*, Berlin, Siedler Verlag, 1987, p. 96.

59 Written personal communication from a government official.

60 Meier and Oldenburg, 'Das deutsch–sowjetische Verhältnis', p. 51.

61 Ibid., p. 53.

62 Ibid., p. 51.

63 Ibid., p. 54.

64 Fred Oldenburg and Christian Meier, 'Die deutsch–sowjetischen Beziehungen im Zeichen des Breschnew-Besuchs', *Osteuropa*, no. 10, October 1978, p. 865.

65 F. Pleitgen interview with G. Gaus in ARD-Tagesschau, 12 June 1978, 17.50 pm and 20.00 pm and A. Beth interview with G. Gaus in Deutschlandfunk 12 June 1978, cited in Meier and Oldenburg, 'Das deutsch–sowjetische Verhältnis', p. 55.

66 Peter J. Winters, 'Ein Schritt auf dem Wege der Normalisierung', *Europa-Archiv*, 9, 1979, pp. 270–1.

67 Report by the Federal Ministry for Intra-German Relations in *Jahresbericht der Bundesregierung 1979*, Presse- und Informationsamt der Bundesregierung, p. 497.

68 Statement by the then government press spokesman, State Secretary Bölling, cited in Jäger and Link, *Republik im Wandel*, p. 369.

69 Jäger and Link, *Republik im Wandel*, p. 369.

70 Ibid.

71 Ibid., pp. 371–2.

72 Johannes Kuppe, 'Deutsch–deutsche Beziehungen im Schatten der Weltpolitik', *Deutschland Archiv*, 2, 1980, p. 115.

73 For the text of the Basic Treaty, see Presse- und Informationsamt der Bundesregierung, *Documentation Relating to the Federal Government's Policy of Détente*, pp. 178–81.

74 Ilse Spittman, 'Der Deutsche Aspekt in Breschnew's Offerte', *Deutschland Archiv*, 11, 1979, p. 1122.

75 Report by the Federal Ministry for Intra-German Relations, *Jahresbericht der*

Bundesregieriung 1980, Presse- und Informationsamt der Bundesregierung, pp. 428–9.

76 Honecker in an interview with Robert Maxwell, *Neues Deutschland*, 5/6 July 1980, p. 1, cited in Dettmar Cramer, 'Der Kanzler im Kreml: Moskau 1970 und Moskau 1980', *Deutschland Archiv*, 8, 1980, p. 787.

77 'Die Bundesrepublik Deutschland 1974–1983', *Informationen zur Politischen Bildung*, no. 202, 1984, p. 25.

78 Jäger and Link, *Republik im Wandel*, p. 372; Johannes Kupper, 'Deutsch–deutsche Beziehungen im Schatten der Weltpolitik', *Deutschland Archiv*, 2, 1980, p. 116.

79 An analysis of official statements from the GDR in the two months preceding the cancellation shows that the party leadership clearly wanted to keep to the meeting. The cancellation thus appears to have been due to Soviet intervention. See Johannes Kuppe, 'Deutsch–deutsche Beziehungen im Schatten der Weltpolitik', *Deutschland Archiv*, 2, 1980, p. 116. The fact that the cancellation followed immediately after Honecker's return from Moscow (see p. 89–90) also speaks for this.

80 Philip Windsor, 'Germany and the Western Alliance: lessons from the 1980 crisis', *Adelphi Papers*, 170, p. 14.

81 See Ilse Spittman, 'Die Rolle der DDR in Moskaus Strategie', *Deutschland Archiv*, 6, 1980, pp. 561–3.

82 Jäger and Link, *Republik im Wandel*, p. 372.

83 Agreements on the exemption of lorries and coaches from motor vehicle tax, on the settlement of the road toll for passenger cars and on co-operation in veterinary matters.

84 Jäger and Link, *Republik im Wandel*, pp. 372–3.

85 Bölling, *Die Fernen Nachbarn*, p. 179.

86 Ibid., p. 79.

87 Ibid., p. 78.

88 Ibid., p. 179.

89 Ibid., p. 78.

90 Erklärung der Bundesregierung zur Konferenz in Venedig und zu den Gesprächen in Moskau in der 229. Sitzung des Deutschen Bundestages am 3. Juli, 1980, *Deutschland Archiv*, Dokumentation, 1980, vol. II, p. 888.

91 See Dettmar Cramer's article, 'Der Kanzler im Kreml: Moskau 1970 und Moskau 1980', *Deutschland Archiv*, 8, 1980, pp. 785–7.

92 Oldenburg, *Sowjetunion 1980/81*, p. 225.

93 Nawrocki, *Relations between the Two States*, p. 120.

94 Ibid., p. 119.

95 Erklärung der Regierung der Deutschen Demokratischen Republik zur Durchführung des Reise- und Besuchsverkehrs von Personen mit ständigem Wohnsitz in Berlin (West). For text see Presse- und Informationsamt der Bundesregierung, *Verträge, Abkommen und Vereinbarungen zwischen der Bundesrepublik Deutschland und der Demokratischen Republik*, p. 257.

96 Arrangement between the Senate and the Government of the German Democratic Republic concerning the Facilitation and Improvement of Travel and Visitor Traffic dated 20 December 1971. For text see Press and

Information Office of the Government of the Federal Republic of Germany, *Documentation Relating to the Federal Government's Policy of Détente*, p. 132.

97 Soviet sources cited (but not named) in Nawrocki, *Relations between the Two States*, p. 59.

98 Report by the Federal Ministry for Intra-German Relations in *Jahresbericht der Bundesregierung 1980*, p. 429.

99 Antwort der Bundesregierung auf die Grosse Anfrage der CDU/CSU zur Deutschlandpolitik, *Bundestagsdrucksache*, 9/ 678, 20 July 1981.

100 Bölling, *Die Fernen Nachbarn*, p. 80.

101 Presse- und Informationsamt der Bundesregierung, *Bulletin*, no. 124, 25 November 1980, p. 1052.

102 Hans-Dietrich Genscher, Bundesvorsitzender der FDP, 'Entspannungspolitik in Krisenzeiten: Von der gemeinsamen Verantwortung der beiden deutschen Staaten', Pressedienst der Freien Demokratischen Partei, Ausgabe 335, 26 October 1980.

103 See, for example, Jäger and Link, *Republik im Wandel*, p. 375.

104 Peter J. Winters, 'Kurswechsel Ost-Berlins gegenüber Bonn. Zum Stand der innerdeutschen Beziehungen', *Europa-Archiv*, 1, 1981, p. 37.

105 Cited in Winters, 'Kurswechsel Ost-Berlins gegenüber Bonn, p. 38.

106 Neues Deutschland 12 April 1981. Cited in Fred Oldenburg and Christian Meier, 'Sowjetische Deutschland-Politik zu Beginn der achtziger Jahre', *Osteuropa*, September/October, 1981, p. 878.

107 Bölling, *Die Fernen Nachbarn*, p. 141.

108 Gerhard Wettig, 'The Soviet view', in *Germany between East and West*, ed. Edwina Moreton, Cambridge University Press, 1987, pp. 41–2.

109 Bruns, *Deutsch-Deutsche Beziehungen*, p. 126.

110 Presse- und Informationsamt der Bundesregierung, *Bulletin*, no. 123, 21 December 1981, p. 1054.

111 Report by the Federal Ministry for Intra-German Relations, in *Jahresbericht der Bundesregierung 1980*, p. 429.

112 Oldenburg, *Sowjetunion 1982/83*, p. 252.

113 Ibid., p. 253.

114 Presse- und Informationsamt der Bundesregierung, *Bulletin*, no. 112, 26 November 1981, p. 962.

115 Ibid.

116 Bölling, *Die Fernen Nachbarn*, p. 116.

117 Report by the Federal Ministry for Intra-German Relations in *Jahresbericht der Bundesregierung 1981*, Presse- und Informationsamt der Bundesregierung, p. 396.

118 Jonathan Carr, *Helmut Schmidt: Helmsman of Germany*, Weidenfeld and Nicolson, 1985, p. 171.

119 'Die Bundesrepublik Deutschland 1974–1983', *Informationen zur Politischen Bildung*, no. 202, 1984, p. 34.

120 Ibid.

121 Bölling, *Die Fernen Nachbarn*, p. 115.

122 Patricia Clough, 'Two Germanies hoping for closer links at Summit', *The Times*, 11 December 1981, p. 6.
123 Report by the Federal Ministry for Intra-German Relations, *Jahresbericht der Bundesregierung 1981*, pp. 396–7.
124 Carr, *Helmut Schmidt*, p. 172.
125 Bölling, *Die Fernen Nachbarn*, p. 54.
126 Carr, *Helmut Schmidt*, p. 173.
127 Bölling, *Die Fernen Nachbarn*, p. 170.
128 Ibid., pp. 155–6.
129 Report by the Federal Ministry for Intra-German Relations, *Jahresbericht der Bundesregierung 1981*, p. 397.
130 Presse- und Informationsamt der Bundesregierung, *Bulletin*, no. 123, 21 December 1981, p. 1054.
131 Foreign Office report, *Jahresbericht der Bundesregierung 1981*, p. 28.
132 Carr, *Helmut Schmidt*, pp. 173–4.
133 Bölling, *Die Fernen Nachbarn*, p. 136.
134 Ibid., p. 138.
135 Ibid., pp. 172–3.
136 Ibid., p. 173.
137 *Daily Express*, 27 March 1982, p. 8.
138 Presse- und Informationsamt der Bundesregierung, *Bulletin*, no. 83, 11 September 1982, p. 741.
139 Ibid., p. 745.
140 Wettig, 'The Soviet view', p. 42.
141 Ilse Spittman, 'Frostschutz gefragt', *Deutschland Archiv*, 12, 1980, p. 1233.
142 See Gaus, *Wo Deutschland liegt: Eine Ortsbestimmung*, pp. 194–5.

5 INF, Afghanistan and the post-Afghanistan period

1 Hans Georg Lehmann, *Öffnung nach Osten: Die Ostreisen Helmut Schmidts und die Entstehung der Ost- und Entspannungspolitik*, Bonn, Verlag Neue Gesellschaft, 1984, p. 192.
2 Presse-und Informationsamt der Bundesregierung, *Bulletin*, no. 8, 18 January 1980. Erklärung der Bundesregierung zur Internationalen Lage, 17 January 1980.
3 See, for example, 'Herr Schmidt in the middle', *The Times*, 23 November 1981, where Schmidt is described as having the task of acting as an interpreter between East and West.
4 In her treatment of the question 'Chancellor Schmidt – mediator/ interpreter between East and West?' the author felt that accounts of her interviews should be given in full as this is a generally held view which has never actually been properly investigated. The interviews were all with people who had expert knowledge not available to the author, i.e. they had access to classified documents, were present at top-level talks or were long-term observers. As such they represent interesting and informed comments. The interviews were, also, a way of probing Schmidt's mind

without actually doing just that. Schmidt himself was not available to be probed in this way and even had he been open to being interviewed, he would not necessarily have been candid. By interviewing those around him the author was able to build up a fairly convincing pen portrait of how he saw himself and what he was actually up to. Having traced actual first-hand references by Schmidt, the author was then able to make a comparison with Schmidt's own statements and draw her own conclusions. All interviews were conducted on a confidential basis, otherwise the author would have been told very little. As a result, the reporting of the contents of these interviews has inevitably a clumsy appearance but one which the author nevertheless considers to be a price worth paying for the material obtained.

5 Fred Oldenburg, 'Das Verhältnis UdSSR – Bundesrepublik Deutschland', *Sowjetunion 1982/83*, Bundesinstitut für ostwissenschaftliche und internationale Studien, Munich, Carl Hanser Verlag, 1983, p. 251.

6 Karl Kaiser, 'The New Ostpolitik', in *West German Foreign Policy: 1949–1979*, ed. Wolfram F. Hanrieder, Boulder, CO, Westview Press, 1980, pp. 151–2.

7 Presse und Informationsamt der Bundesregierung, *Bulletin*, no. 107, 19 November 1981.

8 BPA-Nachrichtenabt., Ref. II R 3, Rundf.-Ausw. Deutschland, DFS/26 November 1981 MS-GE/Sch, Die Fernseh-Diskussion, 'Bonn nach dem Breschnew-Besuch'. Discussion with Chancellor Helmut Schmidt and journalists Ernst Dieter Lüg WDR, Dieter Wild, *Der Spiegel*, Herbert Kremp, *Die Welt*, with Leitung von Rudolf Mühlfenzl.

9 *Chambers Twentieth Century Dictionary*, revised 1973 edn, ed. A. M. Macdonald, Chambers, 1974, p. 814.

10 Presse- und Informationsamt der Bundesregierung, *Bulletin*, no. 116, 4 December 1981. Erklärung der Bundesregierung zur Sicherheits- und Friedenspolitik, 3 December 1981.

11 Thomas Risse-Kappen, '"Fahrplan zur Abrüstung?" Zur INF-Politik der Bundesrepublik Deutschland 1970–1983', *Forschungsbericht der Hessischen Stiftung Friedens- und Konfliktforschung*, January 1985, p. 8.

12 Ibid.

13 Ibid., p. 9.

14 Ibid., p. 8.

15 Ibid., p. 9.

16 See also Hans Günter Brauch on this in *Die Raketen kommen! Vom Nato-Doppelbeschluss bis zur Stationierung*, Cologne, Bund-Verlag, 1983, p. 14.

17 Risse-Kappen, 'Fahrplan zur Abrüstung?', p. 9.

18 Presse- und Informationsamt der Bundesregierung, *Aspekte der Friedenspolitik: Argumente zum Doppelbeschluss des Nordatlantischen Bündnisses*, Bonn, June 1981, p. 15.

19 Ibid.

20 Information given to the author during an interview with a party official.

21 Presse- und Informationsamt der Bundesregierung, *Aspekte der Friedenspolitik*, p. 15.

22 Ibid., p. 16.

23 Jonathan Carr, *Helmut Schmidt: Helmsman of Germany*, London, Weidenfeld and Nicolson, 1985, p. 128.

24 Ibid.

25 Helmut Schmidt, *Menschen und Mächte*, Berlin, Siedler Verlag, 1987, p. 102.

26 Stockholm International Peace Research Institute, *World Armaments and disarmament, SIPRI Yearbook 1980*, p. 178.

27 Helga Haftendorn, *Sicherheit und Entspannung: zur Aussenpolitik der Bundesrepublik Deutschland 1955–1982*, Baden-Baden, Nomos Verlagsgesellschaft, 1983, p. 245.

28 Ibid.

29 Carr, *Helmut Schmidt*, p. 132.

30 Simon Lunn, 'Cruise missiles and the prospects for arms control', *ADIU Report*, vol. 3, no. 5, September/October 1981, part II, main edn, 11 February 1982, pp. 7-F–8-F.

31 See Risse-Kappen, 'Fahrplan zur Abrüstung?', pp. 5–7.

32 Helmut Schmidt, The 1977 Alastair Buchan Memorial Lecture, *Survival*, vol. 20, no. 1, January/February 1978, pp. 3–4.

33 Ibid., p. 4.

34 Interview given by Helmut Schmidt in July 1982 to a small circle of selected Californian journalists, cited in Brauch, *Die Raketen kommen!*, p. 14.

35 Risse-Kappen, 'Fahrplan zur Abrüstung?', p. 18–19.

36 H. Schmidt, *Verteidigung oder Vergeltung*, Stuttgart, Seewald, 1961, p. 159.

37 Thomas Risse-Kappen, 'Fahrplan zur Abrüstung?', pp. 18–19.

38 Gerhard Wettig, 'The role of West Germany in Soviet Policies toward Western Europe', *Sonderveröffentlichung des Bundesinstituts für ostwissenschaftliche und internationale Studien*, June 1982, pp. 3–5.

39 V. Shaposhnikov, 'Onekotorykh problemakh sovremennogo antivoennogo dvizheniia', in *Morovaia ekonomika i mezhdunarodnye otnosheniia*, no. 12, 1981, p. 23, cited in Wettig, 'The Role of West Germany', p. 3.

40 Gerhard Wettig, 'The Relations of the USSR with the Federal Republic of Germany', *Berichte des Bundesinstituts für ostwissenschaftliche und internationale Studien*, 12, 1982, p. 25.

41 Haftendorn, *Sicherheit und Entspannung*, p. 240.

42 Brauch, *Die Raketen kommen!*, p. 74.

43 Ibid., p. 76.

44 Oldenburg, *Sowjetunion 1982/83*, p. 254.

45 Auswärtiges Amt, Referat für Öffentlichkeitsarbeit, *Es geht um unsere Sicherheit: Bündnis, Verteidigung, Rüstungskontrolle*, Bonn, November 1982, p. 64.

46 Carr, *Helmut Schmidt*, p. 132.

47 Foreign Office report, *Jahresbericht der Bundesregierung 1979*, Presse- und Informationsamt der Bundesregierung, p. 42.

48 Christian Meier and Fred Oldenburg, 'Der XXVI KpdSU-Kongress und die Beziehungen der Sowjetunion zu beiden deutschen Staaten', *Berichte des Bundesinstituts für ostwissenschaftliche und internationale Studien*, 26, 1981, p. 23.

49 *Frankfurter Allgemeine Zeitung*, 31 May 1980, cited in Roland Smith, 'Soviet policy towards West Germany', *Adelphi Papers*, no. 203, p. 17.

50 Marion Dönhoff, *Foe into Friend: The Makers of the New Germany from Konrad Adenauer to Helmut Schmidt*, Weidenfeld and Nicholson, 1982, p. 184.
51 Haftendorn, *Sicherheit und Entspannung*, p. 250.
52 Dönhoff, *Foe into Friend*, p. 184.
53 Ibid., p. 185.
54 Carr, *Helmut Schmidt*, p. 133.
55 Meier and Oldenburg, 'Der XXVI KPdSU-Kongress', pp. 14–15.
56 Ibid., p. 15.
57 Ibid.
58 Ibid.
59 Ibid.
60 Ibid.
61 Ibid.
62 Ibid.
63 Ibid., p. 16.
64 Oldenburg, *Sowjetunion 1980/81*, p. 224.
65 Information given to the author during an interview with a government official.
66 Ibid., p. 16.
67 Oldenburg, *Sowjetunion 1982/83*, p. 251.
68 Oldenburg, *Sowjetunion 1980/81*, p. 224.
69 Carr, *Helmut Schmidt*, p. 135.
70 Ibid., p. 134.
71 Brauch, *Die Raketen kommen!*, p. 205.
72 Ibid.
73 Carr, *Helmut Schmidt*, p. 134.
74 Ibid.
75 Ibid., p. 135.
76 Dönhoff, *Foe into Friend*, p. 186.
77 Carr, *Helmut Schmidt*, p. 135.
78 Personal communication from a party official whose information was based on later conversations with Schmidt.
79 Carr, *Helmut Schmidt*, p. 136.
80 Dönhoff, *Foe into Friend*, pp. 186–7.
81 Ibid., p. 187.
82 Brauch, *Die Raketen kommen!*, p. 206.
83 Carr, *Helmut Schmidt*, p. 136.
84 Presse- und Informationsamt der Bundesregierung, *Bulletin*, no. 80, 4 July 1980. Erklärung der Bundesregierung zur Konferenz in Venedig und zu den Gesprächen in Moskau, 3 July 1980.
85 See Dettmar Cramer, 'Der Kanzler im Kreml: Moskau 1970 und Moskau 1980', *Deutschland Archiv*, 8, 1980, pp. 785–7 and Klaus Mehnert, 'Bundeskanzler Schmidt in Moskau', *Osteuropa*, 10, October 1980, pp. 1081–92. Klaus Mehnert was in Moscow for Konrad Adenauer's visit in 1955, Willy Brandt's in 1970 and Helmut Schmidt's in 1974 and 1980.
86 Klaus Mehnert, 'Mit Bundeskanzler Schmidt in Moskau', *Osteuropa*, 10, October 1980, pp. 1083–4.

87 Dokumentation, *Deutschland Archiv*, 1980, vol. 2, pp. 881.

88 Oldenburg, *Sowjetunion 1982/83*, p. 252.

89 Carr, *Helmut Schmidt*, p. 136.

90 'The talking starts', *The Times*, 30 November, 1981, p. 11.

91 Risse-Kappen, 'Fahrplan zur Abrüstung?' p. 56.

92 Ibid., pp. 56–7.

93 Haftendorn, *Sicherheit und Entspannung*, p. 262.

94 Risse-Kappen, 'Fahrplan zur Abrüstung?' pp. 61–3.

95 See p. 106 of this chapter and note 8.

96 Patricia Clough, 'Schmidt's future depends on results', *The Times*, 1 December 1981, p. 6.

97 Foreign Office report, *Jahresbericht der Bundesregierung 1981*, Presse- und Informationsamt der Bundesregierung, p. 40.

98 Ibid.

99 Oldenburg, *Sowjetunion 1980/81*, p. 226.

100 Ibid., pp. 226–7.

101 Foreign Office report, *Jahresbericht der Bundesregierung* 1981, Presse- und Informationsamt der Bundesregierung, p. 41.

102 Oldenburg, *Sowjetunion 1982/83*, p. 252.

103 Ibid., pp. 252–3.

104 Ibid., p. 253.

105 Haftendorn, *Sicherheit und Entspannung*, p. 410.

106 Ibid.

107 'To hell with Europe?' *The Economist*, 9 January 1982, p. 35.

108 Carr, *Helmut Schmidt*, p. 176.

109 Ibid., pp. 176–7.

110 Peter Wilsher, 'Pipe of peace?' *The Sunday Times*, 10 January, 1982, p. 16.

111 Deutsches Institut für Wirtschaftsforschung, *Wochenbericht* (Berlin), no. 15, 1980, cited in Angela Stent, *From Embargo to Ostpolitik: The Political Economy of West German-Soviet Relations 1955–1980*, Cambridge University Press, 1981, p. 213.

112 Ibid., p. 213.

113 *Der Spiegel*, no. 26, 1980, cited in Stent, *From Embargo to Ostpolitik*, p. 298.

114 Wilsher, 'Pipe of peace?' p. 16.

115 Statement by Laurence Brady, US assistant secretary for trade, made several weeks before martial law was declared in Poland, cited in Wilsher, 'Pipe of peace?' p. 16.

116 Chancellor Schmidt, July 1982 in the United States, cited in Carr, *Helmut Schmidt*, p. 178.

117 Wilsher, 'Pipe of peace?' p. 16.

118 Ibid.

119 Carr, *Helmut Schmidt*, p. 177.

120 Interview information and personal communication from a party official and source close to Chancellor Schmidt. This source was unable to tell the author whether, in fact, Schmidt in particular, as opposed to the other European allies, was frozen out of information, but did put forward one explanation if indeed this had been the case: it is possible that Genscher

had secretly given the hint to the Americans that there would be changes in
the coalition in 1982 and therefore the possibility cannot be excluded that
the Americans took into consideration that they could be consulting with a
government which might shortly be no longer in place. Certainly Genscher
had supplied such a hint of a split in the coalition to the Hungarians.

121 It should be pointed out that none of the European governments (with the
possible exception of Great Britain) which would have been affected by
the proposal were kept informed (see Schmidt, *Menschen und Mächte*,
p. 333). Indeed it is possible, even probable, that Nitze and Kvitsinski did
not even properly inform their own governments.

122 Schmidt, *Menschen und Mächte*, pp. 181–2.

123 This version given to the author by a party official and source close to the
Chancellor. According to Strobe Talbott, however, the plan came to
nothing because it was killed off on the American side by Caspar Weinber-
ger and Richard Perle and rejected by the Politburo (Strobe Talbott, *Deadly
Gambits: The Reagan Administration and the Stalemate in Nuclear Arms Control*,
Pan Books, 1985, p. 141 and 146). See also Hans Günter Brauch who blames
'the hawks in the Kremlin and the White House' Brauch, *Die Raketen
kommen!*, p. 227).

6 Assessment of the Federal Republic of Germany's relations with the Soviet Union, 1974–1982

1 Henri Ménudier, 'La Politique à l'Est de Bonn: une relance limitée', *Défence
Nationale*, no. 11, November 1977, p. 62.

2 Author's interview with a close party colleague and long-term observer of
Helmut Schmidt.

3 Marion Dönhoff, *Foe into Friend: The Makers of the New Germany from Konrad
Adenauer to Helmut Schmidt*, London, Weidenfeld and Nicolson, 1982,
pp. 167–8.

4 Helmut Schmidt, '"Die nüchterne Leidenschaft zur praktischen Ver-
nunft". Bilanz und Vermächtnis des Abgeordneten und früheren Bun-
deskanzlers Helmut Schmidt/Auszüge aus seiner Rede', *Frankfurter Allgemeine Zeitung*, 11 September 1986, p. 9.

5 Interview with SPD party official. See also the similar point made by Hans
Georg Lehmann, private archivist to Schmidt, in his book *Öffnung nach
Osten: Die Ostreisen Helmut Schmidts und die Entstehung der Ost- und Entspan-
nungspolitik*, Bonn, Verlag Neue Gesellschaft, 1984, pp. 185–6.

6 William E. Griffith, *Die Ostpolitik der Bundesrepublik Deutschland*, Stuttgart,
Klett-Cotta, 1981, p. 300.

7 Klaus Mehnert, 'Mit Bundeskanzler Schmidt in der UdSSR', *Osteuropa*, 1,
January 1975, pp. 9–10.

8 Author's interview with a party official and source close to Schmidt. 'Mild
in der Art, aber ganz hart in der Sache' (Mild in manner but very hard in
substance) was apparently a saying of Schmidt's.

9 Author's interview with a government official.

10 View expressed to the author by a government official.

11 Text of interview released on 2 May 1978. Source of English copy ('Leonid Brezhnev answers questions put by a West German newspaper'): Soviet Studies Research Centre, The Royal Military Academy, Sandhurst.

12 Translation of speech by Chancellor Schmidt in Moscow on 30 June 1980. English version released by West German Foreign Office.

13 Roland Smith, 'Soviet policy towards West Germany', *Adelphi Papers*, no. 203, 1985, p. 14.

14 Ibid.

15 Translation of speech by Chancellor Schmidt in Moscow on 30 June 1980. English version released by West German Foreign Office.

16 Karl D. Bredthauer, 'Entwarnung? Zur Lage nach Schmidts Moskaureise', *Blätter für deutsche und internationale Politik*, 7, 1980, p. 774.

17 Translation of speech by Chancellor Schmidt in Moscow on 30 June 1980. English version released by West German Foreign Office.

18 R. Russell, 'Are human rights violations compatible with détente? A case study on the East–West conflict of interests over the dissidents in the Soviet Union and the GDR in 1978, and the differences within the West on the appropriate reaction', *Revue de Droit International de Sciences Diplomatiques et Politiques*, July–September 1980, no. 3, p. 207.

19 Author's interview with a government official.

20 Roger Morgan, 'West Germany's foreign policy agenda', *The Washington Papers*, vol. 6, p. 17.

21 Author's interview with a government official.

22 Helmut Schmidt, *Menschen und Mächte*, Berlin, Siedler Verlag, 1987, p. 20.

23 'Herr Schmidt in the middle', *The Times*, 23 November 1981.

24 Gerhard Wettig, *Das Vier-Mächte-Abkommen in der Bewährungsprobe: Berlin im Spannungsfeld von Ost und West*, Berlin, Berlin Verlag, 1981, p. 244.

25 Ibid., pp. 244–5.

26 Ibid., p. 245.

27 Russell, 'Are human rights violations compatible with détente?', pp. 212–13.

28 Ibid., p. 207.

29 Ibid., p. 213.

30 Ibid., pp. 213–14.

31 Jonathan Carr, *Helmut Schmidt: Helmsman of Germany*, London, Weidenfeld and Nicolson, 1985, pp. 124–5. See also Russell, 'Are human rights violations compatible with détente?', pp. 212–17 for a detailed discussion of the FRG's position on human rights in the East and her underlying reasons. R. Russell writes similarly to Jonathan Carr on this point.

32 Russell, 'Are human rights violations compatible with détente?', p. 216.

33 Confirmed to the author by a government official.

7 The Federal Republic of Germany's political relations with the Soviet Union after 1982

1 Figures from the Foreign Office reports in Presse- und Informationsamt der Bundesregierung, *Jahresbericht der Bundesregierung 1985*, p. 62; 1986, p. 48; 1987, p. 70; 1988, p. 44.

2 Source of information: 'Die Russlanddeutschen zwischen Assimilierung und Aussiedlung', paper given by Anton Bosch, Referent für Familien-zusammenführung der Landsmannschaft der Deutschen aus Russland e.V. (specialist on family reunification for the Organisation of Germans from Russia), on 22 October 1988 at the one-day conference 'The German minori-ties in the Soviet Union' held by the Institute of German, Austrian and Swiss Affairs, University of Nottingham (published in translation by the Institute of German, Austrian and Swiss Affairs: Anton Bosch, 'The Germans in Russia: between assimilation and evacuation', *Politics and Society in Germany, Austria and Switzerland*, vol. 1, 2, Winter 1988, pp. 12–20); also author's interview with Anton Bosch. It is interesting to note, in the context of the underlying reasons for the decline in emigration during the years 1977–82 (specifically: loss of skilled workers which cannot be immedi-ately replaced by domestic labour force; damage to agriculture in Kazakh-stan; the desire to avoid setting an example for others to follow – see pp. 27–30) that (i) there is now planned unemployment of 1 million Soviet citizens in industry as part of perestroika, the official plan by year 2000 is to have 2 million unemployed for the restructuring of industries; (ii) special-ised agricultural workers from Kazakhstan are still not allowed to emigrate; (iii) the numbers of Armenians and Jews being let out have also increased.

3 Patrick Cockburn, 'Ethnic politics', in *Getting Russia Wrong: The End of Kremlinology*, London, Verso, 1989, p. 65. On pp. 65–77 Patrick Cockburn presents an interesting analysis of the national problems which have emerged under Gorbachev.

4 See David Goodhart, 'Soviet German republic plan', *Financial Times*, 31 July 1989, p. 2.

5 Figures supplied to the author by an FRG government official.

6 Ibid.

7 See Fred Oldenburg, 'Das Verhältnis UdSSR – Bundesrepublik Deutsch-land', *Sowjetunion 1984/85*, Bundesinstitut für ostwissenschaftliche und internationale Studien, Munich, Carl Hanser Verlag, 1985, p. 269; and Wolfgang Berner, Christian Meier, Dieter Bingen, Gyula Józsa, Fred Olden-burg and Wolf Oschlies, 'Sowjetische Vormachtpolitik und die Autoritäts-krise in Osteuropa', *Sowjetunion 1984/85*, p. 294.

8 See Oldenburg, *Sowjetunion 1984/85*, p. 268.

9 International Institute for Strategic Studies, 'Western Europe facing a new challenge', *Strategic Survey, 1988–89*, Brassey's, 1989, p. 81.

10 Gerhard Wettig, 'Perestroika der Aussen- und Sicherheitspolitik', *Sowjet-union 1988/89*, pp. 218–19; and International Institute for Strategic Studies, 'The winds of change in Eastern Europe', *Strategic Survey 1988–89*, pp. 90–1.

11 Oldenburg, *Sowjetunion 1982/83*, p. 253.

12 Oldenburg, *Sowjetunion 1984/85*, p. 269.

13 Ibid., p. 267.

14 Ibid., p. 266–9; and also Foreign Office report, *Jahresbericht der Bundesregier-ung 1984*, Presse- und Informationsamt der Bundesregierung, pp. 37–38.

15 Oldenburg, *Sowjetunion 1984/85*, pp. 268–9, 271; also information supplied to author by a government official. For an example of the revanchism

campaign see the FRG government reprint of a *Pravda* article (27 July, 1984) published in *Neues Deutschland* (28/9 July 1984): 'Raketenstationierung und Deutschlandpolitik in sowjetischer Sicht', *Innerdeutsche Beziehungen: Die Entwicklung der Beziehungen zwischen der Bundesrepublik Deutschland und der Deutschen Demokratischen Republik 1980–86. Eine Dokumentation*, Bundesministerium für innerdeutsche Beziehungen, pp. 180–3.

16 Oldenburg, *Sowjetunion 1986/87*, pp. 254–5.

17 *Pravda*, 15 March 1985, cited in Oldenburg, *Sowjetunion 1984/85*, p. 275.

18 See Heinz Timmermann, 'Die sowjetische Politik gegenüber Westeuropa', *Sowjetunion 1986/87*, Bundesinstitut für ostwissenschaftliche und internationale Studien, p. 251; and Oldenburg, *Sowjetunion 1986/87*, p. 257.

19 Oldenburg, *Sowjetunion 1986/87*, pp. 257–8.

20 Foreign Office report, *Jahresbericht der Bundesregierung 1986*, Presse- und Informationsamt der Bundesregierung, p. 47.

21 *Newsweek*, 27 October 1986, cited in Oldenburg, *Sowjetunion 1986/87*, p. 264, note 17.

22 Foreign Office report, *Jahresbericht der Bundesregierung 1987*, Presse- und Informationsamt der Bundesregierung, p. 70.

23 Foreign Office report, *Jahresbericht der Bundesregierung 1988*, Presse- und Informationsamt der Bundesregierung, p. 44.

24 Ibid.

25 International Institute for Strategic Studies, 'Western Europe facing a new challenge', *Strategic Survey 1988–1989*, p. 81.

26 Cited in ibid., p. 81.

27 Ibid.

28 David Marsh, 'Gorbachev visit to West Germany will aim for European harmony', *Financial Times*, 12 June 1989, p. 20.

29 See extracts taken from the Joint Declaration made by President Gorbachev and Helmut Kohl in 'Leaders spell out new thinking to meet challenges ahead', *The Times*, 14 June 1989, p. 9; and also David Marsh 'Moscow in wide pact with Bonn', *Financial Times*, 14 June 1989, p. 1.

30 'CDU/CSU–Wähler: Gorbatschow besser als Kohl', *Der Spiegel*, no. 23, 5 June 1989, p. 161.

31 For an account see, for example, Nigel Hawkes, ed., *Tearing Down the Curtain: The People's Revolution in Eastern Europe by a team from the Observer*, London, Hodder and Stoughton, 1990. For accounts specifically related to events in the GDR see also Micha Wimmer et al., eds., *'Wir sind das Volk!' Die DDR im Aufbruch. Eine Chronik in Dokumenten und Bildern*, Munich, W. Heyne Verlag, 1990; and Christoph Links, Hannes Bahrmann, *Wir sind das Volk: Die DDR im Aufbruch: Eine Chronik*, Reinbek bei Hamburg, Rowohlt, 1990.

32 Hawkes, 'Tearing down the Curtain', p. 72.

33 See, for example, Anne McElvoy and Ian Murray, 'Hammering down the Wall: Kohl says we belong together', *The Times*, 11 November 1989, p. 1; also statements made by Gorbachev to a Moscow students' meeting cited in Peter Hitchens, 'Niet to a united Germany', *Daily Express*, 16 November 1989, p. 10; also statements made by Gorbachev to visitors from Bonn such

as Rita Süssmuth and Egon Bahr cited in 'Der Druck von Unten wächst', *Der Spiegel*, no. 48, 27 November 1989, p. 15.

34 Anne McElvoy et al., 'The Iron Curtain torn open', *The Times*, 10 November 1989, p. 1.

35 The ten point programme is set out in translation in 'Overcoming the division', *Scala*, no. 1, January–February 1990, pp. 10–11.

36 See statements made by the Soviet foreign office cited in 'Scharfe Kritik aus Moskau', *Frankfurter Allgemeine Zeitung*, 30 November 1989, p. 3.

37 See John Ellison, 'Soviets back single Germany', *Daily Express*, 31 January 1990, p. 24; Jonathan Steele, David Gow and John Palmer, 'Gorbachev softens on unified Germany', *The Guardian*, 31 January 1990, p. 24; and Hawkes, *Tearing Down the Curtain*, pp. 81–2.

38 David Gow, 'Worries in Bonn over cost of unity', *The Guardian*, 10 February 1990, p. 1.

39 David Gow and Jonathan Steele, 'Moscow accepts Germany will unite this year', *The Guardian*, 12 February 1990, p. 20.

40 Mary Dejevsky, 'Germans able to decide their own future', *The Times*, 12 February 1990, p. 10.

41 Ian Murray, 'Triumphant Kohl wins Gorbachev approval for unity', *The Times*, 12 February 1990, p. 10.

42 Article I(1) of the Warsaw Treaty states that 'the existing boundary line ... shall constitute the western State frontier of the People's Republic of Poland'. In articles I(2) and II(3) the two states affirm 'the inviolability of their existing frontiers now and in the future' and declare that 'they have no territorial claims whatsoever against each other and that they will not assert such claims in the future.' See text to the Warsaw Treaty in Presse- und Informationsamt der Bundesregierung, *Documentation Relating to the Federal Government's Policy of Détente*, pp. 28–30.

43 See Peter Stothard, 'US seeks unity formula to allay Kremlin fears', *The Times*, 3 May 1990, p. 8; and David Gow, 'Moscow still against Germany in Nato', *The Guardian*, 5 May 1990, p. 24.

44 See Gow, 'Moscow still against Germany in Nato', p. 24; and Ian Murray, 'Moscow demands guarantees over Germany in Nato', *The Times*, 7 May 1990, p. 8.

45 Murray, 'Moscow demands guarantees over Germany in Nato'.

46 Ian Murray, '£7 billion deal for Germany to stay in Nato', *The Times*, 11 June 1990, p. 1.

47 See John Rettie, 'Kohl and Gorbachev near breakthrough on Nato', *The Guardian*, 16 July 1990, p. 1; Peter Hitchens, 'Gorbachev gives way over Nato Germany', *Daily Express*, 17 July 1990, p. 10; and Bruce W. Nelan, 'Kohl wins his way', *Time*, 30 July 1990, pp. 10–15.

48 Ian Mather and Roman Rollnick, 'Peace breaks out over Poland', *The European*, 20–2 July 1990, p. 3.

49 Mary Dejevsky, 'Conquerors sign pact of German unity', *The Times*, 13 September 1990, p. 24.

50 Hella Pick, 'Kohl plans pact with Moscow', *The Guardian*, 23 May 1990, p. 7.

51 See Oldenburg, *Sowjetunion 1984/85*, p. 267.

52 See Timmermann, *Sowjetunion 1986/87*, p. 251.
53 Oldenburg, *Sowjetunion 1988/89*, p. 244.
54 Wettig, *Sowjetunion 1988/89*, p. 217.
55 Hella Pick, 'Thatcher gets US reassurances', *The Guardian*, 12 December 1989, p. 9.
56 Ibid.

Appendix A. The Federal Republic of Germany's economic relations with the Soviet Union

1 Statement by the Federal Government on the results of the visit by Head of State of the Soviet Union, General Secretary Brezhnev. Deutscher Bundestag, 90. Sitzung, Bonn, Thursday 11 May 1978, Plenarprotokoll 8/90 7065D–7066A.

2 J. P. Young, 'Quantification of Western exports of high technology products to communist nations,' US Department of Commerce, Washington, GPO, 1977, pp. 15–16, cited in Angela Stent, *From Embargo to Ostpolitik: The Political Economy of West German–Soviet Relations*, 1955–1980, Cambridge University Press, 1981, p. 210.

3 Klaus Bolz, Herman Clement and Petra Pissula, 'Die Wirtschaftsbeziehungen zwischen der BRD und der Sowjetunion', Hamburg, Weltarchiv, 1976, pp. 263–5, cited in Stent, *From Embargo to Ostpolitik*, p. 210.

4 In 1931, the Soviet share in German exports was over 10 per cent. It has never been achieved since. See Werner Beitel, Jürgen Nötzold, 'Entwicklungstendenzen und Perspektiven der Wirtschaftsbeziehungen der Bundesrepublik Deutschland mit der Sowjetunion', *Osteuropa Wirtschaft*, 3, September 1979, p. 152.

5 To 11 milliard DM in 1978. See Paul Noack and Reiner Eger, 'Der Fortgang der Deutschen Ostpolitik: Innerdeutsche Beziehungen und die Berlin-Frage', *Die Internationale Politik 1977/78*, eds. Wolfgang Wagner, Marion Gräfin Dönhoff, Gerhard Fels, Karl Kaiser, Paul Noack, p. 159.

6 Die Zeit, 5 May 1978, cited in Noack and Eger, 'Der Fortgang', p. 159. See also F. Stephen Larrabee, 'Soviet–West German relations: normalization and beyond', RL 203/75, May 16, 1975, p. 2.

7 Noack and Eger, 'Der Fortgang', p. 159. For further reasons see also Beitel and Nötzold, 'Die Wirtschaftsbeziehungen', p. 152.

8 See also Timothy Garton Ash, 'What future for Ostpolitik?' *Spectator*, 23 January 1982, p. 7.

9 Trade with the USSR accounts for some 2.6 per cent of total FRG trade, see Roland Smith, 'Soviet policy towards West Germany', Adelphi Paper, no. 203, 1985, p. 16.

10 Ibid.

11 Ibid.

12 Some 6.5 per cent of West Germany's exports went to Comecon countries in 1980, followed by France with 4 per cent; for Britain the figure was 2.3 per cent. See Garton Ash, 'What future for Ostpolitik?' p. 7.

13 Ibid.

14 *Der Spiegel*, 18, 1978, p. 27.
15 Auswärtiges Amt, Sonderdruck aus dem Jahresbericht 1978 der Bundesregierung, p. 4. Hauptziele der Aussenpolitik der Bundesregierung im Jahr 1978.
16 Karl Hardach, 'The economy of the Federal Republic of Germany: structure, performance, and world position', in *Contemporary Germany: Politics and Culture*, eds. Charles Burdick, Hans-Adolf Jacobsen, Winifried Kudszus, Boulder, CO, Westview Press, 1984, p. 123.
17 H. Schmidt, The Alastair Buchan Memorial Lecture, *Survival*, vol. 20, no. 1, January–February 1978, p. 9.
18 Deutsches Institut für Wirstchaftsforschung (DIW) Wochenbericht (Berlin), no. 15 (1980), cited in Stent, *From Embargo to Ostpolitik*, p. 209.
19 Smith, 'Soviet policy', p. 17.
20 Ibid.
21 Stent, *From Embargo to Ostpolitik*, p. 240.
22 Ibid.
23 Ibid., p. 241.
24 Hans-Dietrich Genscher, 'Towards an overall Western strategy for peace, freedom and progress', *Foreign Affairs*, vol. 61, no. 1, 1982, pp. 53–4. Genscher's view on how dependent the Soviets were or allowed themselves to be on Western trade contrasts with the view that became, at least since the end of Carter's presidency, increasingly dominant in the United States: that is that if trade, particularly but not only, in high technology were denied the Soviet Union, then somehow it would become a politically weaker force.
25 Ibid., pp. 56–7.
26 Smith, 'Soviet policy', p. 18.
27 The author believes that the passage referred to by the party official is the following: 'As nature wisely separates nations which the will of each state, sanctioned even by the principles of international law, would gladly unite under its own sway by stratagem or force; in the same way, on the other hand, she unites nations whom the principle of a cosmopolitan right would not have secured against violence and war. And this union she brings about through an appeal to their mutual interests. The commercial spirit cannot co-exist with war, and sooner or later it takes possession of every nation. For, of all the forces which lie at the command of a state, the power of money is probably the most reliable. Hence states find themselves compelled – not, it is true, exactly from motives of morality – to further the noble end of peace and to avert war, by means of mediation, wherever it threatens to break out, just as if they had made a permanent league for this purpose.' (Immanuel Kant, *Perpetual Peace: A Philosophical Essay*, trans. M. Campbell Smith, George Allen and Unwin, 1903, p. 157)
28 After-dinner speech by Chancellor Schmidt, 5 May 1978, cited in Renata Fritsch-Bournazel, *Die Sowjetunion und die deutsche Teilung: Die sowjetische Deutschlandpolitik 1945–1979*, Opladen, Westdeutscher Verlag, 1979, p. 157.
29 Jonathan Carr, *Helmut Schmidt: Helmsman of Germany*, London, Weidenfeld and Nicolson, 1985, p. 85.
30 H. Schmidt, 'Political action aimed at fostering understanding: speech to

the Congress on "Kant in our time"' (12 March 1982), in *Helmut Schmidt: Perspectives on Politics*, ed. Wolfram F. Hanrieder, Boulder, CO, Westview Press, 1980, p. 193.

31 Michael Binyon, Patricia Clough, 'What will Brezhnev do to keep his best friend in the West?' *The Times*, 21 November 1981.

32 Taking trade figures from 1858, 1914 was the best year for Russian imports from Germany and Russian exports to Germany – see Jürgen Kuczynski and Grete Wittkowski, *Die deutschrussischen Handelsbeziehungen in den letzten 150 Jahren*, Berlin, Verlag Die Wirtschaft, 1947, cited in Stent, *From Embargo to Ostpolitik*, pp. 9 and 253, note 8. The Soviet share in FRG exports only began to reach 1930s levels in the first half of the 1970s. See Werner Beitel and Jürgen Nötzold, 'Entwicklungstendenzen und Perspektiven der deutsch-sowjetischen Wirtschaftsbeziehungen', *Polarität und Interdependenz*, ed. Stiftung Wissenschaft und Politik, Baden-Baden, Nomos Verlagsgesellschaft, 1978, p. 107.

33 Fred Oldenburg, 'Das Verhältnis UdSSR – Bundesrepublik Deutschland', *Sowjetunion 1982/83*, p. 258.

34 Oldenburg, *Sowjetunion 1986/87*, p. 263.

35 Oldenburg, *Sowjetunion 1988/89*, p. 243.

36 Mary Dejevsky, 'Moscow is threatened with food rationing', *The Times*, 2 November 1990, p. 9.

Appendix B. The 'Agreement of 6 May 1978'

1 Press Conference on 7 May 1978, Hamburg-Fuhlsbüttel, nach Stenographischer Dienst, Büro der Regierungssprecher, Presse- und Informationsamt der Bundesregierung, hektographiertes Material, S.2, cited in Christian Meier, Fred Oldenburg, 'Das deutsch–sowjetische Verhältnis nach dem zweiten Brezhnev–Besuch,' *Berichte des Bundesinstituts für ostwissenschaftliche und internationale Studien*, 40, 1978, p. 37.

2 Meier and Oldenburg, 'Das deutsch–sowjetische Verhältnis,' p. 37.

3 For text of the agreement see Presse- und Informationsamt der Bundesregierung, *Bulletin*, no. 44, 9 May 1978, pp. 431–2.

4 Juergen Nötzold, 'Zum Abkommen über die langfristige Zusammenarbeit zwischen Bonn und Moskau,' *Osteuropa*, 10, October 1978, p. 878.

5 Ibid., pp. 878–9.

6 Ibid., p. 879.

7 Meier and Oldenburg, 'Das deutsch–sowjetische Verhältnis', p. 39.

8 Presse- und Informationsamt der Bundesregierung, *Bulletin*, no. 47, 12 May 1978, p. 456.

9 *New York Times*, 7 May 1978, cited in Angela Stent, *From Embargo to Ostpolitik: The Political Economy of West German–Soviet Relations, 1955–1980*, Cambridge University Press, 1981, p. 206.

10 Nötzold, 'Zum Abkommen', p. 876.

11 Deutscher Bundestag, 90. Sitzung, Bonn, Donnerstag, den 11. Mai 1978, Plenarprotokoll 8/90, Hoppe FDP, 7084B.

12 Carl-Christian Kaiser, 'Kein Expander, kein Trampolin. Nach Breschnjews Besuch: Behutsamkeit in der Berlin-Frage,' *Die Zeit*, 20, 12 May 1978.

Select bibliography

FRG government publications and documents

Auswärtiges Amt, Referat für Öffentlichkeitsarbeit und Bundesministerium der Verteidigung, Informations- und Pressestab-Öffentlichkeitsarbeit. *Es geht um unsere Sicherheit: Bündnis, Verteidigung, Rüstungskontrolle.* Bonn: November 1982.

Translation of speech by Chancellor Schmidt in Moscow on 30 June 1980. English version released by West German Foreign Office.

Der Bundesminister des Innern. *Betrifft: Eingliederung der Vertriebenen, Flüchtlinge und Kriegsgeschädigten in der Bundesrepublik Deutschland.* Bonn: November 1982.

Bundesministerium für innerdeutsche Beziehungen. *Innerdeutsche Beziehungen: Die Entwicklung der Beziehungen zwischen der Bundesrepublik Deutschland und der Deutschen Demokratischen Republik 1980–86. Eine Dokumentation.* Bonn: August 1986.

Bundeszentrale für politische Bildung. 'Die Bundesrepublik Deutschland 1966–1974', *Informationen zur Politischen Bildung*, 191. Bonn: November 1981.

'Die Bundesrepublik Deutschland 1974–1983', *Informationen zur Politischen Bildung*, 202, Bonn: July 1984.

'Die Russen: Nachdenken über einen fernen Nachbarn', *Politische Zeitung*, 35. Bonn: December 1983.

Deutscher Bundestag. *Bundestagsdrucksache.* Bonn.

Plenarprotokoll. Bonn

Gesamtdeutsches Institut. 'Die Berlin Regelung', *Seminarmaterial des Gesamtdeutschen Instituts.* Bonn: March 1985.

Presse- und Informationsamt der Bundesregierung. *Aspekte der Friedenspolitik: Argumente zum Doppelbeschluss des Nordatlantischen Bündnisses.* Bonn: June 1981.

Bulletin. Bonn.

Documentation Relating to the Federal Government's Policy of Détente. Bonn: 1978.

Jahresbericht der Bundesregierung 1974–1989, Bonn

Ein Land lebt nicht für sich allein: Zur Aussenpolitik und zu den internationalen Beziehungen der Bundesrepublik Deutschland. Bonn: April 1980.

Verträge, Abkommen und Vereinbarungen zwischen der Bundesrepublik Deutschland und der Deutschen Demokratischen Republik. Bonn: February 1973.

'Zehn Jahre Aussenpolitik der Sozialliberalen Koalition'. Zusammengestellt vom Auswärtigen Amt, *Material für die Presse*. Bonn: 19 October 1979.
BPA-Nachrichtenabteilung, Ref. II R 3, Rundf.-Ausw. Deutschland, DFS/26.11.81/20.15/MS-GE/Sch – Die Fernseh-Diskussion – 'Bonn nach dem Breschnew-Besuch'. Discussion with Chancellor Helmut Schmidt and journalists Ernst Dieter Lüg, WDR, Dieter Wild, *Der Spiegel*, Herbert Kremp, *Die Welt*, chaired by Rudolf Mühlfenzl.
DLF/26.11.81/06.45 Uhr/Hy. Dr Hans-Jochen Vogel, Vorsitzender der SPD-Fraktion im Berliner Abgeordnetenhaus, zu den deutsch-sowjetischen und innerdeutschen Beziehungen.

Deutschland Archiv. Dokumentation (documentation)

'Bundeskanzler Schmidt und Aussenminister Genscher in Moskau', *Deutschland Archiv.*, vol. II, 1980, pp. 881–90. (visit of Chancellor Schmidt and Foreign Minister Genscher to Moscow, 30 June – 1 July 1980: Gemeinsames Kommuniqué 1 July 1980 (Joint Communiqué); Erklärung der Bundesregierung zur Konferenz in Venedig und zu den Gesprächen in Moskau 3 July 1980 (statement by the Federal Government on the conference in Venice and on the talks in Moscow).

Europa-Archiv. Dokumentation (documentation)

D.334–8, *Europa-Archiv*, 12, 1973 (visit by Brezhnev to Bonn, 18–22 May, joint communiqué).

Pressedienst der Freien Demokratischen Partei (FDP news service)

Genscher, Hans-Dietrich, Bundesvorsitzender der FDP. 'Entspannungspolitik in Krisenzeiten: Von der gemeinsamen Verantwortung der beiden deutschen Staaten', Pressedienst der Freien Demokratischen Partei, Ausgabe 335, 26 October 1980.

Bundesinstitut für ostwissenschaftliche und internationale Studien (Federal Institute for Eastern and International Studies), Cologne

Bundesinstitut für ostwissenschaftliche und internationale Studien. *Sowjetunion 1974/75 to 1988/89*. Munich: Carl Hanser Verlag, 1975–89.
Meier, Christian and Fred Oldenburg. 'Das deutsch-sowjetische Verhältnis nach dem zweiten Breschnew-Besuch', *Berichte des Bundesinstituts für ostwissenschaftliche und internationale Studien*, 40, 1978.
'Der XXVI KPdSU-Kongress und die Beziehungen der Sowjetunion zu beiden deutschen Staaten', *Berichte des Bundesinstituts für ostwissenschaftliche und internationale Studien*, 26, 1981.
Wettig, Gerhard. 'Die Bindungen West-Berlins seit dem Vier-Mächte-Abkommen', *Berichte des Bundesinstituts für ostwissenschaftliche und internationale Studien*, 34, 1978.

'The relations of the USSR with the Federal Republic of Germany', *Berichte des Bundesinstituts für ostwissenschaftliche und internationale Studien*, 12, 1982.
'The role of West Germany in Soviet policies towards Western Europe', *Sonderveröffentlichungen des Bundesinstituts für ostwissenschaffliche und international Studien*, June 1982.

Deutsche Gesellschaft für Auswärtige Politik (German Association for Foreign Affairs), Bonn

Wagner, Wolfgang, *et al.*, eds. *Die Internationale Politik 1973/74, 1977/78, 1983/84.* Munich, Vienna: R. Oldenburg Verlag, 1980, 1982, 1986.

Hessische Stiftung Friedens- und Konfliktforschung (Peace Research Institute Frankfurt)

Risse-Kappen, Thomas. '"Fahrplan zur Abrüstung?" Zur INF-Politik der Bundesrepublik Deutschland 1970–1983', *Forschungsbericht der Hessischen Stiftung Friedens- and Konfliktforschung (HSFK), January 1985.*

International Institute for Strategic Studies, London

Berlin press files.
Strategic Survey 1988–1989. Brasseys, 1989.

Soviet Studies Research Centre, The Royal Military Academy, Sandhurst

'Leonid Brezhnev answers questions put by a West German newspaper'. Text released on 2 May 1978 of an interview given by Brezhnev to the West German Social Democratic Party newspaper *Vorwärts* during his 1978 visit to Bonn.

Stiftung Wissenschaft und Politik (Foundation for Science and Politics, Research Institute for International Politics and Security), Ebenhausen

Stiftung Wissenschaft und Politik. *Polarität und Interdependenz.* Baden-Baden: Nomos Verlagsgesellschaft, 1978.

Articles

Bahr, Egon. 'Von Moskau über Helsinki nach Wien', *Deutschland Archiv*, 12, 1975, pp. 1334–40.
Beitel, Werner and Jürgen Nötzold. 'Entwicklungstendenzen und Perspektiven der Wirtschaftsbeziehungen der Bundesrepublik Deutschland mit der Sowjetunion', *Osteuropa Wirtschaft*, 3, September 1979, pp. 151–83.
Böhm, Anton. 'Aus dem Osten nichts Neues: die deutsch-sowjetischen Beziehungen nach Breschnews Besuch', *Die Politische Meinung*, 178, May/June 1978, pp. 47–52.

Bosch, Anton. 'The Germans in Russia: between assimilation and evacuation', *Politics and Society in Germany, Austria and Switzerland*, vol. 1, no. 2, Winter 1988, pp. 12–20.

Brandt, Willy, Erwin Essl, Petra K. Kelly, Herbert Mies, Jürgen Müllermann, Martin Niemöller, Gerhard Weber. 'Zehn Jahre Moskauer Vertrag: Beiträge zu Stand und Perspektiven der deutsch-sowjetischen Beziehungen', *Blätter für Deutsche und Internationale Politik*, 7, 1980, pp. 909–40.

Bredthauer, Karl D., 'Entwarnung? Zur Lage nach Schmidts Moskaureise', *Blätter für Deutsche und Internationale Politik*, 7, 1980, pp. 772–6.

Cramer, Dettmar. 'Gewinner sind beide Seiten: zur Unterzeichnung des Verkehrspaketes', *Deutschland Archiv*, 12, 1978, pp. 1233–4.

'Der Kanzler im Kreml: Moskau 1970 und Moskau 1980', *Deutschland Archiv*, 8, 1980, pp. 785–7.

Fritsch-Bournazel, Renata. 'La RFA et l'Europe de l'Est: voie royale ou impasse?', *Politique Internationale*, 15, Spring 1982, pp. 81–100.

Gelman, Harry. 'Rise and fall of détente', *Problems of Communism*, vol. 34, March–April 1985, pp. 51–72.

Genscher, Hans-Dietrich. 'Towards an overall Western strategy for peace, freedom and progress', *Foreign Affairs*, vol. 61, no. 1, Fall 1982, pp. 42–66.

Gitelman, Zvi. 'Are nations merging in the USSR?' *Problems of Communism*, vol. 32, September–October 1983, pp. 35–47.

Goble, Paul A. 'Managing the multinational USSR', *Problems of Communism*, vol. 34, July–August 1985, pp. 79–83.

Haftendorn, Helga. 'Ostpolitik revisited 1976', *The World Today*, vol. 32, no. 6, June 1976, pp. 222–9.

Jacobsen, Hans-Adolf. 'Deutsch-sowjetische Beziehungen: Kontinuität und Wandel 1945 bis 1987', *Aus Politik und Zeitgeschichte*, B3, 15 January 1988, pp. 28–44.

Joffe, Josef. 'All Quiet on the Eastern Front', *Foreign Policy*, 37, Winter 1979–80, pp. 161–75.

Karpat, Kemal. 'Moscow and the "Muslim Question"', *Problems of Communism*, vol. 32, November–December 1983, pp. 71–9.

Kuppe, Johannes. 'Deutsch-deutsche Beziehungen im Schatten der Weltpolitik', *Deutschland Archiv*, 2, 1980, pp. 113–17.

Kupper, Siegfried. 'Festhalten an der Entspannung: Das Verhältnis der beiden deutschen Staaten nach Afghanistan', *Deutschland Archiv*, 10, 1983, pp. 1045–65.

Larrabee, F. Stephen, 'Soviet–West German relations: normalisation and beyond', Radio Liberty Research, 203/75, 16 May 1975, Munich.

Lunn, Simon, 'Cruise missiles and the prospects for arms control', *ADIU Report*, vol. 3, 5 September/October 1981, part II, Main Edition, 11 February 1982, pp. 7-F–11-F.

Mehnert, Klaus, 'Bundeskanzler Schmidt in Moskau', *Osteuropa*, 10, October 1980, pp. 1081–92.

'Mit Bundeskanzler Schmidt in der UdSSR', *Osteuropa*, 1, January 1975, pp. 3–18.

'Mit dem Bundespräsidenten in der UdSSR: Gedanken nach einer Reise, *Osteuropa*, 1, January 1976, pp. 3–10.

Meier, Christian and Fred Oldenburg. 'Sowjetische Deutschland-Politik Mitte der 1970er Jahre', *Osteuropa*, 8/9, August–September, 1976, pp. 779–90.

Meissner, Boris. 'Stalins Ebbe und Flut: Das Verhältnis der Sowjetunion zur Bundesrepublik, *Die Politische Meinung*, 190, May/June 1980, pp. 23–35.

Ménudier, Henri. 'La Politique à l'Est de Bonn: une relance limitée', *Defense Nationale*, 1, November 1977, pp. 61–70.

Mertes, Alois. 'Bilanz der Entspannungspolitik', *Aus Politik und Zeitgeschichte*, B50, 18 December 1982, pp. 3–9.

Misiunas, Romuald J. 'Baltic identity and Sovietization', *Problems of Communism*, vol. 31, March–April 1982, pp. 37–41.

Morgan, Roger. 'West Germany's foreign policy agenda', *The Washington Papers*, vol. 6, 54, Beverly Hills and London: Sage Publications, 1978.

Morgan, Roger and Caroline Bray. 'Berlin in the post-détente era', *The World Today*, vol. 38, January–December 1982, pp. 81–9.

Nötzold, Juergen, 'Zum Abkommen über die langfristige Zusammenarbeit zwischen Bonn und Moskau', *Osteuropa*, 10, October 1978, pp. 876–82.

Oldenburg, Fred and Christian Meier. 'Die deutsch-sowjetischen Beziehungen im Zeichen des Breshnew-Besuchs', *Osteuropa*, 10, October 1978, pp. 855–75.

Sowjetische Deutschland-Politik zu Beginn der achtziger Jahre', *Osteuropa*, September–October 1981, pp. 874–87.

Porter, Bruce, 'The USSR's relations with West Germany, France and Great Britain since 1979', Radio Liberty Research, 195/82, 12 May 1982.

Rakowska-Harmstone, Teresa, 'The dialectics of nationalism in the USSR', *Problems of Communism*, vol. 23, May–June 1974, pp. 1–22.

Russell, R. 'Are human rights violations compatible with détente? A case study on the East–West conflict of interests over the dissidents in the Soviet Union and the GDR in 1978, and the differences within the West on the appropriate reaction', *Revue de Droit International de Sciences Diplomatiques et Politiques*, July–September 1980, 3, pp. 196–224.

Schmidt, Helmut, 'The 1977 Alastair Buchan Memorial Lecture', *Survival*, Vol. 20, 1, January–February 1978, pp. 2–10.

'Politik der verlässlichen Partnerschaft: Europäer und Amerikaner vor den Aufgaben der achtziger Jahre', *Europa-Archiv*, 7, 1981, pp. 197–208.

Simon, G. 'Nationalitätenprobleme und Regierbarkeit der Sowjetunion', *Osteuropa*, 10, October 1984, pp. 759–68.

Smith, Roland, 'Soviet Policy Towards West Germany', *Adelphi Papers*, no. 203. International Institute for Strategic Studies, 1985.

Spittmann, Ilse, 'Der deutsche Aspekt in Breschnew's Offerte', *Deutschland Archiv*, 11, 1979, pp. 1121–2.

Spittmann, Ilse, 'Frostschutz gefragt', *Deutschland Archiv*, 12, 1980, pp. 1233–6.

'Die Rolle der DDR in Moskaus Strategie', *Deutschland Archiv*, 6, 1980, pp. 561–3.

Stent, Angela, 'The USSR and Germany', *Problems of Communism*, vol. 30, September–October, 1981, pp. 1–24.

van Well, Günther. 'Die Teilnahme Berlins am internationalen Geschehen: ein dringender Punkt auf der Ost-West-Tagesordnung', *Europa-Archiv*, 20, 1976, pp. 647–56.

Wettig, Gerhard. 'Die Bindungen West-Berlins als Verhandlungs- und Vertragsgegenstand der vier Mächte 1970/71, *Deutschland Archiv*, 3, 1979, pp. 278–90.

'Das Problem der Bindungen West-Berlins bei der Anwendung des Viermächteabkommens', *Deutschland Archiv*, 9, 1979, pp. 920–37.

'Die Transformation des Berlin-Konflikts seit dem Inkrafttreten des Vier-Mächte-Abkommens', *Deutsche Studien*, 68, December 1979, pp. 317–31.

Windsor, Philip. 'Germany and the Western Alliance: lessons from the 1980 crises', *Adelphi Papers*, no. 170. International Institute for Strategic Studies, 1981.

Winters, Peter Jochen. 'Kurswechsel Ost-Berlins gegenüber Bonn:\zum Stand der innerdeutschen Beziehungen', *Europa-Archiv*, 1, 1981, pp. 31–8.

'Ein Schritt auf dem Wege der Normalisierung: zu den Verkehrs-und Finanzvereinbarungen der beiden Staaten in Deutschland', *Europa-Archiv*, 9, 1979, pp. 269–78.

Wischnewski, Hans-Jürgen. 'Vom Feindstaat zum Vertragspartner: Bilanz der Entspannungspolitik gegenüber Osteuropa und der Sowjetunion', *Aus Politik und Zeitgeschichte*, B.50, 18 December 1982, pp. 11–16.

Newspapers and magazines

Daily Express
The Economist
The European
Financial Times
Frankfurter Allgemeine Zeitung
The Guardian
Scala
Spectator
Der Spiegel
The Sunday Times
Time
The Times
Die Welt
Die Zeit

Books

Bölling, Klaus. *Die Fernen Nachbarn: Erfahrungen in der DDR*. Hamburg: STERN-Buch im Verlag Grüner und Jahr, 1983.

Brauch, Hans Günter. *Die Raketen kommen! Vom Nato-Doppelbeschluss bis zur Stationierung*. Cologne: Bund-Verlag, 1983.

Bruns, Wilhelm. *Deutsche-Deutsche Beziehungen: Prämissen, Probleme, Perspektiven*, 4th edn, Opladen: Leske and Budrich, 1984.

Bütow, Hellmuth G. (ed.). *Länderbericht Sowjetunion*. Bonn: Bundeszentrale für politische Bilding, 1986.

Burdick, Charles, Hans-Adolph Jacobson, Winifried Kudszus (eds.). *Contemporary Germany: Politics and Culture*. Boulder, CO: Westview Press, 1984.

Cambridge Encyclopedia of Russia and the Soviet Union, The, General eds. Archie Brown, John Fennell, Michael Kaser, H. T. Willetts. Cambridge University Press, 1982.

Carr, Jonathan. *Helmut Schmidt: Helmsman of Germany*. London: Weidenfeld and Nicolson, 1985.

Chambers Twentieth Century Dictionary. Ed. A. M. Macdonald. Chambers, rev. edn 1974.

Cockburn, Patrick. *Getting Russia Wrong: The End of Kremlinology*. London, Verso, 1989.

Delbrück, Jost., et al. (eds.). *Grünbuch zu den Folgewirkungen der KSZE*. DGFK – Veröffentlichungen, Bd. 3. Cologne: Wissenschaft und Politik, 1977.

Dönhoff, Marion. *Foe into Friend: The Makers of the New Germany from Konrad Adenauer to Helmut Schmidt*. London: Weidenfeld and Nicolson, 1982.

Fritsch-Bournazel, Renata. *Die Sowjetunion und die deutsche Teilung: Die sowjetische Deutschlandpolitik 1945–1979*. Opladen: Westdeutscher Verlag, 1979.

Gaus, Günter. *Wo Deutschland liegt: Eine Ortsbestimmung*. Munich: Deutscher Taschenbuch Verlag, 1986.

Griffith, William E. *The Ostpolitik of the Federal Republic of Germany*. Cambridge, MA and London: The MIT Press, 1978.

Die Ostpolitik der Bundesrepublik Deutschland. Stuttgart: Klett-Cotta, 1981. (ch. 6 of German edition enlarged and brought up to date.)

Haftendorn, Helga. *Sicherheit und Entspannung: Zur Aussenpolitik der Bundesrepublik Deutschland 1955–1982*. Baden-Baden: Nomos Verlagsgesellschaft, 1983.

Hanrieder, Wolfram (ed.). *West German Foreign Policy: 1949–1979*. Boulder, CO: Westview Press, 1980.

Helmut Schmidt: Perspectives on Politics. Boulder, CO: Westview Press, 1982.

Hawkes, Nigel (ed.), *Tearing Down the Curtain: The People's Revolution in Eastern Europe by a Team from The Observer*. London: Hodder and Stoughton, 1990.

Hillenbrand, Martin J. (ed.). *The Future of Berlin*, Montclair, New Jersey: Allanheld, Osmun, 1980.

Jäger, Wolfgang and Werner Link. *Republik im Wandel 1974–1982: Die Ära Schmidt*. Stuttgart: Deutsche Verlags-Anstalt, 1987.

Kaiser, Karl. and Hans-Peter Schwarz, (eds.). *Weltpolitik: Strukturen-Akteure-Perspektiven*. Bonn: Bundeszentrale für politische Bildung, 1985.

Kant, Immanuel. *Perpetual Peace: A Philosophical Essay*, trans. M. Campbell Smith. London: George Allen and Unwin, 1903.

Knapp, Guido, (ed.). *Wir und die Russen: Fakten, Chancen, Illusionen*. Aschaffenburg: Paul Pattloch Verlag, 1983.

Lehmann, Hans Georg. *Öffnung nach Osten: Die Ostreisen Helmut Schmidts und die Entstehung der Ost- und Entspannungspolitik*. Bonn: Verlag Neue Gesellschaft, 1984.

Meissner, B. (ed.). *Moskau–Bonn: Die Beziehungen zwischen der Sowjetunion und der Bundesrepublik Deutschland 1955–1973, Dokumentation*. Dokumente zur Aussenpolitik, Bd. III/1. Cologne: Verlag Wissenschaft und Politik, 1975.

Moreton, Edwina (ed.). *Germany between East and West*. Cambridge University Press, 1987.

Nawrocki, Joachim. *Relations between the Two States in Germany: Trends, Prospects and Limitations*. Bonn: Verlag Bonn Aktuell, 1985.

Pfetsch, Frank R. *Die Aussenpolitik der BRD 1949–1980*. Munich: Wilhelm Fink Verlag, 1981.

Schmidt, Helmut. *Menschen und Mächte*, Berlin: Siedler Verlag, 1987.

Schmidt, Helmut and Willy Brandt. *Deutschland 1976 – Zwei Sozialdemokraten im Gespräch*. Hamburg: rororo aktuell, 1976.

Schmidt, Helmut, and Willy Brandt, et al. *Zwischenbilanz: Zur Entwicklung der Beziehungen der Bundesrepublik Deutschland und der Sowjetunion*. Cologne: Pahl-Rugenstein Verlag, 1978.

Stent, Angela. *From Embargo to Ostpolitik: The Political Economy of West German–Soviet Relations, 1955–1980*. Cambridge University Press, 1981.

Stockholm International Peace Research Institute. *World Armaments and Disarmament, SIPRI Yearbook 1980*. Taylor and Francis, 1980.

Talbott, Strobe. *Deadly Gambits: The Reagan Administration and the Stalemate in Nuclear Arms Control*. London: Pan Books, 1985.

Wettig, Gerhard. *Das Vier-Mächte-Abkommen in der Bewährungsprobe: Berlin im Spannungsfeld von Ost und West*. Berlin: Berlin Verlag, 1981.

Index

The following series titles are now out of print:

1   ANDREA BOLTHO
    Foreign trade criteria in socialist economies

2   SHEILA FITZPATRICK
    The commissariat of enlightenment
    Soviet organization of education and the arts under Lunacharsky, October 1917–1921

3   DONALD J. MALE
    Russian peasant organisation before collectivisation
    A study of commune and gathering 1925–1930

4   P. WILES (ED.)
    The production of communist economic performance

5   VLADIMIR V. KUSIN
    The intellectual origins of the Prague Spring
    The development of reformist ideas in Czechoslovakia 1956–1967

6   GALIA GOLAN
    The Czechoslovak reform movement

7   NAUN JASNY
    Soviet economists of the twenties
    Names to be remembered

8   ASHA L. DATAR
    India's economic relations with the USSR and Eastern Europe, 1953–1969

9   T. M. PODOLSKI
    Socialist banking and monetary control
    The experience of Poland

10 SHMUEL GALAI
    The liberation movement in Russia 1900–1905

11 GALIA GOLAN
    Reform rule in Czechoslovakia
    The Dubček era 1968–1969

12 GEOFFREY A. HOSKING
    The Russian constitutional experiment
    Government and Duma 1907–1914

13 RICHARD B. DAY
    Leon Trotsky and the politics of economic isolation

14 RUDOLF BIĆANIĆ
    Economic policy in socialist Yugoslavia

15 JAN M. CIECHANOWSKI
    The Warsaw rising of 1944

16 EDWARD A. HEWITT
    Foreign trade prices in the Council for Mutual Economic Assistance

17 ALICE TEICHOVA
    An economic background to Munich
    International business and Czechoslovakia 1918–1938

Printed in the United States
73043LV00005B/226

9 780521 893336